The UK Stock Market

Almanac

2016

Stephen Eckett

HARRIMAN HOUSE LTD
18 College Street
Petersfield
Hampshire
GU31 4AD
GREAT BRITAIN
Tel: +44 (0)1730 233870
Email: enquiries@harriman-house.com
Website: www.harriman-house.com

First edition published in Great Britain in 2004
This 9th edition published in 2015
Copyright © Harriman House Ltd

The right of Stephen Eckett to be identified as the author has been asserted in accordance with the Copyright, Design and Patents Act 1988.

Print ISBN: 978-0-85719-505-0
eBook ISBN: 978-0-85719-506-7

British Library Cataloguing in Publication Data
A CIP catalogue record for this book can be obtained from the British Library.

Whilst every effort has been made to ensure that information in this book is accurate, no liability can be accepted for any loss incurred in any way whatsoever by any person relying solely on the information contained herein.

No responsibility for loss occasioned to any person or corporate body acting or refraining to act as a result of reading material in this book can be accepted by the Publisher, by the Author, or by the employers of the Author.

CONTENTS

INTRODUCTION

Welcome to the 2016 edition of the *UK Stock Market Almanac*, where we celebrate the Efficient Market Theory – that is, the failure of the theory. This book could alternatively be titled *The Inefficient Almanac*, as it revels in the trends and anomalies of the market that the Efficient Market Theory says shouldn't exist.

New in the 2016 Almanac

The Almanac comprises updates on previous strategies and studies covered in previous editions, and also new research.

New research

New strategies and studies in this Almanac include:

- **Nonfarm payrolls** – what impact does the Nonfarm payroll report have on equities in the days around the announcement? [page 82]

- **MSCI Index reviews** – how the share price behaves when a company is added to the MSCI United Kingdom Index. [page 106]

- **Flotations** – what is the performance of recently floated companies? [page 60]

- **Equally weighted indices** – which index should you be tracking? [page 10]

- **Day of the month** – what is the historic behaviour of the market on each of the days in a month? [page 102]

- **Monthly seasonality of oil** – which months have been historically strong or weak for the oil price? [page 94]

- **Monthly seasonality of silver** – which months have been historically strong or weak for the silver price? [page 28]

- **Olympic Games** – how do the stock markets of Olympic host nations perform in the year of the Games? [page 66]

- **Very large one-day market falls** – how do equity prices react in the days following a large fall? [page 86]

US presidential election

Possibly the most significant known event for the markets in 2016 will be the presidential election in the US. To mark this the Almanac includes:

- **Stock market in election years** – charts displaying the performance of the FTSE All-Share index in the 14 presidential election years since 1960. [page 8]

- **Stock market around elections** – analysis of the behaviour of share prices in the days around presidential elections. [page 92]

- **Presidential election cycle** – analysis of the effect of the four-year presidential cycles on UK stock prices. [page 50]

- **Presidential election portfolios** – is it better for investors if there is a Democrat or Republican in the White House? [page 68]

Updated strategies and studies

The 2016 Almanac updates some of the studies of seasonality trends and anomalies that have featured in previous editions, including:

- **Sell in May** – this extraordinary effect remains as strong as ever: since 1982 the market in the winter months has outperformed the market in the summer months by an average of 8.6 percentage points annually. In the year since the last edition of the Almanac the outperformance was 4.2 percentage points. [page 34]

- **Day Of The Week Strategy** – a strategy exploiting the day of the week anomaly that significantly outperforms the FTSE 100. [page 42, with day of the week analysis also on page 115]

- **FTSE 100/250 Monthly Switching Strategy** – on the back of research into the comparative monthly performance of the two indices, a strategy of switching between the two markets is found that greatly outperforms either index individually. [page 16]

- **FTSE 100/S&P 500 Switching Strategy** – the strong/weak months for the FTSE 100 relative to the S&P 500 are identified; and a strategy of switching between the two markets is found that produces twice the returns of either market individually. [page 56]

- **Low/high Share Price Strategy** – a portfolio of the 20 lowest priced shares in the market has outperformed a portfolio of the 20 highest priced shares by an average 38.7 percentage points each year since 2002. [page 40]

- **Quarterly Sector Strategy** – the strongest/weakest sectors for each quarter are identified; and the Quarterly Sector Strategy continues to beat the market. [page 84]

- **Monthly Share Momentum Strategy** – a monthly rebalanced momentum portfolio of FTSE 100 stocks beats the market. [page 44]

- **Tuesday Reverses Monday Strategy** – since year 2000, market returns on Tuesdays have been the reverse of those on Mondays. A strategy using this effect has significantly outperformed the FTSE 100 over this period. [page 18]

- **Quarterly sector momentum strategy** – a portfolio comprising the best FTSE 350 sector from the previous quarter, and rebalanced quarterly, outperforms the FTSE All-Share by an average of 2.7 percentage points per month. A variant – buying the worst sector of the previous quarter – has performed even better. [page 48]

- **Bounceback Portfolio** – a strategy that buys the worst performing shares in a year, and then sells them after three months into the new year; the strategy has beaten the market every year since 2003 except one year. [page 100]

- **FTSE 100 quarterly reviews** – as before, it is found that share prices tend to rise immediately before a company joins the FTSE 100 and are then flat or fall back. Before a company leaves the index, share prices tend to fall and then rise after the exit. [page 22 and page 70]

- **FTSE 100 and FTSE 250** – the trend continues for the FTSE 100 to greatly underperform the mid-cap index in January and February and outperform it in September and October. [page 120]

- **Holidays and the market** – in recent years the market has been significantly strong on the days immediately before and after holidays and weak four days before and three days after holidays. [page 26]

- **Summer portfolio** – a portfolio of eight (summer) stocks has outperformed the FTSE 350 in nine of the last ten years with an average annual outperformance of 6.4 percentage points. [page 52]

- **Market seasonality (day/week/month)** – December is still the strongest month in the year for the stock market, while September is the weakest. Analysis is also updated for weekly and daily performance of the market (Sinclair Numbers). [page 164]

- **The January Effect** – analysis suggests that performance in January is inversely proportional to company size (i.e. small companies like January). [page 6]

- **Day of the week performance** – Wednesday is the new weakest day of the week (Monday used to be), and the strongest days are now Tuesday and Thursday. [page 115]

- **Turn of the month** – the market tends to be weak a few days either side of the turn of the month, but abnormally strong on the first trading day of the new month (except in December). [page 129]

- **First/last trading day of the month** – the first trading days of April and July are found to be unusually strong, while that of December is weak. The last trading day of October is found to be the year's strongest, while the weakest are those for February and November. [page 122 and page 123]

- **Trading around Christmas and New Year** – how do share prices behave in the days around Christmas and New Year? [page 104]

- **Market momentum grid** – a reference grid is presented giving the historic tendency of the market to rise (fall) following a series of consecutive daily/weekly/monthly/yearly rises (falls). As before, it is found that trends become more established the longer they last, and the market displays greater momentum for longer frequencies. [page 126 and page 127]

- **UK and US markets** – the correlation between the UK and US markets has been increasing since the 1950s, and in the years since 2010 has been stronger than ever. [page 156]

- **Correlation between UK and international markets** – analysis of the correlation of the UK with six overseas stock markets to answer the question: where should investors seek diversification? [page 157]

- **The Long-Term Formula** – the formula that describes the long-term trend of the stock market and gives a forecast for the FTSE 100 in December 2040. [page 158]

- **MPC meetings** – how does the monthly MPC announcement on interest rates affect share prices? [page 76]

- **Correlation of UK equity markets** – if you want to diversify away from the FTSE 100, how effective will this be investing in the FTSE 250, FTSE Small Cap, FTSE Fledgling or FTSE AIM All-Share indices? [page 125]

- **Daylight saving effect** – what is the effect on financial markets of the switches to and from daylight saving time? [page 88]

- **The Market's Decennial Cycle** – can analysis of the market's performance in the equivalent years of decades reveal any pattern of behaviour? [page 159]

- **The average market month** – by taking the average performance of the market on each day of a month, it is possible to create a chart of the average performance of the market for that month, and then to combine the 12 charts to produce a chart of the average behaviour of the market in all months. [page 78]

- **The average market year** – the performance and volatility of the market for an average year. [page 4]

In addition to the above, analysis is also updated for the standard Almanac features, including: comparative performance of UK equity indices, company ranking by financial and price behaviour criteria, price history profile of the FTSE All-Share, sector profiles of the FTSE 100 and 250, annual performance of sectors, etc.

The Diary

The core of the Almanac is the 52-week diary which lists financial and other events for each week in 2016 that should be of interest to investors and traders. An explanation of the information on the diary pages can be found in the section 'Understanding the Diary Pages' (page x).

Month summary pages

The diary section has a summary page for each month highlighting the major investment and seasonality characteristics of the month (e.g. January's is on page 2). Some features of these summary pages are:

1. There are two charts: the left chart plots the performance of the FTSE 100 in the month for every year since 1980, the right chart plots the average performance chart for the month. This latter chart is calculated by taking the average performance of the market on each day in the month since 1985 and using these to create a cumulative performance chart for the month to give an idea of the behaviour of the market over the 22 or so trading days of each month. [More information on this can be found on page 78.]

2. In the summary table, the first row gives the three main statistics that describe the historic performance of the market in that month: the average return, the percentage of months where the return is positive and the month's ranking among the 12 months.

3. In the summary table, the second row displays the FTSE 350 sectors that have been historically strong and weak that month.

4. In the summary table, the third row displays the FTSE 350 shares that have been historically strong and weak that month.

Quantitative analysis

It should be noted that the type of quantitative analysis contained in the Almanac in some cases is best exploited by an arbitraged or hedged strategy, not a simple long position. For example, to exploit the strong shares identified for January, it would be best to short the FTSE 100, or the weak shares, against a portfolio of long positions in the strong shares.

Outlook for 2016

So, what can we look forward to in 2016?

Well, 2016 will be the International Year of Pulses and polymer banknotes are due to be introduced by the Bank of England. And there will be synchronised swimming in Rio de Janeiro. So, it's shaping up to be quite a year.

Elsewhere in 2016, we'll be celebrating the 100th anniversary of the toggle light switch and the 900th anniversary of the modern book of separate pages stitched together (invented in China). And then there's the 2200-year anniversary of Cato the Elder being elected censor in Rome. Cato, as a stout defender of the austere Roman way of life, inaugurated a puritanical campaign to combat degenerate Greek influences. He passed measures increasing taxes, cracking down on abuses by tax collectors, and he sought to control who could stand as law-makers. But that was all 2200 years ago...

Onto the stock market, what is 2016 likely to bring for investors?

The Decennial Cycle is not that encouraging for investors: since 1800, the average performance of the FTSE All-Share in the sixth year of the decade has been a lowly 1.6%. And the longer Centennial Cycle is inconclusive; in 1716, 1816 and 1916 the respective market returns were +13%, -12%, +1%. In the Chinese calendar it will be the year of the monkey, which is a middling animal market-wise: since 1950 the S&P 500 has returned an average 7.3% in monkey years. However, the Long-Term Formula (see page 158) forecasts a very bullish FTSE 100 value of 11,197 by December 2016.

The most significant predictable event in 2016 is the US presidential election – what can we learn from previous such elections? Generally, the fourth years in the four-year election cycle are good ones for stocks in the US and UK. In fact, since 1948, the UK market has risen 9 times out of 17 (53%) in US election years, with an average annual return in those years of 5%.

Overall, the historic signs are moderately bullish for stocks in 2016.

Stephen Eckett

PREFACE

What the book covers

Topics in the Almanac cover a wide spectrum. The Diary includes essential information on upcoming company announcements and financial events such as exchange holidays and economic releases. There are also the results of a unique seasonality analysis of historic market performance for every day and week of the year – our Sinclair Numbers. Besides this, there is information of a lighter nature, such as important social and sporting occasions and notable events in history.

Accompanying the Diary is a series of articles about the stock market. Many of these focus on seasonality effects, such as the likely performance of the market in each month, momentum effects, and the difference in market performance between summer and winter.

In short, the Almanac is a unique work providing everything from essential reference information to informative and entertaining articles on the UK stock market.

How the book is structured

The *Almanac* has three major parts:

1. **Diary**: A week-per-page format. (See the next page for a detailed explanation of the layout of each Diary page.) Opposite each Diary page is a short strategy-oriented article about the stock market – they aim to reveal trading patterns and anomalies that investors and traders can exploit to make money.

2. **Statistics**: This section contains further seasonality and anomaly studies as well as background information on the profile characteristics of the market – the indices, sectors and companies.

3. **Reference**: This section includes background information about UK and international stock indices, and a look at the original constituents of the FT 30 of 1935 and the FTSE 100 of 1984.

Supporting website

The website supporting this book can be found at stockmarketalmanac.co.uk.

Follow the Almanac on Twitter

@UKAlmanac

Free eBook

Every owner of a physical copy of **The UK Stock Market Almanac 2016** can download the eBook edition for free direct from us at Harriman House, in a format that can be read on any eReader, tablet or smartphone.

Simply head to **ebooks.harriman-house.com/almanac2016** to get your copy now.

UNDERSTANDING THE DIARY PAGES

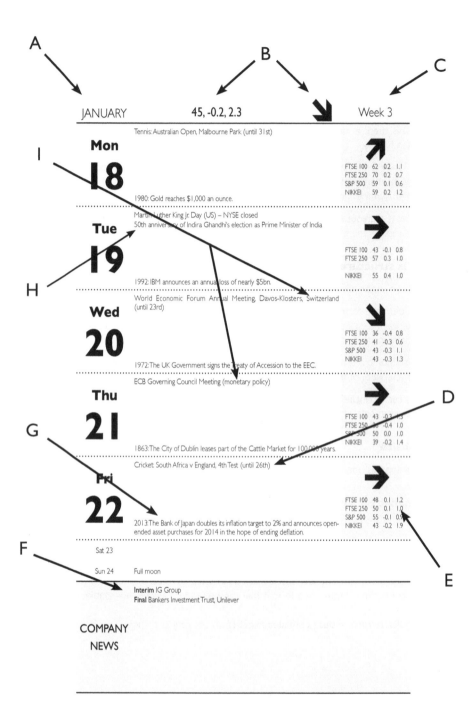

A

B

C

JANUARY   45, -0.2, 2.3   ↘   Week 3

Tennis: Australian Open, Malbourne Park (until 31st)

I

Mon

18   ↗

FTSE 100	62	0.2	1.1
FTSE 250	70	0.2	0.7
S&P 500	59	0.1	0.6
NIKKEI	59	0.2	1.2

1980: Gold reaches $1,000 an ounce.

Martin Luther King Jr. Day (US) – NYSE closed
50th anniversary of Indira Ghandhi's election as Prime Minister of India

Tue

19   →

FTSE 100	43	-0.1	0.8
FTSE 250	57	0.3	1.0
NIKKEI	55	0.4	1.0

H

1992: IBM announces an annual loss of nearly $5bn.

World Economic Forum Annual Meeting, Davos-Klosters, Switzerland (until 23rd)

Wed

20   ↘

FTSE 100	36	-0.4	0.8
FTSE 250	41	-0.3	0.6
S&P 500	43	-0.3	1.1
NIKKEI	43	-0.3	1.3

1972: The UK Government signs the Treaty of Accession to the EEC.

ECB Governing Council Meeting (monetary policy)

Thu

21   →

FTSE 100	43	-0.3	1.3
FTSE 250	36	-0.4	1.0
S&P 500	50	0.0	1.0
NIKKEI	39	-0.2	1.4

D

G

1863: The City of Dublin leases part of the Cattle Market for 100,000 years.

Cricket: South Africa v England, 4th Test (until 26th)

Fri

22   →

FTSE 100	48	0.1	1.2
FTSE 250	50	0.1	1.0
S&P 500	55	-0.1	0.9
NIKKEI	43	-0.2	1.9

2013: The Bank of Japan doubles its inflation target to 2% and announces open-ended asset purchases for 2014 in the hope of ending deflation.

F

Sat 23

Sun 24   Full moon

E

Interim IG Group
Final Bankers Investment Trust, Unilever

COMPANY
NEWS

A – Diary page title

The Diary is a week-per-page format.

B – Weekly performance analysis (Sinclair Numbers)

These figures and arrow show the results of the analysis on the historic performance of the FTSE 100 during this week. The ten best and ten worst performing weeks are marked by the figures being in bold. [See the next page for further explanation and the Statistics section (page 164) for more detail and full data tables of FTSE 100 daily, weekly and monthly Sinclair Numbers.]

C – Week number

The week number within the year.

D – Social and sporting events

Notable social and sporting events, including public holidays, are included each day.

E – Daily performance analysis (Sinclair Numbers)

These figures and arrow show the results of the analysis on the historic performance of four world stock indices on this calendar day. The ten best and ten worst performing days for the FTSE 100 are marked by the figures being in bold. [See the next page for further explanation and the Statistics section (page 164) for more detail and full data tables of FTSE 100 daily, weekly and monthly Sinclair Numbers.]

F – Likely company announcements

A list of companies expected to announce interim or final results during the week. The list is provisional, using the date of announcements in previous years as a guide.

G – On this day

Events that happened on this calendar day in history.

H – Anniversaries

Significant anniversaries that occur on this day.

I – Financial events

Indicates days of financial and economic significance. For example, exchange holidays and important economic releases.

Abbreviations

FOMC – Federal Open Market Committee

MPC – Monetary Policy Committee

SINCLAIR NUMBERS – MARKET PERFORMANCE ANALYSIS

Sinclair Numbers

Beginning on page 164 you will find an explanation of the Almanac's unique analysis of the historic performance of four stock indices – the FTSE 100, FTSE 250, S&P 500 and Nikkei 225 – for each day, week and month of the year.

In order to understand the Diary pages, it will also be useful to read the following explanation of the Sinclair arrows.

Sinclair arrows

The figures for Up (%) are displayed for the respective days and weeks on the Diary pages employing the following arrow symbols:

Daily arrows

↑	the Positive (%) is over 75%
↗	the Positive (%) is 64% to 75%
→	the Positive (%) is 43% to 63%
↘	the Positive (%) is 31% to 42%
↓	the Positive (%) is under 31%

Weekly arrows

↑	the Positive (%) is over 70%
↗	the Positive (%) is 60% to 69%
→	the Positive (%) is 50% to 59%
↘	the Positive (%) is 40% to 49%
↓	the Positive (%) is under 40%

These daily ranges were calculated on the following basis: the average Positive (%) for all days in the year is 53% and the standard deviation is 11. Adding two standard deviations to the average gives 75, adding one standard deviation gives 64, subtracting one standard deviation gives 42 and subtracting two standard deviations gives 31. The weekly ranges have been modified slightly from these figures so as to present the data with more variation.

The top ten days and weeks – with the highest Positive (%) – and the weakest ten days and weeks – with the lowest Positive (%) – are highlighted in bold.

See the Statistics section, beginning on page 164, for full data tables of FTSE 100 Sinclair Numbers.

I.
DIARY

JANUARY MARKET

Market performance this month

From 1984 to 1999, January was easily the strongest month of the year, but the dot-com crash seems to have knocked the stuffing out of it. Since 2000, January has been the second weakest month of the year, with an average return in the month of -1.9%. For the period since 1984, January has a ranking of 8th among months.

As can be seen from the average January chart below, historically the euphoria of December (the strongest month of the year) carries over into the first few days of January as the market continues to climb for the first couple of days. But by around the fourth trading day the exhilaration is wearing off and the market then falls for the next two weeks – the second week of January has been the weakest week for the market in the whole year. Then, around the middle of the third week, the market has tended to rebound sharply.

The month is better for mid-cap and small-cap stocks. On average since 2000, the FTSE 250 has outperformed the FTSE 100 by 2.0 percentage points in January – the best outperformance (with February) of all months. Small caps do even better (called the *January Effect*), outperforming the FTSE 100 by an average 2.7 percentage points.

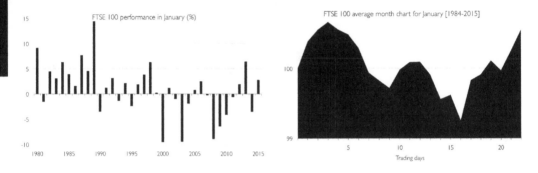

January summary

Market performance	Avg return: 0.4%		Positive: 58%	Ranking: 8th
Sector performance	*Strong* Construction & Materials, Electronic & Electrical Equipment, Equity Investment Instruments, Financial Services, General Industrials, Health Care Equipment & Services, Industrial Metals, Media, Software & Computer Services, Support Services		*Weak* Beverages, Food & Drug Retailers, Food Producers	
Share performance	*Strong* CSR, Computacenter, Electra Private Equity, Euromoney Institutional Investor, St James's Place		*Weak* Berkeley Group Holdings (The), Dairy Crest Group, GlaxoSmithKline, Tesco, Unilever	
Main features	Small-cap stocks often outperform large-cap stocks (January Effect) The FTSE 250 is particularly strong relative to the FTSE 100 FTSE 100 often underperforms the S&P 500 Strong month for silver First trading day average return: 0.38%; positive: 58% Last trading day average return: 0.14%; positive: 58% 11 Jan: start of the weakest week in the year 26 Jan: 4th strongest market day of the year			
Significant dates	01 Jan: LSE, NYSE, TSE, HKEX closed 08 Jan: US Nonfarm payroll report (anticipated) 13 Jan: Beige Book published; ECB Governing Council Meeting (non-monetary policy) 14 Jan: MPC interest rate announcement at 12 noon (anticipated) 19 Jan: Martin Luther King Day (US) – NYSE closed 21 Jan: ECB Governing Council Meeting (monetary policy) 26 Jan: Two-day FOMC meeting starts Don't forget: the last date to file your 2014/15 tax return online is 31 January			

DEC/JAN

Mon
28

1694: Queen Mary II of England dies after five years of joint rule with her husband, King William III.

FTSE 100	62	0.2	0.5
FTSE 250	85	0.3	0.3
S&P 500	58	0.0	0.6
NIKKEI	52	-0.1	1.3

Tue
29

1860: The HMS Warrior, Britain's first seagoing iron-hulled warship, is launched.

FTSE 100	76	0.4	1.1
FTSE 250	81	0.3	0.9
S&P 500	54	0.2	0.7
NIKKEI	67	0.2	0.5

Wed
30

2006: Former President of Iraq Saddam Hussein is executed.

FTSE 100	55	0.1	0.9
FTSE 250	67	0.3	0.6
S&P 500	62	0.2	0.7
NIKKEI	50	0.2	1.4

Thu
31

New Year's Eve
LSE closes early at 12h30; TSE closed

1600: The British East India Company is chartered.

FTSE 100	57	0.1	1.0
FTSE 250	74	0.1	0.6
S&P 500	68	0.2	0.7

Fri
1

New Year's Day
LSE, NYSE, TSE, HKEX closed
45th anniversary of the LSE flotation of Yule Catto & Co

1998: The European Central Bank is established.

Sat 2   Cricket: South Africa v England, 2nd Test (until 6th)

Sun 3

COMPANY
RESULTS

AN AVERAGE YEAR

What does an average year for the FTSE 100 look like?

The monthly summary pages in the diary section carry charts that show the average cumulative behaviour of the market day-by-day. These charts are produced by calculating the daily mean return for each day in the trading year over a specific period (in this case from 1984).

For example, if we take the index returns on the first trading of January for the 29 years since 1985, we can calculate the average return to be 0.38%. With this we can say that on average the FTSE 100 increased 0.38% on the first trading day of January over the period 1985-2015. We can repeat this process for the second trading day of January, and the third, etc., until we have a set of average returns for all the trading days of January.

With this set of returns we can plot an average index for the market in January (we will set the index to start at 100). For example, the average return for the market on the first trading day is 0.38%, and so the average index would close at 100.38 on the first trading day of January.

By concatenating the average index data for each month, we can create an average index chart for the whole year. This is shown in the following chart.

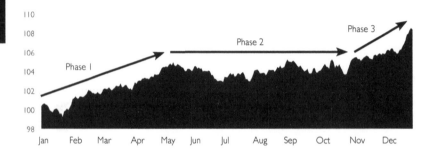

In the above chart we can see that, on average, the year appears to have three phases:

1. **Phase 1**: after a weak three weeks, the market is strong until May, then

2. **Phase 2**: from May to October the market is fairly flat, and then

3. **Phase 3**: it rises strongly in the final two months of the year.

This annual market behaviour profile concurs with what we already knew about the market, but it is illustrated simply and efficiently in this one chart.

Beyond simple mean returns, it is also useful to look at the volatility. The following chart shows the five-day moving average of the standard deviation of the daily returns throughout the year for the FTSE 100 from 1984 to 2015. In plain English: the chart plots the range of daily fluctuations of the FTSE 100 for each trading day throughout the year.

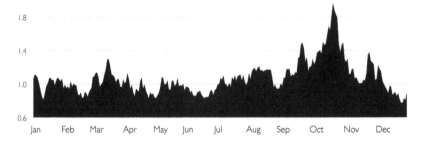

It can be seen that the volatility of daily returns is fairly even for the first eight months; it then starts to increase in September and peaks in October before trailing off for the remainder of the year. So, according to this study of daily returns throughout the year, October is indeed the most volatile month.

Mon

4

FTSE 100	57	0.2	1.3
FTSE 250	70	0.4	1.0
S&P 500	55	0.1	1.2
NIKKEI	67	0.4	1.8

1865: The New York Stock Exchange opens its first permanent headquarters at 10-12 Broad near Wall Street in New York City.

Tue

5

FTSE 100	43	-0.1	1.0
FTSE 250	57	0.1	0.9
S&P 500	67	0.1	1.0
NIKKEI	43	-0.1	1.2

1993: The oil tanker MV Braer runs aground on the coast of the Shetland Islands, spilling 84,700 tons of crude oil.

Epiphany (Twelfth Night)

Wed

6

FTSE 100	57	0.3	0.9
FTSE 250	82	0.4	0.6
S&P 500	60	0.1	0.8
NIKKEI	61	0.3	1.8

1974: In response to the oil crisis, daylight saving time commences nearly four months early in the United States.

Thu

7

FTSE 100	35	-0.2	0.9
FTSE 250	64	0.1	0.8
S&P 500	43	-0.1	0.9
NIKKEI	43	-0.2	0.9

1975: OPEC agrees to raise crude oil prices by 10%, which begins a time of world economic inflation.

Nonfarm payroll report (anticipated)

Fri

8

FTSE 100	43	0.0	0.8
FTSE 250	45	0.0	0.7
S&P 500	43	-0.3	1.3
NIKKEI	43	-0.6	1.6

1835: The United States national debt is zero – for the only time in history.

Sat 9

Sun 10 New moon

Final Elementis

COMPANY
RESULTS

THE JANUARY EFFECT

In 1976 an academic paper[1] found that equally weighted indices of all the stocks on the NYSE had significantly higher returns in January than in the other 11 months over the period 1904-1974. This indicated that small capitalisation stocks outperformed larger stocks in January. Over the following years many further papers were written confirming this finding. In 2006 a paper[2] tested this effect (now called the *January Effect*) on data from 1802 and found it was consistent up to the present time.

Does the January Effect work for UK stocks?

The following chart shows the cumulative performance from 1995 to mid-2015 of four stock indices in just the month of January. The four indices are:

1. FTSE 100

2. FTSE 250

3. FTSE SmallCap

4. FTSE Fledgling

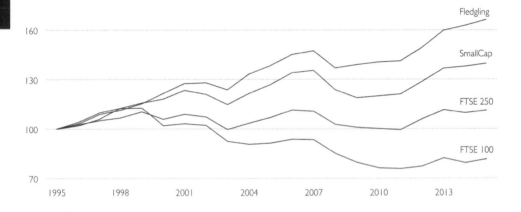

A portfolio investing in the FTSE 100 in just the Januaries since 1995 would have fallen 18.4% in value by mid-2015. By contrast, similar portfolios investing in the FTSE 250, SmallCap and Fledgling indices would have returned 11.2%, 39.5% and 66.1% respectively.

This suggests that not only does the January Effect hold for UK equities but also that, to a certain extent, performance in January is inversely proportional to company size (down to the level of companies in the Fledging index at least).

Other January Effects

In academic literature the term *January Effect* usually refers to the anomaly described above. However, the term is occasionally used in another couple of ways:

1. The returns in January indicate the returns for the rest of the year. If January market returns are positive, then returns for the whole year will be positive (and vice versa). This is sometimes called the *January Predictor* or *January Barometer*. A variant of this effect has it that returns for the whole year can be predicted by the direction of the market in just the first five days of the year.

2. In 1942 Sidney B. Wachtel wrote a paper, 'Certain Observations on Seasonal Movements in Stock Prices', in which he proposed that stocks rose in January as investors began buying again after the year-end tax-induced sell-off.

1. Rozeff and Kinney, 'Capital market seasonality: The case of stock returns', *Journal of Financial Economics* 3 (1976), 379-402.
2. Haug, M. and Hirschey, M., 'The January Effect', *Financial Analysts Journal* 62:5 (2006), 78-88.

Mon

11

Coming of Age Day (Japan) – TSE closed

FTSE 100	38	-0.2	0.7
FTSE 250	65	0.1	0.7
S&P 500	60	0.0	0.8

1569: The first English lottery is held.

Tue

12

FTSE 100	43	-0.3	0.7
FTSE 250	43	-0.1	0.7
S&P 500	51	-0.1	0.8
NIKKEI	50	-0.1	1.0

1998: Nineteen European nations agree to forbid human cloning.

Wed

13

Beige Book published
ECB Governing Council Meeting (non-monetary policy)

FTSE 100	41	-0.2	0.8
FTSE 250	55	0.0	0.8
S&P 500	43	0.0	0.6
NIKKEI	48	-0.3	1.7

2000: Bill Gates resigns as CEO of Microsoft.

Thu

14

MPC interest rate announcement at 12h00
Cricket: South Africa v England, 3rd Test (until 18th)

FTSE 100	57	-0.2	1.5
FTSE 250	45	-0.1	1.0
S&P 500	72	0.2	0.9
NIKKEI	65	0.4	1.3

1954: The Hudson Motor Car Company merges with Nash-Kelvinator Corporation forming the American Motors Corporation.

Fri

15

FTSE 100	65	0.3	1.2
FTSE 250	52	-0.1	1.0
S&P 500	64	0.1	0.9
NIKKEI	64	-0.1	2.1

1797: The first top hat is worn, by John Etherington of London.

Sat 16

Sun 17

COMPANY
RESULTS

US PRESIDENTIAL ELECTION YEARS

On page 156 it can be seen how closely correlated the UK and US markets are. As a result, the most important predictable event affecting the UK market in 2016 will be the US presidential election.

The 14 charts below show the performance of the FTSE All-Share index over the 12 months of a US election year. For example, the first chart shows the January-December performance of the UK market in 1960, the year John Kennedy was elected President of the United States. The dashed line in each chart indicates the date of the election.

Since 1948, the UK market has risen 9 times out of 17 (53%) in US election years, with an average annual return in those years of 5%. Generally, the UK market tends to rise in the few weeks leading up to the election.

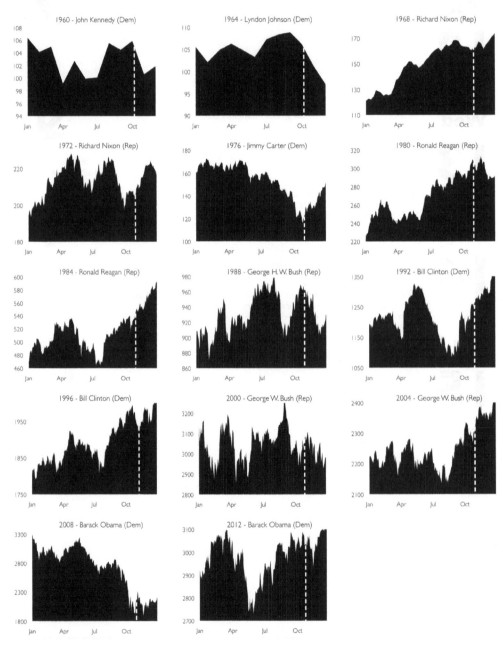

Mon

18

Tennis: Australian Open, Malbourne Park (until 31st)

FTSE 100	62	0.2	1.1
FTSE 250	70	0.2	0.7
S&P 500	59	0.1	0.6
NIKKEI	59	0.2	1.2

1980: Gold reaches $1,000 an ounce.

Tue

19

Martin Luther King Jr. Day (US) – NYSE closed
50th anniversary of Indira Ghandhi's election as Prime Minister of India

FTSE 100	43	-0.1	0.8
FTSE 250	57	0.3	1.0
NIKKEI	55	0.4	1.0

1992: IBM announces an annual loss of nearly $5bn.

Wed

20

World Economic Forum Annual Meeting, Davos-Klosters, Switzerland (until 23rd)

FTSE 100	36	-0.4	0.8
FTSE 250	41	-0.3	0.6
S&P 500	43	-0.3	1.1
NIKKEI	43	-0.3	1.3

1972: The UK Government signs the Treaty of Accession to the EEC.

Thu

21

ECB Governing Council Meeting (monetary policy)

FTSE 100	43	-0.3	1.3
FTSE 250	36	-0.4	1.0
S&P 500	50	0.0	1.0
NIKKEI	39	-0.2	1.4

1863: The City of Dublin leases part of the Cattle Market for 100,000 years.

Fri

22

Cricket: South Africa v England, 4th Test (until 26th)

FTSE 100	48	0.1	1.2
FTSE 250	50	0.1	1.0
S&P 500	55	-0.1	0.9
NIKKEI	43	-0.2	1.9

2013: The Bank of Japan doubles its inflation target to 2% and announces open-ended asset purchases for 2014 in the hope of ending deflation.

Sat 23

Sun 24   Full moon

Interim IG Group
Final Bankers Investment Trust, Unilever

COMPANY
RESULTS

WHICH INDEX SHOULD YOU BE TRACKING?

How do you calculate the average performance of a stock market?

This is a harder question to answer than it may at first seem. For example, the FTSE 100 is a measure of the aggregate market capitalisation of the 100 companies in the index. The problem is that the index is greatly influenced by the larger companies in it (the five largest companies in the index account for 24% of the total market capitalisation, while the 21 smallest companies in the index account for only 5% of total capitalisation).

So, how representative is the FTSE 100 of the average performance of the 100 component companies?

In the following chart, the columns show the proportion of FTSE 100 companies that outperformed the index in each year for the period 2005-2014 (left axis), and for reference the line plots the index price (right axis). For example, in 2005 55% of the FTSE 100 companies outperformed the index.

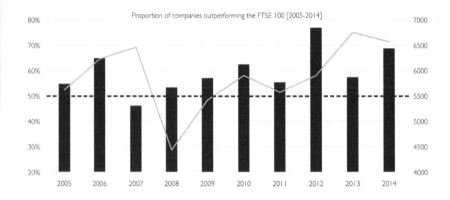

Proportion of companies outperforming the FTSE 100 [2005-2014]

As can be seen, there is quite a range of annual behaviour here: in 2007 46% of companies outperformed the index, while in 2012, fully 77% of companies outperformed. In other words, tracking the index in 2012 resulted in underperforming 77% of the individual stock performance. The only year where fewer than 50% of the 100 shares outperformed the index was 2007.

For comparison, the following is a similar chart, but this time for the FTSE 250.

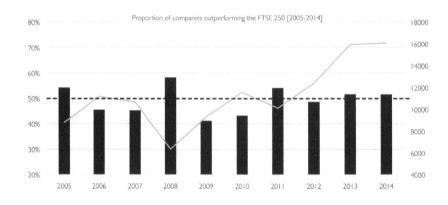

Proportion of companies outperforming the FTSE 250 [2005-2014]

As can be seen, for the mid-cap index the variability of the proportion of outperformers is far less than for the large-cap index, and the years of individual companies out- and underperformance are evenly matched.

Interestingly, in 2015 the indexing company FTSE Russell introduced a new FTSE 100 Semi Annual Equally Weighted Index (and Deutsche Bank launched an ETF tracking this index, ticker: XFEW). If the above trend of FTSE 100 behaviour continues, we could expect the equally-weighted index to outperform the market-capitalisation weighted index.

Mon

25

Burns Night
70th anniversary of the LSE flotation of Weir Group

FTSE 100	38	-0.2	0.7
FTSE 250	40	-0.1	0.6
S&P 500	59	0.1	0.7
NIKKEI	68	0.6	1.2

1900: Newcastle Badminton Club, the world's oldest, is formed in England.

Tue

26

Two-day FOMC meeting starts
Australia Day

FTSE 100	**81**	**0.7**	**1.0**
FTSE 250	62	0.4	0.8
S&P 500	45	0.1	0.6
NIKKEI	50	0.3	1.0

1995: Cadbury Schweppes takes over Dr. Pepper/Seven-Up.

Wed

27

FTSE 100	45	0.1	1.2
FTSE 250	50	0.1	1.0
S&P 500	52	0.2	0.8
NIKKEI	52	0.2	1.6

1606: The trial of Guy Fawkes and his fellow conspirators begins. They are executed on 31 January.

Thu

28

FTSE 100	61	0.1	1.0
FTSE 250	50	0.2	0.9
S&P 500	61	0.1	1.1
NIKKEI	52	0.2	1.4

1998: Michelangelo's *Christ and the Woman of Samaria* sells for $7.4m.

Fri

29

FTSE 100	39	-0.2	0.9
FTSE 250	50	-0.1	1.0
S&P 500	55	0.1	1.0
NIKKEI	57	0.3	1.4

Sat 30

Sun 31   Deadline for self-assessment tax return for 2014/15 tax year

Interim Diageo, PZ Cussons, Rank Group, Renishaw
Final Aberforth Smaller Companies Trust, Crest Nicholson, Royal Dutch Shell

COMPANY
RESULTS

FEBRUARY MARKET

Market performance this month

February is the third strongest month; but it hasn't always been so strong, as just seven years ago it was ranked ninth. The market has risen in February in 61% of all years, with an average return of 1.1%. In fact, the market has only fallen twice in February in the last 13 years – and is currently on a six-year winning streak (the longest for any month). The average chart shows that the market tends to rise for the first two-and-a-half weeks and then drifts lower for the rest of the month.

With January, February is the best month for mid-cap stocks relative to the large caps. Since 2000, on average the FTSE 250 has outperformed the FTSE 100 by 1.7 percentage points in this month.

This is one of the four months that the FTSE 100 has historically outperformed the S&P 500, although the outperformance is attenuated once currency is taken into account as GBPUSD is historically weak in February.

This is the busiest month for FTSE 100 results announcements – 39 companies announce their prelims in February (as do 56 FTSE 250 companies).

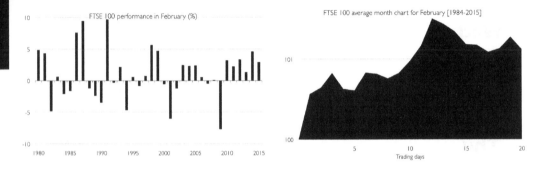

FTSE 100 performance in February (%)

FTSE 100 average month chart for February [1984-2015]

February summary

Market performance	Avg return: 1.1%		Positive: 61%	Ranking: 3rd
Sector performance	*Strong* Chemicals, Construction & Materials, General Retailers, Household Goods, Mining, Oil Equipment, Services & Distribution		*Weak* Electronic & Electrical Equipment, Financial Services, Fixed Line Telecommunications, Mobile Telecommunications, Technology Hardware & Equipment	
Share performance	*Strong* Bunzl, Croda International, Electra Private Equity, Fidessa Group, Jardine Lloyd Thompson Group		*Weak* AstraZeneca, Carnival, Vodafone Group	
Main features	The FTSE 250 is particularly strong relative to the FTSE 100 in this month GBPUSD historically weak this month Busiest month for FTSE 250 preliminary results announcements Strong month for gold Strong month for silver First trading day average return: 0.56%; positive: 58% (year's 3rd strongest) Last trading day average return: -0.06%; positive: 42% (year's 3rd weakest) 02 Feb: 10th strongest market day of the year 15 Feb: start of the 4th strongest week in the year 17 Feb: 7th strongest market day of the year			
Significant dates	03 Feb: ECB Governing Council Meeting (non-monetary policy) 04 Feb: MPC interest rate announcement at 12 noon (anticipated) 05 Feb: US Nonfarm payroll report (anticipated) 08 Feb: Chinese New Year (Year of the Monkey) 11 Feb: MSCI Quarterly Index Review Announcement date 16 Feb: Presidents' Day (US) – NYSE closed 17 Feb: ECB Governing Council Meeting (non-monetary policy)			

Mon
1

Imbolc

FTSE 100	67	0.7	1.0
FTSE 250	85	0.8	0.9
S&P 500	61	0.1	0.8
NIKKEI	55	-0.1	0.7

1984: The half penny coin ceases to be legal tender.

Tue
2

FTSE 100	76	0.3	0.8
FTSE 250	81	0.3	1.0
S&P 500	64	0.2	0.7
NIKKEI	55	0.2	0.9

1989: The Sky Television Satellite Service is launched by Rupert Murdoch's News International.

Wed
3

ECB Governing Council Meeting (non-monetary policy)

FTSE 100	50	0.3	1.1
FTSE 250	59	0.3	0.7
S&P 500	64	0.2	0.8
NIKKEI	35	-0.2	0.9

1637: Tulip mania collapses in the United Provinces (the Netherlands) as sellers can no longer find buyers for their bulb contracts.

Thu
4

MPC interest rate announcement at 12h00

FTSE 100	39	-0.3	1.0
FTSE 250	50	0.1	0.9
S&P 500	43	-0.2	1.0
NIKKEI	48	0.1	1.4

2003: Yugoslavia is formerly dissolved and replaced with a union of Serbia and Montenegro.

Fri
5

Nonfarm payroll report (anticipated)

FTSE 100	52	-0.1	1.2
FTSE 250	64	-0.1	1.0
S&P 500	45	-0.1	0.9
NIKKEI	30	-0.5	1.2

1982: Pioneering budget airline Laker Airways collapses, owing £270 million to banks and other creditors.

Sat 6 — Rugby: Six Nations (until 19th March)

Sun 7 — American football: Superbowl 50, Levi's Stadium, Santa Clara

---

Interim Hargreaves Lansdown, Sky
Final AstraZeneca, Beazley, BG Group, BP, GlaxoSmithKline, Ocado Group, Smith & Nephew, St Modwen Properties

COMPANY
RESULTS

CHINESE CALENDAR AND THE STOCK MARKET

When we look at the annual performance of the stock market we naturally take our start and end points as 1 January and 31 December. For example, a long-term chart of an index will normally plot the index values on 31 December for each year.

But using different start and end points may be interesting. While the overall performance of the market will obviously not change, the path to the final point may show up differently, and thus possibly reveal a pattern of behaviour not previously noticed.

The start of the Chinese Year moves around (on the Western calendar) from year to year, but always falls between 21 January and 21 February. The calculation of the actual date of the Chinese New Year is sinologically complex. For example:

> Rule 5: In a leap suì, the first month that does not contain a zhongqì is the leap month, rùnyuè. The leap month takes the same number as the previous month.

That quote comes from a 52-page academic paper, *The Mathematics of the Chinese Calendar*.[1] However, we shall skip lightly over such details and focus on a key aspect of the Chinese calendar, which is the sexagenary cycle. This is a combination of ten heavenly stems and the 12 earthly branches. The branches are often associated with the sequence of 12 animals. (At last – the animals!) Cutting to the chase, the Chinese calendar encompasses a 12-year cycle where each year is associated with an animal.

Can we detect any significant behavioural patterns in the stock market correlated with the sexagenary cycle? In other words, are there monkey years in the market?

The following chart plots the average performance of the stock market[2] for each animal year since 1950. For example, Ox years started in 1961, 1973, 1985, 1997 and 2009; and the average performance of the market in those (Chinese) years was +14.0%.

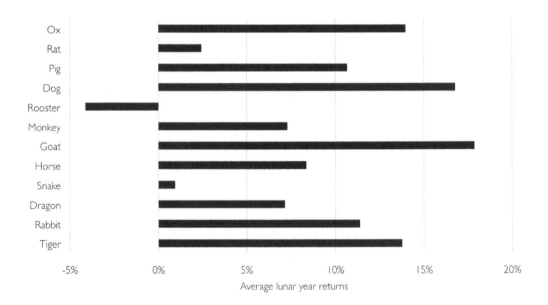

Average lunar year returns

As can be seen, the best performing market animals have been the goat and dog. And, coincidentally (or, is it?), the worst performing animals have been the rooster (perhaps a mistranslation for turkey?) and snake.

The Chinese New Year starting on 8 February is the Year of the Monkey, and in monkey years the S&P 500 has had an average return of 7.3%.

1. Aslaksen, H., *The Mathematics of the Chinese Calendar*, www.math.nus.edu.sg/aslaksen (2010).
2. The S&P 500 index was used for this study. The correlation between the US and UK markets is so high that the US index is a sufficient proxy for the UK market for the purposes here.

Mon 8

Chinese New Year (Year of the Monkey) – HKEX closed
New moon

FTSE 100	57	0.2	0.9
FTSE 250	65	0.0	0.9
S&P 500	48	-0.1	0.8
NIKKEI	59	-0.1	1.1

2013: India announces a bank for women in its national budget. The bank will employ women and lend mostly to women.

Tue 9

HKEX closed

FTSE 100	52	0.0	0.7
FTSE 250	57	0.2	0.7
S&P 500	40	-0.3	0.9
NIKKEI	36	-0.2	1.0

2000: Sage shares reach an all-time high of 930.5, having risen 77 times in the previous five years. (Two years later the price is below 100.)

Wed 10

HKEX closed
Shrove Tuesday (Pancake Day)
Fat Tuesday (Mardi Gras)

FTSE 100	36	-0.3	0.8
FTSE 250	45	-0.2	0.7
S&P 500	52	0.0	1.0
NIKKEI	59	0.1	0.8

2004: Coca-Cola launches a new bottled water called Dasani in the UK. It is soon revealed that it is just tap water.

Thu 11

National Foundation Day (Japan) – TSE closed
MSCI quarterly index review (announcement date)
Ash Wednesday (Lent begins)
35th anniversary of the LSE flotation of BAE Systems

FTSE 100	61	0.4	0.9
FTSE 250	77	0.3	0.6
S&P 500	53	0.1	0.9

1990: Nelson Mandela is freed.

Fri 12

Vasant Panchami

FTSE 100	45	-0.1	1.1
FTSE 250	59	0.1	0.8
S&P 500	53	0.1	0.7
NIKKEI	79	0.5	1.3

1958: The first Trans-Atlantic passenger jetliner service begins with flights between London and New York on the BOAC Comet Jet Airliner.

Sat 13

Sun 14   St Valentine's Day

Interim Dunelm Group, Redrow
Final ARM, Indivior, Informa, Lancashire, Millennium & Copthorne Hotels, Morgan Advanced Materials, Randgold Resources, Reckitt Benckiser, Rio Tinto, Shire, Telecity Group, Tullow Oil

COMPANY RESULTS

THE FTSE 100/250 MONTHLY SWITCHING STRATEGY

Analysis of the historic data shows that although the FTSE 250 has greatly outperformed the FTSE 100 in the long term (since 2000 the FTSE 100 has fallen 3% compared with an increase of 174% for the FTSE 250), there are certain months for which the large-cap index on average outperforms the mid-cap index.

The previous edition of the Almanac presented a strategy that exploited this feature; this page updates the performance of the strategy in the last year.

The following chart shows the average outperformance of the FTSE 100 over the FTSE 250 by month for the period 2000-2015. For example, on average the FTSE 100 has outperformed the FTSE 250 by -2.0 percentage points in January since year 2000.

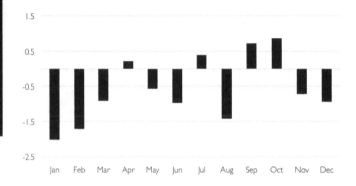

As can be seen, there are only two months, September and October, in which the FTSE 100 convincingly outperforms the FTSE 250.

The FTSE 100/FTSE 250 monthly switching strategy

The above results suggest a strategy of investing in the FTSE 250 for the year but switching into the FTSE 100 for just the two-month period September-October. In other words, the portfolio would be invested in the FTSE 250 from January to August, at the end of August it switches out of the FTSE 250 and into the FTSE 100 for two months, then back into the FTSE 250 until the end of August the following year.

The following chart shows the result of operating such a strategy from 2000. For comparison, the chart also includes the portfolio returns from continuous investments in the base FTSE 100 and FTSE 250. All the data series have been rebased to start at 100.

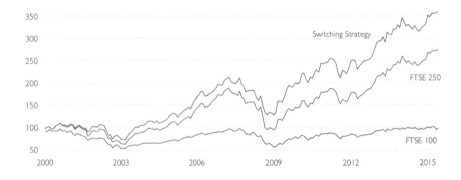

The result: from 2000 to 2015 the FTSE 100 portfolio would have grown -3% and the FTSE 250 174%, but the FTSE 100/FTSE 250 monthly switching portfolio would have increased 260%.

Switching between the indices each year would have incurred transaction costs, but these would have been relatively negligible relative to the overall returns.

Mon
15

Nirvana Day
10th anniversary of the LSE flotation of QinetiQ Group

FTSE 100	62	0.1	0.6
FTSE 250	60	0.0	0.6
S&P 500	54	0.1	0.6
NIKKEI	55	0.0	1.0

1971: Decimal currency is launched in the UK.

Tue
16

Washington's Birthday (Presidents' Day) – NYSE closed

FTSE 100	43	0.1	1.0
FTSE 250	57	0.1	0.6
NIKKEI	41	0.0	0.7

1937: DuPont Corp patents nylon, which has been developed by employee Wallace H. Carothers.

Wed
17

ECB Governing Council Meeting (non-monetary policy)

FTSE 100	**77**	**0.4**	**0.9**
FTSE 250	82	0.3	0.9
S&P 500	44	-0.1	1.0
NIKKEI	74	0.4	1.0

2008: Kosovo declares independence from Serbia.

Thu
18

FTSE 100	43	0.1	0.7
FTSE 250	68	0.4	0.7
S&P 500	54	0.1	0.8
NIKKEI	55	0.3	1.4

2014: Shares of automobile manufacturer Tesla rise above $200 after reports that Apple executives have met with Tesla CEO Elon Musk, potentially to discuss an acquisition.

Fri
19

FTSE 100	48	0.0	1.0
FTSE 250	59	0.1	0.6
S&P 500	46	-0.1	0.8
NIKKEI	52	-0.1	0.9

2004: Former Enron chief executive Jeffrey Skilling is charged with fraud and insider trading.

Sat 20

Sun 21

Interim City of London Investment Trust, Galliford Try, Go-Ahead Group, Petra Diamonds
Final Acacia Mining, Aldermore Group, Anglo American, BAE Systems, Centrica, Coca-Cola HBC AG, Fidessa Group, Hammerson, InterContinental Hotels, Rathbone Brothers, Rexam, Riverstone Energy, Rolls-Royce Group, Segro, Wood Group (John)

COMPANY
RESULTS

TUESDAY REVERSES MONDAY

Some traders believe that Tuesday's market reverses Monday's. In other words, if the market rises on Monday it will fall the following day, and vice versa.

Is this true?

The first chart on the right shows the change in the FTSE 100 on:

1. Tuesdays when the market has **risen** the previous day (*Monday up*), and

2. Tuesdays when market has **fallen** the previous day (*Monday down*).

The data analysed covers two periods: 1984-2015 and 2000-2015.

For example, in the period 2000-2015, the market fell on average 0.07% on Tuesdays following a Monday increase.

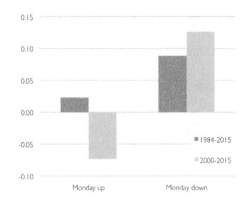

As can be seen, for the longer period of 1984-2014 the theory that Tuesday reverses Monday does not fully hold. For this period, when the market falls on Monday the return is positive the next day (which is fine), but when the market rises on Monday the average Tuesday returns are positive as well (i.e. no reversal).

However, since 2000 the theory appears to be working rather well. Tuesday returns have on average been the reverse of Monday. In fact, when the market is down on Monday, the average returns the following day have been five times greater than the average returns on all days since 2000.

How can this be exploited?

The next chart on the right shows the value of three portfolios since 2000 (all starting with a value of 100):

1. **Portfolio 1**: tracks the FTSE 100

2. **Portfolio 2**: if the market is down on Monday this portfolio goes long the market at the end of Monday and closes the position at the end of Tuesday (for four days out of five the portfolio is in cash)

3. **Portfolio 3**: similar to the above, with the addition that it also goes short the market on Tuesday if Monday was up

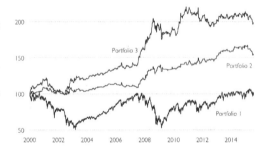

By mid-2015 the Portfolio 1 value would be 101, Portfolio 2 would be worth 155 and Portfolio 3 would be worth 198. As can be seen, the profitability of the strategies has dipped in the past year. However, it's interesting to look at the final chart, which suggests a refinement of the strategy. This replicates the first chart, but adds a filter to only consider Tuesday returns following Monday moves that have been greater than 1 standard deviation from the average.

The Tuesday reverses Monday effect would appear to be far stronger with this filter applied (i.e. only considering large Monday moves).

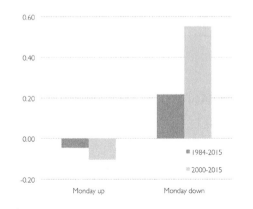

Mon
22

Full moon

→

FTSE 100	43	-0.1	0.6
FTSE 250	60	-0.1	0.6
S&P 500	45	0.0	1.0
NIKKEI	50	0.1	1.0

2013: The UK's bond credit rating is downgraded for the first time in history. Moody's changes the rating from AAA to AA1.

Tue
23

→

FTSE 100	43	-0.2	0.9
FTSE 250	52	-0.1	0.6
S&P 500	41	-0.1	0.7
NIKKEI	50	0.1	1.1

1955: First meeting of the Southeast Asia Treaty Organization (SEATO).

Wed
24

→

FTSE 100	45	0.0	0.9
FTSE 250	59	0.1	0.6
S&P 500	57	0.2	1.0
NIKKEI	50	-0.4	1.1

2008: The world's first biofuel-powered commercial aircraft touches down in Amsterdam, having flown from Heathrow.

Thu
25

FTSE 100	65	0.3	1.1
FTSE 250	64	0.4	0.9
S&P 500	50	0.0	0.8
NIKKEI	83	0.7	1.2

1920: It is found that sugar can be obtained from the branches of Douglas Fir trees in British Columbia. The value of the sugar from this tree is $66 per pound (0.5kg).

Fri
26

→

FTSE 100	57	0.2	0.8
FTSE 250	59	0.2	0.6
S&P 500	60	0.1	0.8
NIKKEI	48	-0.1	1.3

1797: The Bank of England issues the first one-pound and two-pound notes.

Sat 27   International Polar Bear Day

Sun 28   Football: League Cup Final, Wembley

COMPANY RESULTS

Interim Ashmore Group, Barratt Developments, BHP Billiton, Dechra Pharmaceuticals, Genesis Emerging, Markets Fund, Genus, Hays, JPMorgan Emerging Markets Inv Trust, Just Retirement Group, Kier Group

Final Bank of Georgia, Barclays, Bodycote, Bovis Homes Group, British American Tobacco, Bunzl, Capita, Capital & Counties Properties, COLT Group SA, Countrywide, CRH, Croda International, Derwent London, Domino's Pizza, Drax Group, Essentra, GKN, Henderson Group, Howden Joinery Group, HSBC, International Personal Finance, Interserve, Jupiter Fund Management, KAZ Minerals, Kennedy Wilson Europe Real Estate, Ladbrokes, Man Group, Meggitt, Merlin Entertainments, Mondi, National Express, NMC Health, Persimmon, Petrofac, Playtech, Premier Oil, Provident Financial, RELX, Rightmove, Royal Bank of Scotland Group, RSA Insurance Group, St James's Place, Standard Life, Synthomer, Temple Bar Investment Trust, Tritax Big Box REIT, UNITE Group, Weir Group

MARCH MARKET

Market performance this month

March ranks 9th in performance of all months of the year. Since 1984, the market has had an average return of 0.4% in this month. Returns are positive in 55% of all years.

As can be seen in the accompanying average month chart, the general trend for the market in March is to rise for the first three weeks and then fall back in the final week – the last week of March has historically been one of the weakest weeks for the market in the whole year.

March marks the end of the three-month period when mid-cap stocks strongly outperform large caps: since 1986 the FTSE 250 has outperformed the FTSE 100 by an average of 0.8 percentage points this month. In fact, the mid-cap index has outperformed the large cap index in every March for the past ten years.

This is another busy month for company announcements: it's the busiest in the year for FTSE 250 companies, with 75 companies announcing their prelims this month (along with 22 FTSE 100 companies).

Aside from equities, March has been historically strong for oil and weak for gold.

FTSE 100 performance in March (%)

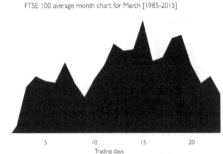
FTSE 100 average month chart for March [1985-2015]

March summary

Market performance	Avg return: 0.4%	Positive: 55%	Ranking: 9th
Sector performance	*Strong* Aerospace & Defense, Financial Services, General Industrials, General Retailers, Industrial Engineering, Oil & Gas Producers, Oil Equipment, Services & Distribution	*Weak* Gas, Water & Multiutilities, Health Care Equipment & Services, Nonlife Insurance	
Share performance	*Strong* Berendsen, Cobham, Intertek Group, Restaurant Group (The), Victrex	*Weak* HSBC Holdings, PZ Cussons, Renishaw, Royal Bank of Scotland Group (The), Smiths Group	
Main features	The FTSE 250 is particularly strong relative to the FTSE 100 in this month Market abnormally strong on day before and day after Easter holiday Busiest month for FTSE 250 preliminary results announcements Weak month for gold Strong month for oil First trading day average return: -0.06%; positive: 55% (2nd weakest in year) Last trading day average return: 0.05%; positive: 48% 21 Mar: start of the 5th weakest week in the year		
Significant dates	02 Mar: FTSE 100 review announced 04 Mar: US Nonfarm payroll report (anticipated) 10 Mar: ECB Governing Council Meeting (monetary policy) 15 Mar: Two-day FOMC meeting starts 16 Mar: Chancellor's Budget (anticipated) 17 Mar: MPC interest rate announcement at 12 noon (anticipated) 18 Mar: Triple Witching 25 Mar: Good Friday, LSE, NYSE closed 28 Mar: Easter Monday, LSE closed		

Mon
29

2012: The Tokyo Skytree construction is completed, making it the tallest tower in the world (634m), and the second tallest man-made structure, after the Burj Khalifa in Dubai.

FTSE 100	40	-0.1	1.2
FTSE 250	25	-0.4	0.6
S&P 500	42	0.0	1.2
NIKKEI	67	0.0	1.2

Tue
1

St David's Day
MSCI quarterly index review (effective date)

FTSE 100	67	0.3	1.0
FTSE 250	75	0.4	0.8
S&P 500	65	0.3	0.7
NIKKEI	50	-0.2	1.7

1977: Bank of America adopts the name VISA for its credit cards.

Wed
2

FTSE 100 quarterly review
Beige Book published

FTSE 100	48	-0.1	1.3
FTSE 250	62	0.1	0.9
S&P 500	57	0.0	0.9
NIKKEI	59	-0.2	1.7

1995: British trader Nick Leeson is arrested following the collapse of Barings Bank.

Thu
3

FTSE 100	50	0.0	1.0
FTSE 250	59	0.1	0.7
S&P 500	67	0.1	0.7
NIKKEI	36	-0.3	1.3

1865: The opening of the Hongkong and Shanghai Banking Corporation, the founding member of the HSBC Group.

Fri
4

Nonfarm payroll report (anticipated)

FTSE 100	61	0.4	1.1
FTSE 250	77	0.5	1.0
S&P 500	54	0.2	0.9
NIKKEI	74	0.5	1.3

1957: The S&P 500 is introduced, replacing the S&P 90.

Sat 5

Sun 6   Mother's Day

COMPANY RESULTS

Final Alent, Amlin, BBA Aviation, Berendsen, Carillion, CLS, Dignity, Direct Line Insurance Group, Fisher (James) & Sons, Foreign & Colonial Investment Trust, Fresnillo, Glencore, Greggs, Hellermann Tyton Group, Hiscox, IMI, International Consolidated Airlines, Intertek Group, Intu Properties, ITV, Jardine Lloyd Thompson, Keller Group, Laird, Legal & General, Lloyds Banking Group, Melrose Industries, Moneysupermarket.com, Old Mutual, Pace, Pearson, Regus, Rentokil Initial, Restaurant Group, RIT Capital Partners, Rotork, Senior, Spectris, Standard Chartered, Taylor Wimpey, Travis Perkins, Tullett Prebon, UBM, Ultra Electronics, Vesuvius, William Hill, Witan Investment Trust, Woodford Patient Capital Trust

FTSE 100 REVIEWS – COMPANIES JOINING THE INDEX

The charts below show the share prices of nine companies that have recently joined the FTSE 100. The time period for each chart is six months, starting from three months before the company joined the index. The vertical line in each chart indicates the announcement date of the company joining the index.

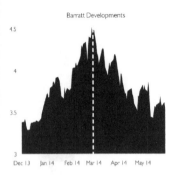

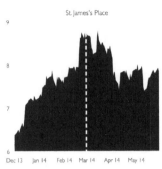

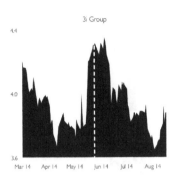

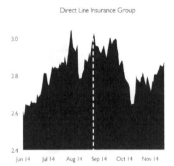

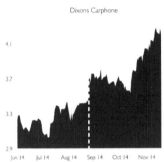

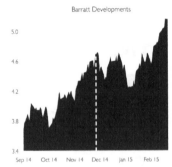

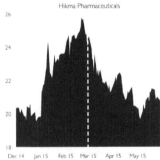

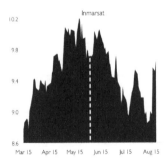

Observation

It can be seen that in most cases the share price rises for several weeks before the announcement of the company joining the FTSE 100. While afterwards the price is often flat or falls back again.

Mon
7

100th anniversary of the founding of German automobile company BMW in Munich

FTSE 100	45	-0.2	0.8
FTSE 250	57	-0.1	0.9
S&P 500	48	-0.2	0.7
NIKKEI	48	-0.3	1.2

1997: Steven Hoffen – the former chief of Towers Financial Corps who sold "worthless" Tower-backed bonds to investors – is given a 20-year jail sentence and ordered to pay out $462m in compensation.

Tue
8

Maha Shivaratri
International Women's Day

FTSE 100	67	0.1	0.7
FTSE 250	55	0.1	0.8
S&P 500	61	0.1	0.9
NIKKEI	50	0.5	1.6

1817: The New York Stock Exchange is founded.

Wed
9

New moon
Total solar eclipse (Australia and Southeast Asia)

FTSE 100	43	0.0	0.7
FTSE 250	43	0.0	0.5
S&P 500	48	0.0	0.8
NIKKEI	59	0.3	1.0

1933: President Franklin D. Roosevelt submits the Emergency Banking Act to Congress, the first of his New Deal policies.

Thu
10

ECB Governing Council Meeting (monetary policy)

FTSE 100	64	0.2	1.4
FTSE 250	59	0.1	1.1
S&P 500	59	0.1	1.3
NIKKEI	50	-0.2	1.0

1876: The first telephone call is made, when Alexander Graham Bell phones Thomas Watson.

Fri
11

Cricket: World Twenty20, India (until 3rd April)

FTSE 100	48	-0.2	0.9
FTSE 250	59	0.0	1.0
S&P 500	57	0.2	0.9
NIKKEI	65	0.0	1.3

1955: The World Bank Institute is established with the support of the Rockefeller and Ford Foundations.

Sat 12

Sun 13

COMPANY RESULTS

Interim Close Brothers Group
Final Admiral Group, Aggreko, Alliance Trust, Aviva, Cairn Energy, Clarkson, Cobham, CSR, esure Group, G4S, Grafton Group, Hansteen, Hunting, Inchcape, Inmarsat, IP Group, London Stock Exchange, Murray International Trust, Prudential, Schroders, Shawbrook Group, Spirax-Sarco Engineering, Virgin Money UK, WPP Group

BUDGET DAY

How do the markets behave on the days around Budget day?

The UK Budget used to be in April, after the start of the fiscal year, but these days it is in March, before the end of the fiscal year. The Chancellor of the Exchequer is expected to give his Budget to Parliament next week, on the 23rd.

Equities

The following chart shows the daily returns since 2005 for the FTSE 100 for the three days around Budget day:

1. **B(-1)**: the day before the Budget

2. **B(0)**: Budget day

3. **B(+1)**: the day after the Budget

For example, in 2005 the Budget was on 16 March, the day before the Budget the FTSE 100 rose 0.5%, on Budget day the index fell 1.3%, and on the day after the index fell 0.3%.

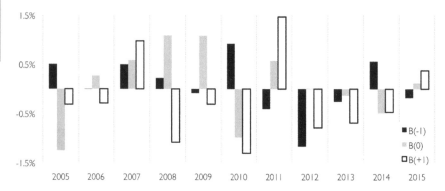

Equities, currencies, gilts

The following chart shows the average daily returns for the three days around the Budget for the FTSE 100, GBPUSD and the 8% Treasury 2021 gilt over the period 2005-2015.

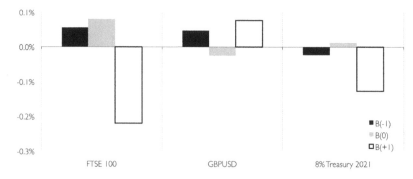

On average since 2005, the equity market has seen mildly positive daily returns on the day before the Budget and on Budget day itself. But the most significant observation is that equities have on average been very weak on the day after the Budget: the average return for the day after the budget is -0.22%.

Sterling tends to be weak on Budget day, but mildly positive either side of it.

Gilts move little on the first two days, but tend to be weak on the day after the Budget.

Mon
14

FTSE 100	59	0.3	1.2
FTSE 250	57	0.0	1.0
S&P 500	48	-0.1	0.9
NIKKEI	52	-0.3	1.8

1900: The Gold Standard Act is ratified, placing the US on the gold standard.

Tue
15

Two-day FOMC meeting starts

FTSE 100	48	0.1	1.0
FTSE 250	55	0.0	1.0
S&P 500	67	0.2	0.7
NIKKEI	82	0.3	2.5

1985: The first Internet domain name is registered (symbolics.com).

Wed
16

UK Chancellor's Budget (anticipated)
ECB Governing Council Meeting (non-monetary policy)

FTSE 100	48	0.1	1.2
FTSE 250	60	0.1	0.7
S&P 500	63	0.3	1.0
NIKKEI	45	0.2	1.6

2000: The DJIA makes the biggest one-day gain in its history, with a 499.19 point increase (almost 5%).

Thu
17

St Patrick's Day
MPC interest rate announcement at 12h00
ECB General Council Meeting

FTSE 100	59	0.0	1.3
FTSE 250	68	0.1	1.0
S&P 500	62	0.2	1.0
NIKKEI	64	0.3	1.4

1975: The Chicago, Rock Island and Pacific railroad enters its third and final bankruptcy.

Fri
18

Triple Witching

FTSE 100	52	0.2	1.1
FTSE 250	55	0.3	0.8
S&P 500	57	0.3	0.9
NIKKEI	65	0.2	1.6

1850: American Express is founded.

Sat 19

Sun 20   Palm Sunday; March equinox; 65th anniversary of the LSE flotation of British Land Co

Interim Smiths Group, Wetherspoon (JD)
Final Antofagasta, Bwin.Party Digital Entertainment, Cineworld Group, Computacenter, Fidelity European Values, Foxtons, Hikma Pharmaceuticals, Just Eat, Michael Page International, Morrison (Wm) Supermarkets, OneSavings Bank, Phoenix Group, Serco Group, SIG

COMPANY
RESULTS

HOLIDAYS AND THE MARKET

How does the market behave around holidays?

In 1990, an academic paper[1] was published with the finding that the trading day prior to holidays in the US market had an average return 14 times greater than the average for the other days in the year. This, and other papers, found that the day immediately before holidays had the highest returns (in the period around holidays), with the third day before the holidays having the next highest return, while the day following the holiday had negative returns.

Does such a holiday effect exist in the UK market?

The following charts show the results of research on the daily returns of the FTSE 100 around holidays. The three trading days immediately prior to holidays, H(-3) to H(-1), and the three trading days after holidays, H(+1) to H(+3) were analysed. A holiday was defined as a minimum three-day period with no trading. The bars in the charts show the average return for each of the six days around holidays. The chart on the left is for the period 1984-2015 and the chart on the right is for the period 2000-2015.

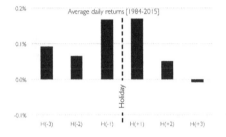

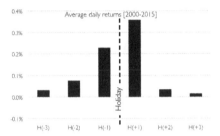

From the chart on the left we can see that, as with the US studies, H(-3) and H(-1) were strong during the holiday periods. Although, unlike the US studies, the day after a holiday, H(+1), was also found to be strong – this day has an average return of 0.17% (six times greater than the average return for all days in the year).

Looking at the chart on the right it can be seen that the UK holiday effect has changed slightly in recent years. In the last ten years or so the market has still been significantly strong on the day immediately before holidays and the day after holidays, but weaker on the third day before holidays.

As Easter is upon us, let's look specifically at the market around the Easter holiday.

Easter

As above, the following charts analyse the market behaviour around holidays, but this time the data is restricted to just Easter holidays.

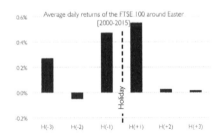

Looking at the chart on the left, the general profile of behaviour around Easter can be seen to be similar to that for all holidays. The main difference is that the average returns for the days immediately before and after Easter are significantly higher than for all holidays. For example, the average return for H(-1) is 0.4% (13 times greater than the average return for all days in the year).

The chart on the right shows that the behaviour of the market around Easter has not changed significantly in recent years.

1. Ariel, R. A., 'High stock returns before holidays: Existence and evidence on possible causes', *Journal of Finance* 45:5 (1990), 1611-1626.

Mon

21

TSE closed
20th anniversary of the LSE flotation of Perpetual Income & Growth Investment Trust

FTSE 100	48	0.0	1.0
FTSE 250	55	0.1	0.8
S&P 500	37	-0.1	0.9

2006: Twitter is created by Jack Dorsey in San Francisco, California.

Tue

22

FTSE 100	43	-0.4	1.1
FTSE 250	35	-0.4	0.8
S&P 500	48	0.0	0.6
NIKKEI	40	-0.3	1.6

2003: Niagara Falls runs out of water because of a drought.

Wed

23

Holi
Full moon
Penumbral lunar eclipse (Australia and Asia)

FTSE 100	48	0.1	0.9
FTSE 250	62	0.0	0.7
S&P 500	59	0.3	1.3
NIKKEI	43	0.0	1.3

1839: The first recorded printed use of "OK" (oll korrect) occurs in Boston's *Morning Post*.

Thu

24

Maundy Thursday

FTSE 100	45	-0.2	1.3
FTSE 250	55	0.0	0.9
S&P 500	48	-0.2	1.1
NIKKEI	45	0.0	1.5

1906: A census of the British Empire shows Great Britain rules one-fifth of the world.

Fri

25

Good Friday
LSE, NYSE, HKEX closed

NIKKEI	65	0.5	1.2

1947: John D. Rockefeller III presents a cheque for $8.5m to the United Nations for the purchase of land for the site of the UN Center.

Sat 26

Sun 27   Easter Sunday; BST begins (clocks go forward); Rowing: Cambridge v Oxford Boat Race

Interim Bellway, Wolseley
Final Balfour Beatty, Barr (AG), BH Macro, Card Factory, Centamin, Jimmy Choo, John Laing Group, John Laing Infrastructure Fund, Next, Nostrum Oil & Gas, Ophir Energy, Premier Farnell, Savills, Spire Healthcare Group, SVG Capital, Ted Baker

COMPANY

RESULTS

SILVER

On 27 March 1980 – 36 years ago last Sunday – the silver market collapsed. Panic swept the financial markets and there was a fear that several brokerage firms may go bust. To avert this, a consortium of banks provided a line of credit of over $1bn to two brothers. The brothers were called Hunt and they had tried to corner the silver market.

Silver may not be as popular as gold as a store of wealth, but come the zombie apocalypse it may well be more useful than gold as a medium of exchange. But how does it stack up as an investment? On this page we will look at two aspects of silver: its seasonality and relationship with the stock market.

The following chart on the left shows the average price returns for silver by month since 1963, while the chart on the right shows the proportion of months that have seen positive returns.

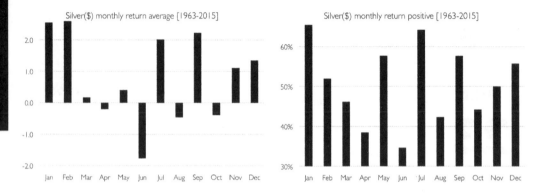

It can be seen that silver has been historically strong in January, February, July and September, and weak in June, August and October. This profile of behaviour would seem to have some persistency as the same pattern can be seen for the period 1990-2013.

Silver and equities

The following chart shows the ratio of the FTSE All-Share index to silver since 1968. (One can regard the chart as the UK equity market priced in silver.)

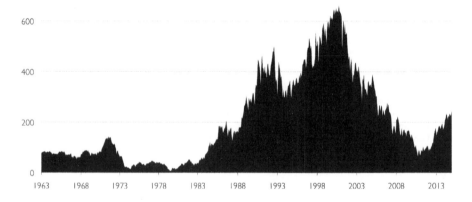

The ratio peaked at 662.60 in April 2001 and then fell to a low of 65.05 in April 2011, since when it has been steadily falling in price against equities. Since 1963 the ratio average is 205.25.

Note: There are several silver ETFs/ETNs listed on the LSE, for example: PHAG($), PHSP(£), SLVR($), XSIL($) and SILG(£).

Mon

28

Easter Monday
LSE, HKEX closed

1994: BBC Radio 5 is closed and replaced with the news and sport station BBC Radio 5 Live.

S&P 500	51	-0.1	0.8
NIKKEI	59	0.3	1.2

Tue

29

1886: Dr. John Pemberton brews the first batch of Coca-Cola in a backyard in Atlanta.

FTSE 100	56	0.2	0.8
FTSE 250	59	0.0	0.5
S&P 500	49	0.1	0.6
NIKKEI	45	-0.2	1.5

Wed

30

1867: Alaska is purchased for $7.2 million, about 2 cents/acre, by US Secretary of State William H. Seward. The media refers to this as Seward's Folly.

FTSE 100	48	-0.4	1.1
FTSE 250	52	-0.2	0.7
S&P 500	35	-0.3	0.9
NIKKEI	45	-0.4	1.6

Thu

31

1986: The Greater London Council is abolished.

FTSE 100	40	0.0	1.4
FTSE 250	35	-0.1	0.8
S&P 500	42	0.0	0.7
NIKKEI	36	-0.5	1.5

Fri

1

Nonfarm payroll report (anticipated)

1989: Margaret Thatcher's new local government tax, the Community Charge (commonly known as the poll tax), is introduced in Scotland.

FTSE 100	**78**	**0.6**	**1.1**
FTSE 250	71	0.4	1.3
S&P 500	68	0.3	0.9
NIKKEI	52	0.2	1.6

Sat 2

Sun 3

Final AA, Al Noor Hospitals Group, Amec Foster Wheeler, International Public Partnership, JPMorgan American Investment Trust, Kingfisher, Mercantile Investment Trust, Polymetal International

COMPANY
RESULTS

APRIL MARKET

Market performance this month

Five years ago, April was the strongest month for the market in the year, but it now ranks second behind December. The two have been switching first and second places for some time – it is odd how the performance of the market in these months tracks so closely.

On average, the market rises 1.8% in this month and the probability of a positive return is 71%. Since 2003 the market has only fallen three times in April. However, this doesn't match the earlier performance: from 1971 the market rose in April every year for 15 years – a recent record for any month.

This is the strongest month for the FTSE 100 relative to the S&P 500 (in sterling terms); the former outperforms the latter by an average of 1.3 percentage points in April (in April 2015 the FTSE 100 outperformed the US index by 5.1 percentage points).

The market often gets off to a strong start in the month – the first trading day of April is the second strongest first trading day of all months. The market then tends to be fairly flat for the middle two weeks before rising strongly in the final week.

The great seasonality significance of April is that it is the last month in the strong part of the six-month cycle (November-April); therefore investors may be reducing their exposure to equities ahead of May.

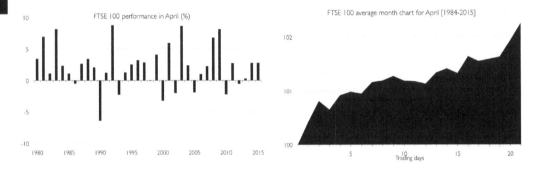

April summary

Market performance	Avg return: 1.8%		Positive: 71%	Ranking: 2nd
Sector performance	Strong Electronic & Electrical Equipment, Industrial Engineering, Personal Goods		Weak Household Goods, Mining, Mobile Telecommunications, Software & Computer Services	
Share performance	Strong Aberdeen Asset Management, Fenner, Royal Dutch Shell, SABMiller, Severn Trent		Weak BAE Systems, Balfour Beatty, Reed Elsevier, UNITE Group	
Main features	FTSE 100 strong relative to S&P 500 this month GBPUSD historically strong this month Strong month for oil First trading day average return: 0.44%; positive: 71% (2nd strongest in year) Last trading day average return: 0.17%; positive: 56% 01 Apr: 5th strongest market day of the year 08 Apr: 2nd weakest market day of the year			
Significant dates	01 Apr: US Nonfarm payroll report (anticipated) 06 Apr: ECB Governing Council Meeting (non-monetary policy) 14 Apr: MPC interest rate announcement at 12 noon (anticipated) 21 Apr: ECB Governing Council Meeting (monetary policy) 26 Apr: Two-day FOMC meetings starts			

APRIL

Mon
4

Ching Ming Festival (China) – HKEX closed

1968: Martin Luther King, Jr. is assassinated by James Earl Ray at a motel in Memphis, Tennessee.

FTSE 100	55	0.1	0.9
FTSE 250	58	-0.2	0.9
S&P 500	53	-0.1	0.6
NIKKEI	43	0.0	1.1

Tue
5

FTSE 100	67	0.2	0.7
FTSE 250	59	0.0	0.7
S&P 500	60	0.3	1.0
NIKKEI	55	0.4	0.9

1896: The first modern Olympic Games officially opens in Athens.

Wed
6

ECB Governing Council Meeting (non-monetary policy)

FTSE 100	63	0.2	0.7
FTSE 250	76	0.4	0.8
S&P 500	56	0.1	0.8
NIKKEI	50	0.2	1.2

1974: ABBA win the Eurovision Song Contest.

Thu
7

Golf: Masters, Augusta (until 10th)
New moon

FTSE 100	45	0.2	1.1
FTSE 250	45	0.0	1.0
S&P 500	52	-0.2	0.8
NIKKEI	68	0.2	1.2

1959: Radar is first bounced off the sun, from Stanford, California.

Fri
8

Ramayana (until 15th)
25th anniversary of the LSE flotation of HSBC Holdings

FTSE 100	**24**	**-0.3**	**0.6**
FTSE 250	43	-0.2	0.6
S&P 500	61	0.2	0.8
NIKKEI	57	0.0	1.5

1904: Longacre Square in Manhattan is renamed Times Square after the *New York Times*.

Sat 9   Horse racing: Grand National, Aintree racecourse

Sun 10

Final Evraz

COMPANY
RESULTS

POLITICS AND FINANCIAL MARKETS

FTSE All-Share index

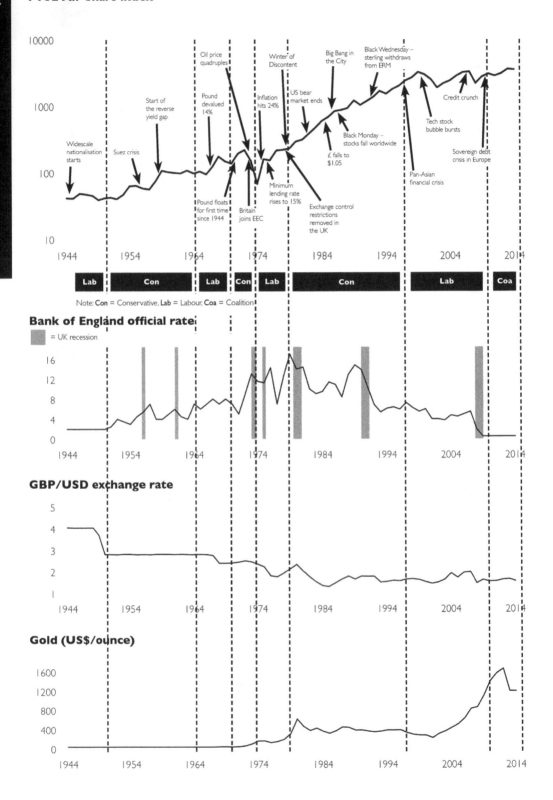

Oil price quadruples

Winter of Discontent

Big Bang in the City

Black Wednesday – sterling withdraws from ERM

Pound devalued 14%

Inflation hits 24%

US bear market ends

Credit crunch

Start of the reverse yield gap

Tech stock bubble bursts

Widescale nationalisation starts

Suez crisis

Black Monday – stocks fall worldwide

Sovereign debt crisis in Europe

£ falls to $1.05

Pound floats for first time since 1944

Britain joins EEC

Minimum lending rate rises to 15%

Pan-Asian financial crisis

Exchange control restrictions removed in the UK

| Lab | Con | Lab | Con | Lab | Con | Lab | Coa |

Note: **Con** = Conservative, **Lab** = Labour, **Coa** = Coalition

Bank of England official rate

= UK recession

GBP/USD exchange rate

Gold (US$/ounce)

Mon
11

FTSE 100	39	-0.2	0.9
FTSE 250	52	-0.1	0.8
S&P 500	49	-0.1	0.8
NIKKEI	48	0.2	1.5

1976: The original Apple computer, the Apple I, is released.

Tue
12

FTSE 100	55	0.1	0.7
FTSE 250	50	0.0	0.6
S&P 500	67	0.3	0.7
NIKKEI	65	-0.1	1.0

1961: The Soviet Union wins the space race, putting the first man into space – Major Yuri Alekseyevich Gagarin.

Wed
13

Beige Book published

FTSE 100	59	0.1	0.6
FTSE 250	59	0.0	0.6
S&P 500	52	-0.1	0.7
NIKKEI	50	0.0	1.5

2007: Google reaches a deal with DoubleClick to buy the company for $3.1bn.

Thu
14

MPC interest rate announcement at 12h00

FTSE 100	35	-0.3	0.9
FTSE 250	45	0.0	0.9
S&P 500	60	0.0	1.4
NIKKEI	45	-0.2	1.1

1994: The top executives of the seven largest American tobacco companies testify in Congress that they do not believe cigarettes are addictive.

Fri
15

FTSE 100	61	0.3	0.9
FTSE 250	68	0.1	0.8
S&P 500	72	0.2	0.7
NIKKEI	52	0.1	1.2

1927: The first Volvo car comes off the production line in Sweden.

Sat 16

Sun 17

Final Bluecrest Allblue Fund, F&C Commercial Property Trust, JD Sports Fashion

COMPANY
RESULTS

SELL IN MAY

An update on the strongest – and strangest – seasonality effect in the market.

When we look at historic time series of asset prices the frequencies we use tend to be day, week, month or year. But new patterns of historic behaviour might be revealed using other time frames.

In this case, we are going to split the year into two six-month periods:

1. **Winter period**: 1 November–30 April
2. **Summer period**: 1 May–31 October

The following chart compares the performance from 1982 of the FTSE All-Share index for the two periods; each bar represents the outperformance of the winter period over the following summer period. For example, from 1 Nov 2013 to 30 Apr 2014 the index rose 1.0%, while during the following period 1 May 2014 to 31 Oct 2014 the index fell 3.2%. The difference in performance was therefore 4.2 percentage points, and that is the figure plotted on the chart for 2014 (the final bar in the chart).

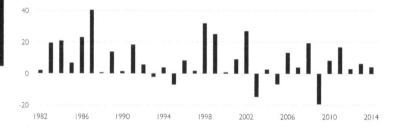

The chart shows a quite remarkable thing, namely that the market seems to perform much better in the six-month winter period than the summer period. To quantify this outperformance:

- In the 33 years since 1982, the winter period has outperformed the summer period 28 times (84%).

- The average annual outperformance since 1982 has been 8.6%!

The behaviour is extraordinary and should not exist in a modern, efficient(ish) market. But exist it does. Indeed, a similar effect also exists in other markets, such as the US.

How long has this effect been operating?

The following chart is identical to that above except the data starts from 1922.

We can see from this chart that during the first half of the 20th century the market performance during the two periods was pretty equally balanced. But the behaviour changed significantly around the beginning of the 1970s.

It may be that the above study is woefully short term in its approach. An academic paper[1] of 2012 found evidence of the Six-Month Effect (also called the Sell in May Effect in the UK and the Halloween Effect in the US) starting from 1694 in the UK. The paper also found the effect was present in 36 of 37 developed and emerging markets.

---

1. Jacobsen, B., Zhang, C.Y., 'Are Monthly Seasonals Real? A Three Century Perspective' (15 February 2012).

Mon
18

FTSE 100	48	0.0	0.9
FTSE 250	53	0.1	0.9
S&P 500	56	0.2	1.1
NIKKEI	61	0.4	1.6

1956: British Chancellor Harold Macmillan unveils the Premium Bond scheme.

Tue
19

FTSE 100	57	0.2	0.7
FTSE 250	65	0.3	0.6
S&P 500	49	-0.1	0.6
NIKKEI	45	-0.1	1.1

1770: Captain James Cook sights Australia.

Wed
20

Ridvan (until 2nd May)

FTSE 100	63	0.0	1.2
FTSE 250	68	0.0	1.2
S&P 500	53	-0.1	1.0
NIKKEI	41	-0.1	1.0

2010: The Deepwater Horizon oil platform explodes in the Gulf of Mexico, resulting in one of the largest oil spills in history.

Thu
21

ECB Governing Council Meeting (monetary policy)

FTSE 100	42	0.0	0.5
FTSE 250	58	0.0	0.5
S&P 500	54	0.3	0.8
NIKKEI	.45	0.0	1.4

1509: Henry VIII ascends to the throne of England on the death of his father, Henry VII.

Fri
22

Passover (until 30th)
Hanuman Jayanti
Theravadin (Buddhist New Year)
Full moon

FTSE 100	45	0.1	0.8
FTSE 250	67	0.2	0.7
S&P 500	43	0.0	1.0
NIKKEI	52	0.0	1.0

1659: The Lord Protector Oliver Cromwell disbands English parliament.

Sat 23   St George's Day; 400th anniversary of the death of William Shakespeare

Sun 24   London Marathon

Interim Debenhams, WH Smith
Final NB Global Floating Rate Income Fund, Tesco, UK Commercial Property Trust

COMPANY
RESULTS

MONTHLY SEASONALITY OF THE FTSE 100

A table of the monthly seasonality of the FTSE 100 can be seen in the Statistics section (page 117). The table below contains the same values as the other table, except this one adds a fourth column (the product of the Positive and Average Return values). The table is ordered by this fourth column to create a revised ranking of monthly performance of the market. Instead of just looking at the number of positive returns in a month this new ranking also adds in the factor of average return and so is slightly more sophisticated.

Month	Positive(%)	Avg Rtn (%)	Std Dev	Positive x Avg Rtn
December	84	2.3	3.0	2.0
April	71	1.8	3.4	1.3
February	61	1.1	3.9	0.7
July	56	1.0	4.2	0.6
October	74	0.7	6.5	0.5
November	58	0.7	3.7	0.4
August	58	0.5	4.5	0.3
January	58	0.4	5.1	0.3
March	55	0.4	3.4	0.2
May	50	-0.2	4.3	-0.1
June	38	-1.0	3.5	-0.4
September	45	-1.0	5.6	-0.5

With this new ranking, December is still found to be the strongest month, but it is now followed by April and then February (which previously were ranked third and fourth respectively). At the bottom of the table, September is now the weakest month (previously it was 11th). The new ranking system has a big impact on October, which falls from 2nd position to 5th.

Changes from the rankings a year ago are that October and July have switched places, and March has fallen from 7th to 9th place.

Cumulative performance by month

The following chart plots the cumulative returns of the FTSE 100 for each of the 12 months from 1979 (e.g. the January line plots the returns a portfolio would see if it only invested in the FTSE 100 in January each year).

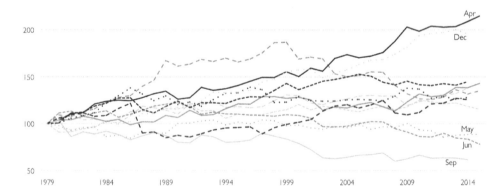

With all 12 months plotted on the chart in this way, it is interesting to note that seven of them are clustered together in the middle of the chart, while there are two outstanding strong performers (April and December) and three obviously poor performers (May, June and September). Apart from that, we can also note that September has been a consistently poor performer since 1980. Up till year 2000 the strongest month had been January, but since then it has suffered a steady decline in performance. Conversely, since 1989 October has been one of the stronger months.

See also: 'Monthly performance of FTSE 100' on page 117.

Mon

25

FTSE 100	59	0.1	0.5
FTSE 250	50	0.0	0.5
S&P 500	57	0.1	0.9
NIKKEI	61	0.1	1.0

2007: The Dow Jones Industrial Average closes above 13,000 (13,089.89) for the first time.

Two-day FOMC meeting starts

Tue

26

FTSE 100	68	0.3	0.6
FTSE 250	70	0.1	0.4
S&P 500	54	0.1	0.6
NIKKEI	55	0.1	0.8

1986: A nuclear reactor accident occurs at the Chernobyl Nuclear Power Plant in the Soviet Union (now Ukraine) – the world's worst nuclear disaster.

Wed

27

FTSE 100	52	-0.2	1.1
FTSE 250	52	-0.2	0.8
S&P 500	51	-0.1	0.8
NIKKEI	50	-0.1	1.3

1981: Xerox PARC introduces the computer mouse.

Thu

28

FTSE 100	50	0.1	1.0
FTSE 250	50	-0.1	0.8
S&P 500	57	0.0	0.7
NIKKEI	45	-0.3	1.1

2008: Mars announces that it is buying the Wm. Wrigley Jr. Company, the world's largest chewing gum manufacturer, in a deal worth $23bn. The deal is partly financed by Warren Buffett's Berkshire Hathaway.

Shōwa Day (Japan) – TSE closed

Fri

29

FTSE 100	50	0.2	0.9
FTSE 250	62	0.5	1.8
S&P 500	52	0.2	0.9

1958: The Broadway musical *My Fair Lady* opens in London.

Sat 30

Sun 1   Beltane

Interim Associated British Foods, Redefine International
Final Allied Minds, Brown (N) Group, Home Retail Group, Whitbread

COMPANY
RESULTS

MAY MARKET

Market performance this month

One of the most famous sayings in the stock market is "Sell in May", so it is no surprise that May is one of the weakest months of the year for shares. There are only three months where, since 1970, the market has an average return of below zero in the month – May is one of them (the others are June and September). On average the market falls -0.2% in the month, and the probability of a positive return is below 50%. Since year 2000 performance has been even worse, with an average return of -0.6% for the month.

May is the start of the weaker half of the year (historically the market over November to April greatly outperforms the period May to October). Some investors therefore tend to reduce exposure to the stock market from May.

On average in May the market trades fairly flat for the first two weeks, and then prices drift lower in the second half of the month (as can be seen in the chart).

Strong sectors relative to the general market in May tend to be Aerospace & Defense, Electricity and Food Producers; while the weaker sectors are General Industrials and Life Insurance.

May is the weakest month of the year for the FTSE 100 relative to the S&P 500; on average the UK index underperforms the US index by 1.9 percentage points in May.

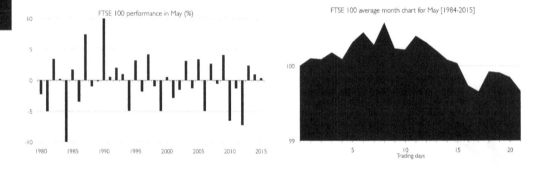

FTSE 100 performance in May (%)

FTSE 100 average month chart for May [1984-2015]

Trading days

May summary

Market performance	Avg return: -0.2%		Positive: 50%	Ranking: 10th
Sector performance	*Strong* Aerospace & Defense, Electricity, Equity Investment Instruments, Food Producers, Gas, Water & Multiutilities		*Weak* General Industrials, Life Insurance	
Share performance	*Strong* 3i Group, Babcock International Group, Cranswick, Severn Trent, United Utilities Group		*Weak* Bellway, Bovis Homes Group, Close Brothers Group, Petra Diamonds Ltd, Workspace Group	
Main features	Sell in May effect: start of the weak six months of the year FTSE 100 often underperforms the S&P 500 in this month First trading day average return: 0.1%; positive: 56% Last trading day average return: 0.00%; positive: 47% 02 May: 6th strongest market day of the year 23 May: start of 3rd weakest market week 30 May: weakest market day of the year			
Significant dates	02 May: Early May bank holiday – LSE closed 04 May: ECB Governing Council Meeting (non-monetary policy) 06 May: US Nonfarm payroll report (anticipated) 12 May: MPC interest rate announcement at 12 noon (anticipated) 12 May: MSCI Semi-Annual Index Review announcement date 18 May: ECB Governing Council Meeting (non-monetary policy) 30 May: Spring bank holiday – LSE, HKSE closed 30 May: Memorial Day (US) – NYSE closed			

Mon 2

May Day bank holiday (UK)
LSE, HKEX closed

S&P 500	66	0.2	0.7
NIKKEI	59	0.5	0.8

1918: General Motors acquires the Chevrolet Motor Company of Delaware.

Tue 3

Constitution Memorial Day (Japan) – TSE closed

FTSE 100	61	-0.2	1.1
FTSE 250	63	0.1	0.4
S&P 500	59	0.1	0.8

1951: London's Royal Festival Hall opens.

Wed 4

Greenery Day (Japan) – TSE closed
Yom HaShoah (until 5th)
ECB Governing Council Meeting (non-monetary policy)

FTSE 100	53	-0.1	1.2
FTSE 250	63	-0.1	1.1
S&P 500	61	0.0	1.0

2001: The Bank of Scotland and Halifax agree terms for a £30bn merger to create a new bank called HBOS.

Thu 5

Children's Day (Japan) – TSE closed

FTSE 100	47	0.0	1.0
FTSE 250	59	0.3	1.1
S&P 500	60	0.2	0.7

1893: A market crash hits the New York Stock Exchange (the Panic of 1893).

Fri 6

Nonfarm payroll report (anticipated)
New moon

FTSE 100	65	0.2	0.9
FTSE 250	67	0.3	0.6
S&P 500	38	-0.1	0.8
NIKKEI	57	0.4	2.0

1937: The German airship Hindenburg explodes and bursts into flames at Lakehurst, NJ.

Sat 7   Horse racing: Kentucky Derby, Louisville

Sun 8   Transit of Mercury

Interim Aberdeen Asset Management, Imperial Tobacco Group, Sage Group
Final Saga, Sainsbury (J)

COMPANY RESULTS

THE LOW-HIGH PRICE PORTFOLIO

Do investors like low share prices?

"Investors like low share prices" is the reason often given for companies having share splits or bonus issues. But surely rational investors understand that price is independent of value?

Apparently not.

The previous edition of the Almanac compared the historic performance of low-priced shares against high-priced ones. This page updates the study to include the last year's data.

To recap, an academic paper[1] in 2008 found that in the US equity market share returns are inversely proportional to share price (i.e. the lower the share price, the higher the future return). In addition, the paper found that a portfolio that was long of stocks under $5 and short of stocks over $20 and rebalanced annually generated average monthly returns of 0.53%. Lengthening the rebalancing period to two years increased the returns and reduced the costs.

To test whether this applies also to the UK market, the performance of two portfolios was compared:

1. **Low-price_20**: this portfolio buys equal amounts of the 20 lowest priced shares in the FTSE All-Share index at close on 31 December, holds the same portfolio for one year, and then rebalances the next 31 December.

2. **High-price_20**: as above, but this portfolio buys the 20 highest priced shares.

The following chart plots the annual outperformance of the Low-price_20 portfolio over High-price_20 for the period 2005-2014. For example, in 2005 the Low-price_20 portfolio increased 45% compared with an increase of 19% for the High-price_20 portfolio, giving an outperformance of 26 percentage points.

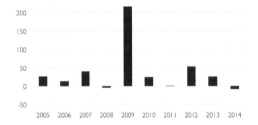

Overall, the Low-price_20 portfolio has outperformed the High-price_20 portfolio every year since 2005, except 2008 and 2014. The average annual return for the Low-price_20 portfolio over the period was 43.2%, and for High-price_20 portfolio it was 4.5%, giving the former an average annual outperformance of 38.7 percentage points.

And, yes, the data for 2009 are correct – when markets rebound low-priced shares can fly.

Share price frequency distribution

The chart below shows the frequency distribution of share prices in the FTSE All-Share as at the end of 2014.

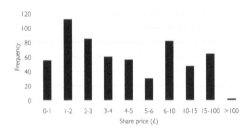

The chart shows that, for example, there are 55 companies with share prices below £1, 112 companies with share prices £1-2 and 64 companies with share prices £15-100.

---

1. Hwang, Soosung and Lu, Chensheng, 'Is Share Price Relevant?' (25 September 2008).

Mon
9

FTSE 100	39	-0.1	0.6
FTSE 250	48	-0.2	0.4
S&P 500	48	-0.1	0.7
NIKKEI	30	-0.5	0.9

1921: US financial weekly *Barron's* sells its first copy.

Tue
10

FTSE 100	45	0.3	1.4
FTSE 250	50	0.2	1.5
S&P 500	48	-0.1	1.1
NIKKEI	45	-0.2	1.4

1955: West Germany is accepted into Nato.

Yom Ha'atzmaut (until 12th)

Wed
11

FTSE 100	50	0.1	1.1
FTSE 250	43	-0.1	0.9
S&P 500	42	-0.1	0.9
NIKKEI	50	-0.2	1.4

1927: The Academy of Motion Picture Arts and Sciences is founded in the USA.

MPC interest rate announcement at 12h00
MSCI semi-annual index review (announcement date)

Thu
12

FTSE 100	55	-0.1	0.9
FTSE 250	59	0.1	0.9
S&P 500	59	0.2	0.7
NIKKEI	45	0.1	1.2

1926: A nine-day general strike by UK trade unions comes to an end.

Fri
13

FTSE 100	61	0.2	0.9
FTSE 250	64	0.0	1.0
S&P 500	49	-0.1	0.8
NIKKEI	48	0.0	1.2

1927: Black Friday on the Berlin Stock Exchange.

Sat 14

Sun 15

Interim Compass Group, Diploma, easyJet, Enterprise Inns, Finsbury Growth & Income Trust, Lonmin, Mitchells & Butlers, TUI AG
Final 3i Infrastructure, BT Group, Experian, SABMiller, Scottish Mortgage Investment Trust

COMPANY
RESULTS

DAY OF THE WEEK STRATEGY

The performance characteristics of the equity market on the five days of the week can be seen in the Statistics section (page 115). To summarise, since 2012 the FTSE 100 has had negative average returns on Monday and Wednesday, and positive average returns on Tuesday, Thursday and Friday.

This suggests a strategy of going short the market for Monday (i.e. shorting at the close the previous Friday), switching to long on Tuesday, back to short on Wednesday, and then long on Thursday and Friday (and back to short at the close of Friday).

The following chart updates the results of implementing this strategy every week from January 2012 to mid-2015 (the time of writing). A spread cost of 1 point on each transaction is included in the performance figures. For comparison, a simple long-only FTSE 100 portfolio is also shown. The portfolios values are rebased to start at 100.

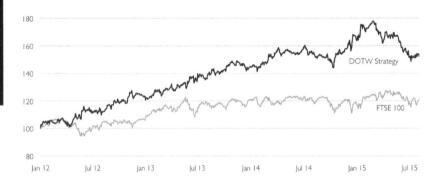

At the end of the period the FTSE 100 portfolio would have increased 20%, while the Day Of The Week Switching Strategy (DOTW Strategy) would have increased 54% (after costs).

Doubling up on Thursday

The previous edition of the Almanac looked at a variant strategy that doubled the unit size of the trade on Tuesdays (to exploit the day's strength). However, the profitability of this strategy has decreased in the last year because of the fall in Tuesday daily returns. So, this time we'll look at doubling the trade size on Thursday.

The following chart shows the performance of a portfolio similar to that above, but it adds this new 2xThursday strategy variant. Again, a spread cost of 1 point per trade is included.

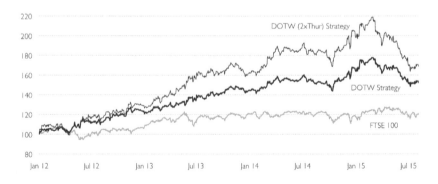

As can be seen, this strategy beats the simple DOTW Strategy. However, there has been a decline in the profitability of this strategy in the last year. Of course, further variants are possible. For example, the unit trade size on Wednesday (going short) could also be doubled.

Mon 16

50th anniversary of the release of Bob Dylan's album *Blonde on Blonde*
50th anniversary of the release of The Beach Boys' album *Pet Sounds*

1532: Sir Thomas More resigns as Lord Chancellor of England, saying he is suffering from ill health.

FTSE 100	43	0.1	0.5
FTSE 250	45	0.0	0.7
S&P 500	47	0.0	0.7
NIKKEI	39	-0.3	1.0

Tue 17

1996: First trading day of the newly privatised Railtrack.

FTSE 100	50	-0.2	1.2
FTSE 250	60	-0.1	1.0
S&P 500	57	-0.1	0.8
NIKKEI	59	-0.3	1.3

Wed 18

ECB Governing Council Meeting (non-monetary policy)
Football: Europa League Final, St Jakob-Park, Basel

1964: Mods and Rockers are jailed after riots in Brighton.

FTSE 100	59	0.2	0.9
FTSE 250	71	0.2	0.7
S&P 500	45	0.0	0.9
NIKKEI	36	-0.5	1.3

Thu 19

1976: Gold ownership is legalised in Australia.

FTSE 100	55	-0.2	1.3
FTSE 250	64	0.1	1.1
S&P 500	53	-0.1	0.8
NIKKEI	55	0.2	1.2

Fri 20

1874: Levi Strauss and Jacob Davis receive a US patent for blue jeans with copper rivets.

FTSE 100	52	-0.1	1.0
FTSE 250	68	-0.2	0.9
S&P 500	43	-0.1	0.9
NIKKEI	52	-0.1	0.9

Sat 21   Football: FA Cup Final, Wembley; Full moon; Blue moon; 100th anniversary of UK Daylight Savings Time

Sun 22   Tennis: French Open, Roland Garros (until 5th June)

COMPANY RESULTS

Interim Britvic, Euromoney Institutional Investor, Grainger, Greencore Group, Marston's, Paragon Group of Companies, Thomas Cook Group, UDG Healthcare, Victrex, Zoopla Property Group
Final 3i Group, Aveva Group, Babcock International Group, Big Yellow Group, British Land Co, BTG, Burberry Group, Cable & Wireless Communications, Cranswick, DCC, Entertainment One Group, Great Portland Estates, Homeserve, ICAP, Intermediate Capital Group, Land Securities Group, Marks & Spencer Group, Mitie Group, Pennon Group, SSE, TalkTalk Telecom Group, Vectura Group, Vedanta Resources, Vodafone Group

MONTHLY SHARE MOMENTUM

Do shares exhibit a momentum effect from one month to the next?

If we selected the best performing shares in one month and created an equally-weighted portfolio of those shares to hold for the following month, would that portfolio outperform the market index? Or, more interestingly, if we did this systematically every month (i.e. our portfolio each month is comprised of the best performing shares in the previous month), would that portfolio outperform the market?

Previous editions of the Almanac analysed this for the companies in the FTSE 100. Here that study is updated, comparing for the first time momentum portfolios comprising each month the five and ten best performing shares from the previous month.

The following chart shows the results of operating such momentum portfolios from 2011-2015 and, for comparison, the FTSE 100 (all three series have been rebased to start at 100). So, to summarise, the two portfolios in the chart are:

1. **MSMP(5)**: a portfolio rebalanced at the end of each month comprising the *five* best performing FTSE 100 shares of the previous month.

2. **MSMP(10)**: as above, but this portfolio contains the *ten* best performing FTSE 100 shares of the previous month.

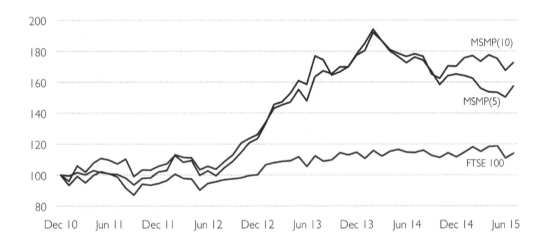

By mid-2015 (the time of writing), the momentum portfolio would have a value of 176 compared with a value of 114 for the FTSE 100. As can be seen in the chart, the portfolios enjoyed a successful run in 2012-2013, but profitability declined in 2014. Then in early 2015 the ten-share portfolio started outperforming the five-share portfolio.

Reversal portfolio

Previous editions of the Almanac have studied reverse momentum portfolios, i.e. portfolios that held the worst performing shares of the previous month.

To summarise quickly here: some form of reversal effect was found (the Reversal Portfolio has outperformed the FTSE 100), but the extent of the outperformance is not significant and would be unlikely to cover the trading costs required to exploit it.

MAY

Mon
23

5th anniversary of the LSE flotation of Rolls-Royce Holdings

FTSE 100	39	-0.4	1.1
FTSE 250	48	-0.1	1.3
S&P 500	43	-0.2	0.8
NIKKEI	52	-0.3	1.8

2003: The Euro exceeds its initial trading value as it hits $1.18 for the first time since its introduction in 1999.

Tue
24

RHS Chelsea Flower Show (until 28th)

FTSE 100	41	-0.1	0.8
FTSE 250	45	-0.2	0.7
S&P 500	50	-0.1	0.9
NIKKEI	62	0.2	0.8

1993: Microsoft unveils Windows NT.

Wed
25

Lag B'Omer (until 26th)

FTSE 100	53	-0.2	1.1
FTSE 250	44	-0.2	1.0
S&P 500	50	-0.1	0.8
NIKKEI	50	-0.2	1.3

1994: Camelot wins the right to run the UK lottery.

Thu
26

Corpus Christi

FTSE 100	53	0.2	0.8
FTSE 250	47	0.4	1.0
S&P 500	51	0.1	0.9
NIKKEI	68	0.2	1.1

1896: Charles Dow publishes the first edition of the Dow Jones Industrial Average.

Fri
27

FTSE 100	47	0.0	1.0
FTSE 250	58	0.2	0.8
S&P 500	49	0.2	1.2
NIKKEI	43	-0.2	1.1

1932: The Sydney Harbour Bridge opens.

Sat 28   Football: Champion's League Final, San Siro, Milan

Sun 29   Motor racing: Indianapolis 500

COMPANY RESULTS

Interim Brewin Dolphin, British Empire Securities & General Trust, Electra Private Equity, GCP Infrastructure Investments, Shaftesbury, SSP Group
Final Booker Group, Caledonia Investments, Dairy Crest Group, Edinburgh Investment Trust, Electrocomponents, HICL Infrastructure Company, Investec, National Grid, QinetiQ Group, Royal Mail Group, Severn Trent, TR Property Investment Trust, United Utilities Group, Wizz Air

JUNE MARKET

Market performance this month

This is not a good period for investors – the weak month of May is followed by the even weaker month of June. On average the market has fallen 1.0% in June; and the probability of a positive return in the month is a lowly 38% – which ranks it 11th of all months in the year.

Since year 2000 the situation has been even worse: the average return in the month has been -2.0%; the market has only risen one June in the past nine years. And, as can be seen in the accompanying chart, the market falls in June can be quite large; the market has fallen over 3% in June in eight years since 1982.

In an average June the market starts strong, hitting its month high on the second or third trading day, but prices then drift down steadily for the rest of the month. Even so, the market ends the month on a positive note – the last trading day is the second strongest in the year.

Events to watch out for this month include the FTSE 100 index review on the 1st and triple witching on the 17th.

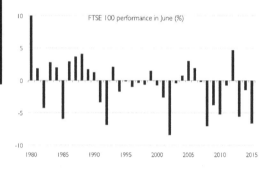

FTSE 100 performance in June (%)

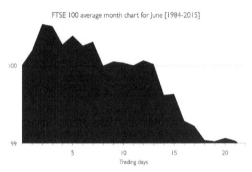

FTSE 100 average month chart for June [1984-2015]

Trading days

June summary

Market performance	Avg return: -1.0%		Positive: 38%	Ranking: 11th
Sector performance	*Strong* Beverages, Oil & Gas Producers, Pharmaceuticals & Biotechnology		*Weak*	
Share performance	*Strong* RPC Group, Synergy Health, Ted Baker		*Weak* Barclays, Bodycote, Morrison (Wm) Supermarkets, Schroders, Travis Perkins	
Main features	Weak month for silver First trading day average return: 0.19%; positive: 53% Last trading day average return: 0.12%; positive: 63% (2nd strongest in year) 20 Jun: start of the 4th weakest market week in the year			
Significant dates	01 Jun: FTSE 100 quarterly review 02 Jun: ECB Governing Council Meeting (monetary policy) 03 Jun: US Nonfarm payroll report (anticipated) 14 Jun: Two-day FOMC meeting starts 16 Jun: MPC interest rate announcement at 12 noon (anticipated) 17 Jun: Triple Witching 22 Jun: ECB Governing Council Meeting (non-monetary policy)			

Mon
30

Spring Bank Holiday – LSE closed
Memorial Day (US) – NYSE closed

2002: South African Breweries seals the takeover of US brewer Miller for $5.6bn, to creating the world's second biggest brewer. The new company, SABMiller, is to produce 12bn litres of beer a year.

NIKKEI	39	-0.3	1.3

Tue
31

FTSE 100	56	0.1	0.6
FTSE 250	75	0.2	0.5
S&P 500	59	0.2	1.0
NIKKEI	62	-0.1	1.2

2003: The final Air France Concorde flight takes place.

Wed
1

FTSE 100 quarterly review
Beige Book published
MSCI semi-annual index review (effective date)

FTSE 100	59	0.3	1.0
FTSE 250	58	0.2	0.9
S&P 500	64	0.2	1.0
NIKKEI	64	0.2	1.1

1954: The TV licence is increased 50% (from £2 to £3).

Thu
2

ECB Governing Council Meeting (monetary policy)

FTSE 100	52	0.1	0.9
FTSE 250	73	0.3	0.7
S&P 500	57	0.1	0.8
NIKKEI	62	0.4	1.0

1985: Tobacco giant R.J. Reynolds buys food producer Nabisco. The $4.9bn merger sets a record for non-oil mergers.

Fri
3

Nonfarm payroll report (anticipated)
Horseracing: The Oaks, Epsom Downs Racecourse

FTSE 100	59	0.1	0.8
FTSE 250	52	0.0	0.6
S&P 500	49	0.0	0.7
NIKKEI	48	-0.3	1.4

1957: Noel Coward returns to Britain from the West Indies, amid criticism he has been living abroad to avoid paying income tax.

Sat 4   Horse racing: The Derby, Epsom Downs Racecourse

Sun 5   New moon

Interim Scottish Investment Trust
Final AO World, B&M European Value Retail SA, Londonmetric Property, PayPoint, Perpetual Income & Growth Investment Trust, Scottish Investment Trust, Synergy Health, Tate & Lyle, Workspace Group

COMPANY
RESULTS

QUARTERLY SECTOR MOMENTUM STRATEGY

Do FTSE 350 sectors display a quarterly momentum behaviour that can be exploited?

This analysis updates the performance of two strategies, defined as:

1. **Strong sector momentum strategy (Strong SMS)**: The portfolio comprises just one FTSE 350 sector, that being the sector with the strongest performance in the previous quarter. So at the end of each quarter, the portfolio is liquidated and a 100% holding is established in the strongest sector of the quarter just finished. This is held for three months (one quarter), before the portfolio is liquidated and re-invested in the new sector. Therefore the strategy will trade four times a year.

2. **Weak sector momentum strategy (Weak SMS)**: As above, but in this case it is the weakest sector of the previous quarter that is held by the portfolio. (Strictly, perhaps, this should be called a *bounceback*, or *reversal*, strategy and not a momentum strategy.)

Only FTSE 350 sectors with at least three component companies are considered. The period studied was from 2005 to the second quarter of 2015.

The accompanying chart compares the performance of the two strategies, and adds the FTSE All-Share index as a benchmark. All series are rebased to start at 100.

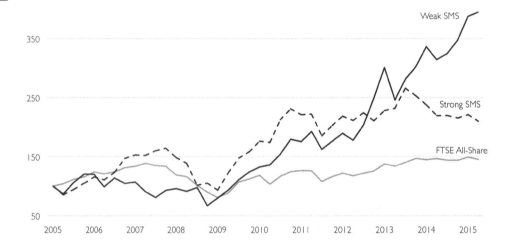

Notes:

1. As can be seen, both the SMS strategies outperformed the index over the period of the study. However, they did so with greater volatility (the standard deviation of the Strong SMS quarterly returns was 0.12, against comparable figures of 0.13 for the Weak SMS and 0.08 for the FTSE All-Share index).

2. From 2012 the reversal portfolio (Weak SMS) started strongly outperforming the Strong SMS.

3. A refinement of the strategy would be to hold the two or three best/worst performing sectors from the previous quarter instead of just the one (which would likely have the effect of reducing volatility).

4. Costs were not taken into account in the study, but given that the portfolio was only traded four times a year costs would not have had a significant impact on the overall performance.

Mon
6

Ramadan (until 5th July)

FTSE 100	57	0.0	1.0
FTSE 250	70	0.0	1.3
S&P 500	55	0.2	1.1
NIKKEI	30	-0.2	0.9

1934: President Roosevelt signs the Securities Exchange Act, creating the SEC to police Wall Street and restore investor confidence.

Tue
7

FTSE 100	50	0.0	0.8
FTSE 250	65	0.1	0.7
S&P 500	46	0.0	0.8
NIKKEI	59	0.1	1.3

1956: Sony unveils the videocassette recorder (VCR).

Wed
8

FTSE 100	38	-0.1	0.8
FTSE 250	48	-0.3	0.9
S&P 500	45	-0.1	0.9
NIKKEI	50	-0.2	1.1

1789: James Madison proposes the Bill of Rights to the American House of Representatives.

Thu
9

Tuen Ng Festival (China) – HKEX closed

FTSE 100	45	0.1	0.8
FTSE 250	62	0.2	0.7
S&P 500	43	-0.2	0.6
NIKKEI	48	-0.3	1.1

1991: The original name of Russia's second largest city, St. Petersburg, is restored, having been changed to Petrograd in 1914 and Leningrad in 1924.

Fri
10

Football: EURO 2016 (until 10th July)

FTSE 100	48	0.0	0.7
FTSE 250	57	0.1	0.6
S&P 500	51	0.1	0.7
NIKKEI	39	0.4	1.5

2003: Disgraced ImClone CEO, Samuel Waksal, is fined $4.3m for insider trading and sentenced to over seven years in prison.

Sat 11   Shavuot (until 13th)

Sun 12

Final FirstGroup, Halfords Group, Johnson Matthey, Monks Investment Trust, Pets at Home Group, RPC Group

COMPANY
RESULTS

UK MARKET AND THE US ELECTION CYCLE

The chart below shows the four-year US presidential cycle superimposed on the FTSE All-Share index from 1956. The vertical bars indicate the timing of the November elections every four years.

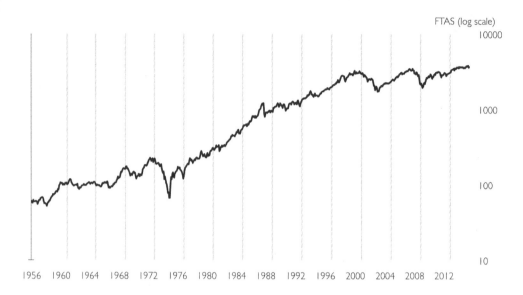

It can be seen that on occasions the US presidential election has (approximately) coincided with significant turning points in the UK market; notably those elections in 1960, 1968, 1972, 1976, 2000 and 2008.

US election results

The table below shows the presidential election results since 1948.

Election date	Elected president	Party	Popular vote (%)	Electoral vote
02 Nov 1948	Harry Truman	Dem	49.6	303
04 Nov 1952	Dwight Eisenhower	Rep	55.2	442
06 Nov 1956	Dwight Eisenhower	Rep	57.4	457
08 Nov 1960	John Kennedy	Dem	49.7	303
03 Nov 1964	Lyndon Johnson	Dem	61.1	486
05 Nov 1968	Richard Nixon	Rep	43.4	301
07 Nov 1972	Richard Nixon	Rep	60.7	520
02 Nov 1976	Jimmy Carter	Dem	50.1	297
04 Nov 1980	Ronald Reagan	Rep	50.7	489
06 Nov 1984	Ronald Reagan	Rep	58.8	525
08 Nov 1988	George H. W. Bush	Rep	53.4	426
03 Nov 1992	Bill Clinton	Dem	43.0	370
05 Nov 1996	Bill Clinton	Dem	49.2	379
07 Nov 2000	George W. Bush	Rep	47.9	271
02 Nov 2004	George W. Bush	Rep	50.7	286
04 Nov 2008	Barack Obama	Dem	46.2	365
06 Nov 2012	Barack Obama	Dem	48.1	332

Mon

13

FTSE 100	52	-0.2	0.8
FTSE 250	33	-0.3	0.5
S&P 500	64	0.1	0.8
NIKKEI	43	-0.5	1.7

1990: The official demolition of the Berlin Wall begins.

Tue

14

Two-day FOMC meeting starts
Horse racing: Royal Ascot (until 18th)
70th anniversary of the LSE flotation of GKN

FTSE 100	45	-0.1	1.0
FTSE 250	55	0.1	1.0
S&P 500	52	-0.1	0.8
NIKKEI	59	0.2	1.0

2015: *Jurassic World* is the first film to make $500m worldwide in its opening weekend.

Wed

15

FTSE 100	45	-0.1	0.9
FTSE 250	45	-0.2	1.1
S&P 500	55	0.0	1.0
NIKKEI	41	-0.4	1.0

1924: The Ford Motor Company announces completion of its 10 millionth motor car.

Thu

16

MPC interest rate announcement at 12h00
Golf: US Open, Oakmont, Pennsylvania (until 19th)

FTSE 100	59	0.1	0.5
FTSE 250	52	0.4	1.8
S&P 500	64	0.1	0.8
NIKKEI	45	0.0	1.4

1903: A one-year old soft drinks company registers its trade name as Pepsi-Cola.

Fri

17

Triple Witching

FTSE 100	65	0.2	0.9
FTSE 250	55	-0.3	2.0
S&P 500	53	0.1	0.8
NIKKEI	48	0.1	1.2

1964: The first purpose-built floating trade fair docks at Tilbury in London, with 22,000 samples of Japanese goods on board.

Sat 18   25th anniversary of the LSE flotation of SSE

Sun 19

Interim Crest Nicholson
Final Ashtead Group, Atkins (WS), Berkeley Group, Betfair Group, Fidelity China Special Situation, Halma, Templeton Emerging Markets Investment Trust

COMPANY
RESULTS

SUMMER SHARE PORTFOLIO

How do shares behave in the summer?

A simple question perhaps, but first it is necessary to define "summer".

When do you think summer begins and ends?

The summer solstice marks the date when the earth's axis is most inclined towards the sun – this results in the longest day of the year (and occurs between 20-22 June in the northern hemisphere). Strictly, this should mark the *middle* of the summer season in the astronomical calendar. However, due to seasonal lag the warmest days of the year tend to occur after this date, and so in the meteorological calendar summer extends for the whole months of June, July and August. But in some countries (e.g. the UK) where the temperature lag can be up to half a season, then summer is taken to start with the summer solstice and end with the autumn equinox (22 September, when the earth is tilted neither towards nor away from the sun).

For the purposes of the analysis here we will take the dates of summer as being 21 June-22 September. The following analysis looked at the performance of the share prices of the companies in the FTSE 350 over summer for the ten years 2005-2014.

Stocks that like summer

The table below shows eight companies whose share prices have risen in at least nine summers in the past ten years. For example, ARM shares rose 5.2% in the summer of 2014, and the shares had an average summer return of 12.6% for the years 2005-2014. BAT and National Grid are the only companies in the FTSE 350 whose shares have increased every summer over this ten-year period.

Company	TIDM	2005	2006	2007	2008	2009	2010	2011	2012	2013	2014	Avg
ARM Holdings	ARM	-3.3	1.9	5.3	21.5	20.7	33.3	4.4	11.4	25.3	5.2	12.6
British American Tobacco	BATS	12.0	8.5	5.4	2.5	14.8	9.8	1.6	0.1	0.3	0.6	5.6
Bunzl	BNZL	7.4	13.2	1.2	4.4	28.2	2.8	2.6	4.7	9.7	-0.1	7.4
Centrica	CNA	12.4	13.5	2.2	5.5	12.2	11.0	-10.9	7.0	11.0	0.1	6.4
National Grid	NG.	3.0	7.4	2.5	4.7	9.3	5.9	7.9	4.6	3.8	5.7	5.5
Rotork	ROR	12.1	21.4	11.9	-17.2	30.9	22.1	2.4	20.4	6.6	5.2	11.6
SABMiller	SAB	21.7	1.3	10.9	2.4	17.8	0.1	-6.2	6.7	5.3	3.4	6.3
Worldwide Healthcare Trust	WWH	12.1	2.5	2.6	15.7	13.8	2.2	-6.7	7.9	12.3	13.0	7.5
average:		9.7	8.3	5.5	5.4	17.9	14.7	1.9	8.9	9.7	5.9	8.8
FTSE 350:		6.3	3.5	-3.3	-6.8	19.2	5.6	-11.8	4.7	7.5	-0.7	2.4
diff:		3.4	4.8	8.8	12.2	-1.3	9.1	13.7	4.2	2.2	6.6	6.4

On average over the last ten years, the FTSE 350 has risen 2.4% over the summer, but an equally-weighted portfolio of these eight stocks rose an average of 8.8% in each summer.

An equally-weighted portfolio of these eight companies would have outperformed the FTSE 350 in nine of the past ten years; the average outperformance each year would have been 6.4% percentage points.

Stocks that don't like summer

In the last ten years there are no stocks that have consistently underperformed the market in the summer.

Mon
20

Full moon
June solstice

FTSE 100	39	-0.4	1.0
FTSE 250	29	-0.6	1.7
S&P 500	47	-0.1	0.8
NIKKEI	57	0.0	0.9

1789: The French Revolution begins.

Tue
21

World Giraffe Day

FTSE 100	55	0.0	0.7
FTSE 250	50	-0.1	0.6
S&P 500	52	0.0	0.8
NIKKEI	64	0.4	1.4

1843: The Royal College of Surgeons is founded in London.

Wed
22

ECB Governing Council Meeting (non-monetary policy)

FTSE 100	45	-0.2	0.9
FTSE 250	33	-0.1	0.6
S&P 500	50	-0.1	0.9
NIKKEI	41	-0.1	1.4

2009: Eastman Kodak Company announces that it will discontinue sales of colour film after 74 years.

Thu
23

ECB General Council Meeting
Motor racing: Goodwood Festival of Speed (until 26th)

FTSE 100	36	-0.3	0.8
FTSE 250	32	-0.3	0.5
S&P 500	40	-0.1	0.8
NIKKEI	50	0.0	1.2

2013: Nik Wallenda becomes the first person to cross a high wire over the Grand Canyon, traversing 1,400 feet of steel cable more than 1,500 feet above the Canyon floor, with no safety net.

Fri
24

FTSE 100	39	-0.4	0.9
FTSE 250	23	-0.5	0.9
S&P 500	45	-0.1	0.8
NIKKEI	61	-0.1	1.0

1441: Eton College is founded by Henry VI.

Sat 25

Sun 26

Interim Bankers Investment Trust, Carnival
Final Auto Trader Group, Poundland Group, Stagecoach, Telecom plus, Worldwide Healthcare Trust

COMPANY
RESULTS

JULY MARKET

Market performance this month

July ranks fourth of all months for performance: on average the market increases 1.0% in July, with a probability of a positive return of 56%. So, after a usually disappointing May and June, shares tend to perform a bit better this month.

July is one of only three months (the others being September and October) where the FTSE 100 tends to outperform the mid-cap FTSE 250, although the outperformance in July is not significantly large. Better is the performance of the FTSE 100 relative to the S&P 500 – in sterling terms July is the second best month for the FTSE 100 (outperforming by an average 1.0% percentage points since 1984).

As can be seen in the accompanying chart, the start of the month tends to be strong: the first trading day (FTD) is the strongest for any month in the year. After that, the market has a propensity to drift lower for a couple of weeks before finishing strongly in the final week of the month.

Although this may not be an exciting month for the overall market, there can be a fair degree of divergence of performance at the sector level. Historically, the sectors that have been strong in July are Chemicals, Personal Goods and Real Estate Investment Trusts, while weak sectors have been Gas, Water & Multiutilities, Support Services and Beverages.

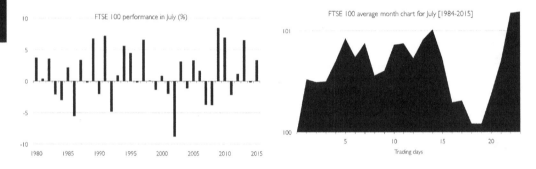

July summary

Market performance	Avg return: 1.0%		Positive: 56%	Ranking: 4th
Sector performance	*Strong* Chemicals, Personal Goods, Real Estate Investment Trusts, Technology Hardware & Equipment		*Weak* Beverages, Gas, Water & Multiutilities, Industrial Transportation, Support Services	
Share performance	*Strong* Brown (N) Group, Elementis, Greene King, Land Securities Group, Shire		*Weak* IP Group, SSE	
Main features	FTSE 100 strong relative to S&P 500 this month 2nd busiest month for FTSE 100 interim results Strong month for silver First trading day average return: 0.52%; positive: 72% (strongest of the year) Last trading day average return: 0.15%; positive: 47% 08 Jul: 6th weakest market day of the year 27 Jul: start of the strongest market week in the year 29 Jul: 8th strongest market day of the year			
Significant dates	01 Jul: US Nonfarm payroll report (anticipated) 03 Jul: Independence Day (US) – NYSE closed 06 Jul: ECB Governing Council Meeting (non-monetary policy) 14 Jul: MPC interest rate announcement at 12 noon (anticipated) 21 Jul: ECB Governing Council Meeting (monetary policy) 26 Jul: Two-day FOMC meeting starts			

Mon
27

Tennis: Wimbledon (until 10th July)

FTSE 100	61	0.2	0.8
FTSE 250	57	0.0	0.6
S&P 500	56	0.0	0.7
NIKKEI	35	-0.2	1.5

1954: The world's first nuclear power station opens in Obninsk, near Moscow.

Tue
28

FTSE 100	64	0.2	0.9
FTSE 250	65	0.2	0.5
S&P 500	54	0.2	0.9
NIKKEI	64	0.5	1.3

1820: The tomato is proved not to be poisonous.

Wed
29

Rowing: Henley Royal Regatta (until 3rd July)

FTSE 100	55	0.0	1.2
FTSE 250	67	0.1	1.1
S&P 500	50	0.0	1.1
NIKKEI	50	0.0	1.3

1905: The AA is formed.

Thu
30

FTSE 100	55	-0.1	0.9
FTSE 250	64	0.2	0.5
S&P 500	50	0.1	0.7
NIKKEI	64	0.3	1.1

2001: ENI of Italy signs a $550m contract to develop Iran's Darquain field, which is expected to produce 160,000 barrels of petroleum per day.

Fri
1

Hong Kong Special Administrative Region Establishment Day – HKEX closed
Nonfarm payroll report (anticipated)

FTSE 100	70	0.4	1.4
FTSE 250	77	0.2	1.0
S&P 500	72	0.2	0.7
NIKKEI	61	0.6	1.4

1987: A stockbroker at Morgan Grenfell becomes the first person to be convicted of insider dealing since it became illegal in 1980.

Sat 2   Cycling: Tour de France (until 24th)

Sun 3

Interim Ocado Group
Final DS Smith, Greene King, Northgate

COMPANY
RESULTS

THE FTSE 100/S&P 500 MONTHLY SWITCHING STRATEGY

A strategy to exploit the monthly comparative returns of the FTSE 100 and S&P 500.

Although since 1984 the S&P 500 has overall greatly outperformed the FTSE 100 (+1176% against +574%), there are months in the year when the FTSE 100 fairly consistently outperforms the S&P 500.

The chart on the right shows the monthly outperformance of the FTSE 100 over the S&P 500 since 1984.

Looking first at the grey bars in the chart, this shows, for example, that on average in January the FTSE 100 has outperformed the S&P 500 by -0.4 percentage points (i.e. the UK index has underperformed the US index). From the chart we can see that the five months that are relatively strong for the FTSE 100 are: February, April, July, August and December. For example, the FTSE 100 has outperformed the S&P 500 in February in 13 of the past 15 years.

Now, turning to the black bars, these display the same average monthly outperformance of the FTSE 100 over the S&P 500, except this time the S&P 500 has been sterling-adjusted. One effect of adjusting for currency moves is to amplify the outperformance of the FTSE 100 index in certain months (April, July and December). Conversely, the FTSE 100 underperformance is amplified in January, May and November.

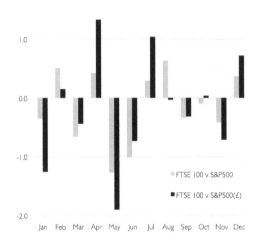

Whereas, before, the relatively strong FTSE 100 months were February, April, July, August and December, we can see that the currency-adjusted strong months are just April, July and December.

The FTSE 100/S&P 500 monthly switching strategy (FSMSP)

The above results suggest a strategy of investing in the UK market (i.e. the FTSE 100) in the months April, July and December, and in the US market (i.e. the S&P 500) for the rest of the year. In other words, the portfolio would be invested in the S&P 500 from January to March, at the end of March it switches out of the S&P 500 into the FTSE 100 for one month, then back into the S&P 500 for two months, into the FTSE 100 for July, back into the S&P 500 for four months, then back into the FTSE 100 for December, and finally back into the S&P 500 to start the next year.

The following chart shows the result of operating such a strategy from 2000 to 2015. For comparison, the chart also includes the portfolio returns from continuous investments in the FTSE 100 and S&P 500.

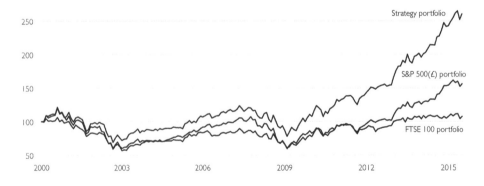

The final result: the FTSE 100 portfolio would have grown 8% and the S&P 500(£) 56%, but the FTSE 100/S&P 500 monthly switching portfolio (FSMSP) would have increased 160%. Switching six times a year would have incurred some commission costs, but these would not have dented performance significantly.

Mon 4

Independence Day (US) – NYSE closed
New moon
NASA's Juno spacecraft is expected to arrive at Jupiter

FTSE 100	57	0.4	1.0
FTSE 250	57	0.1	0.7
NIKKEI	45	-0.1	0.8

1837: The Grand Junction Railway, the world's first long-distance railway, opens between Birmingham and Liverpool.

Tue 5

Eid al-Fitr (end of Ramadan)

FTSE 100	41	0.0	1.0
FTSE 250	45	0.0	0.6
S&P 500	62	0.2	1.1
NIKKEI	59	0.2	0.8

1948: The National Health Service commences.

Wed 6

ECB Governing Council Meeting (non-monetary policy)

FTSE 100	50	0.0	1.0
FTSE 250	57	0.1	0.8
S&P 500	52	0.1	0.9
NIKKEI	36	-0.3	1.2

1957: John Lennon meets Paul McCartney for the first time at a village festival.

Thu 7

Golf: US Women's Open, CordeValle (until 10th)

FTSE 100	55	0.3	1.0
FTSE 250	55	0.1	0.8
S&P 500	57	0.1	1.0
NIKKEI	36	0.3	1.6

1993: In Snowdonia, a gold mine opens to the general public for a £9.50 entry fee. The three-hour trip includes a chance to dig for gold.

Fri 8

FTSE 100	30	-0.2	1.0
FTSE 250	45	-0.1	1.0
S&P 500	53	0.0	0.9
NIKKEI	43	-0.4	1.4

1932: The Dow Jones Industrial Average (DJIA) hit its Great Depression low of 41.22.

Sat 9

Sun 10   Football: EURO 2016 final, Paris; 10th anniversary of the LSE flotation of Standard Life

Final Daejan, Micro Focus International, Polar Capital Technology Trust

COMPANY

RESULTS

SIX-MONTH STRATEGY

On page 34 we looked at the Six-Month Effect. Let's look at how to exploit that effect in practice.

Consider two portfolios:

1. **Winter Portfolio**: this portfolio only invests in the UK stock market in the winter period (1 November-30 April), and for the other six months of the year the portfolio is all in cash.

2. **Summer Portfolio**: does the reverse of the above portfolio – it invests in shares only in the summer period (1 May-31 October) and is in cash for the rest of the time.

For the purposes of this simple study, we'll assume that the portfolios' investments track the FTSE All-Share index. The chart below shows the comparative performance of the two portfolios, each starting with £100, since 1994.

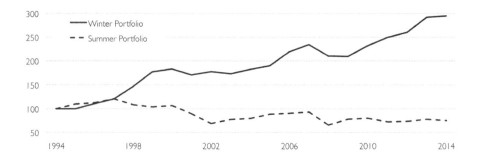

Starting with £100 in 1994, the:

* **Summer Portfolio** would be worth £75 by 2012; but the

* **Winter Portfolio** would be worth £294.

This bizarre effect suggests a strategy of investing in the stock market during the period 1 November-30 April, and then selling up and putting the cash in a deposit account or buying sterling T-bills for the other six months of the year.

The following chart illustrates the result of doing this methodically since 1994, and compares the performance of this strategy to the FTSE 100 Total Return index (i.e. compares it to a strategy of being fully invested in the market all year and receiving dividends).

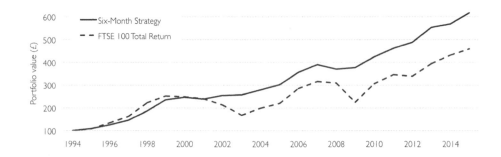

Starting in 1994 with £100, the six-month strategy would have increased in value to £617 by 2015; over the same period a portfolio tracking the FTSE 100 Total Return index year round would have increased to just £459 (including dividends).

NB. There is evidence that the profitability of the strategy can be further enhanced by using an indicator like the MACD (as explained in the 2013 edition of the Almanac) to time the exact entry and exit points for the equity investment. See page 74 for more on this.

Mon

11

FTSE 100	57	-0.2	1.4
FTSE 250	52	-0.3	1.0
S&P 500	57	0.1	0.8
NIKKEI	39	-0.3	1.2

1859: The chimes of Big Ben sound for the first time.

Tue

12

FTSE 100	36	-0.2	0.7
FTSE 250	55	0.1	0.5
S&P 500	49	0.1	1.0
NIKKEI	50	0.1	1.2

927: Æthelstan, King of England, secures a pledge from Constantine II of Scotland that the latter will not ally with Viking kings, beginning the process of unifying Great Britain.

Beige Book published

Wed

13

FTSE 100	73	0.3	0.9
FTSE 250	67	0.3	0.8
S&P 500	53	0.0	0.7
NIKKEI	50	0.0	1.1

2005: Former WorldCom CEO Bernard Ebbers is sentenced to 25 years imprisonment for conspiracy, securities fraud and seven counts of making false SEC filings.

MPC interest rate announcement at 12h00
Golf: Open Championship, Royal Troon, Ayrshire (until 17th)
Bastille Day

Thu

14

FTSE 100	62	0.3	1.0
FTSE 250	52	0.2	0.8
S&P 500	71	0.2	0.7
NIKKEI	62	0.4	1.2

1867: Alfred Nobel demonstrates dynamite for the first time at a quarry in England.

100th anniversary of the incorporation of Pacific Aero Products (later Boeing) by William Boeing in Seattle

Fri

15

FTSE 100	45	-0.1	1.6
FTSE 250	52	-0.1	1.0
S&P 500	54	0.0	0.8
NIKKEI	62	-0.1	0.9

1959: A steel strike begins in the US, leading to the significant importation of foreign steel for the first time in the country's history.

Sat 16

Sun 17

Interim St Modwen Properties
Final Dixons Carphone, Sports Direct International, SuperGroup

COMPANY
RESULTS

FLOTATIONS

The chart below shows the monthly frequency of company flotations (IPOs) and listings on the London Stock Exchange. The black bars show the month frequency for all flotations of companies currently listed on the LSE, and the grey bars are limited to just the 162 companies floated from the beginning of 2010 to the time of writing.

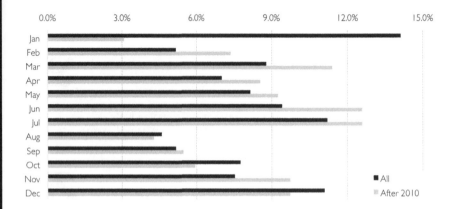

As can be seen, the most popular month for flotations has been January – 14% of all flotations took place in this month. The second most popular month has been July (11%). By contrast, the least popular month is August, followed by February and September.

This profile has changed somewhat in recent years. Since 2010, the two busiest months for flotations have been June and July (13%), followed by March. And, oddly, January is now the least popular month for flotations (3%).

Flotation performance

The following chart plots the performance of an equally-weighted portfolio comprising the 162 companies that have floated since the beginning of 2014. For reference, the FTSE 100 is also shown.

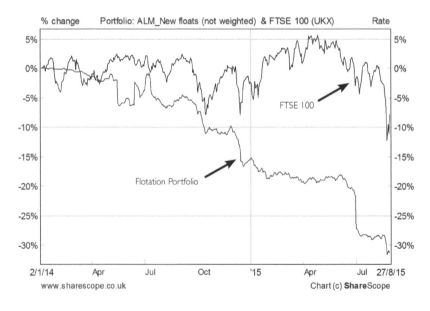

It is not a pretty sight. Since the start of 2014, the FTSE 100 has fallen 8%, but the Flotation Portfolio has declined 31% in value.

Mon
18

Marine Day (Japan) – TSE closed

FTSE 100	43	-0.1	1.0
FTSE 250	48	0.0	0.9
S&P 500	36	-0.1	0.8

1968: N M Electronics is incorporated – later to be renamed Intel.

Tue
19

Guru Purnima; Asalha Puja Day
Full moon

FTSE 100	50	-0.1	1.2
FTSE 250	60	0.3	0.8
S&P 500	51	0.0	0.9
NIKKEI	50	-0.3	1.0

1903: The first Tour de France cycle race is won by Maurice Garin.

Wed
20

15th anniversary of the LSE flotation of London Stock Exchange Group

FTSE 100	43	-0.1	0.8
FTSE 250	45	-0.1	0.7
S&P 500	46	-0.1	0.8
NIKKEI	50	-0.5	1.7

2000: AOL announces it has achieved a profit of $1bn in a single financial year for the first time.

Thu
21

ECB Governing Council Meeting (monetary policy)

FTSE 100	43	-0.2	0.8
FTSE 250	43	0.0	0.7
S&P 500	40	-0.2	0.7
NIKKEI	47	0.0	1.1

1994: The MP for Sedgefield, Tony Blair, is confirmed as the new leader of the Labour Party.

Fri
22

FTSE 100	45	-0.4	1.4
FTSE 250	43	-0.1	0.9
S&P 500	48	-0.1	0.9
NIKKEI	32	-0.5	1.3

2004: Major North American brewers Coors and Molson announce they will go ahead with a proposed merger.

Sat 23

Sun 24

Interim Aberforth Smaller Companies Trust, Alliance Trust, Anglo American, ARM, Beazley, Croda International, CSR, Hammerson, Howden Joinery Group, Morgan Advanced Materials, RELX, Shire, Temple Bar Investment Trust, Unilever
Final IG Group, PZ Cussons

COMPANY
RESULTS

In commemoration this week of the 50th anniversary of England beating Germany 4-2 in the 1966 World Cup final, here is a quick overview of academic papers on the relationship between football and the stock market.

The main focus of research in this area is on whether the results of games have an effect on the share prices of quoted football clubs. For academics, the interest here is that football results provide an easy and quantifiable proxy for mood, and much of this research therefore comes within the ambit of behavioural finance.

Zuber et al (2005)[1] found that the price behaviour of publicly-quoted English Premier League teams was insensitive to game results; they concluded that a new type of investor gained value from mere share ownership. By contrast, Stadtmann (2006)[2] studied the share price of Borussia Dortmund and found that game results were an important driver. The research of Berument et al (2006)[3] was partly consistent with both the preceding in finding that the Turkish team Beşiktaş' win against foreign rivals in the Winner's Cup did increase stock market returns, but that no such effect was found for two other Turkish teams: Fenerbahçe and Galatasaray.

Palomino et al (2009)[4] found that stock prices did react strongly to game results, generating significant abnormal returns and trading volumes; and, further, that winning team share prices experienced a high level of overreaction. Their research also studied the football betting market and found that while betting odds were a good predictor of game outcomes, investors largely ignored these odds, and that betting information predicted stock price overreactions to game results.

The research of Benkraiem et al (2009)[5] was largely consistent with those that found game results had an influence on returns and trading volumes; their analysis further showed that the extent of the share price effect and timing of it was dependent on the type of result (win, draw, lose) and match venue (home, away). Berument et al (2009)[6] argued that the share price effect on football teams quoted on the Istanbul Exchange increased with the fanaticism of the team's supporters. Scholtens and Peenstra's (2009)[7] research was again consistent with the finding that match results affected share prices (significant and positive for victories and negative for defeats); and they further found that the effect was significantly stronger for defeats, and stronger in European than for national competitions.

Like Palomino et al (2009), Bernile and Lyandres (2011)[8] analysed the football betting markets to find that investors are overly optimistic about their teams' prospects before games and disappointed afterwards, which leads to abnormal negative returns after games.

Bell et al (2012)[9] found that share returns were more influenced by important games for English clubs, where "important" was defined as a game having a particular significance for the club's league position. Godinho and Cerqueira (2014)[10] also incorporated the concept of game importance; they built a model for 13 clubs of six different European countries that weights games according to a new measure of match importance and using the betting markets to isolate the unexpected component of match results; this model finds a significant link between the results and share performance.

Berkowitz and Depken (2014)[11] found that share prices reacted asymmetrically to game results: the negative effect being greater and quicker for losers than the positive effect for winners. They suggested the reason for this is that losing is a stronger predictor of future losing (and lower financial performance) than winning is a predictor of future winning.

1. Zuber, R., Yiu, P., Lamb, R. and Gandar, J., 'Investor-fans? An examination of the performance of publicly traded English Premier League teams', *Applied Financial Economics* 15:5 (2005).

2. Stadtmann, G., 'Frequent news and pure signals: the case of a publicly traded football club', *Scottish Journal of Political Economy* 53:4 (2006).

3. Berument, H., Ceylan, N. and Gozpinar, E., 'Performance of soccer on the stock market: Evidence from Turkey', *The Social Science Journal* 43:4 (2006).

4. Palomino, F., Renneboog, L. and Zhang, C., 'Information salience, investor sentiment, and stock returns: The case of British soccer betting', *Journal of Corporate Finance* 15:3 (2009).

5. Benkraiem, R., Louhichi, W. and Marques, P., 'Market reaction to sporting results: The case of European listed football clubs', *Management Decision* 47:1 2009.

6. Berument, H., Ceylan, N. and Ogut-Eker, G., 'Soccer, stock returns and fanaticism: Evidence from Turkey', *The Social Science Journal* 46:3 (2009).

7. Scholtens, B. and Peenstra, W., 'Scoring on the stock exchange? The effect of football matches on stock market returns: an event study', *Applied Economics* 41:25 (2009).

8. Bernile, G. and Lyandres, E., 'Understanding Investor Sentiment: The Case of Soccer', *Financial Management* 40:2 (2011).

9. Bell, A., Brooks, C., Matthews, D. and Sutcliffe, C., 'Over the moon or sick as a parrot? The effects of football results on a club's share price', *Applied Economics* 44:26 (2012).

10. Godinho, P. and Cerqueira, P., 'The Impact of Expectations, Match Importance and Results in the Stock Prices of European Football Teams', GEMF Working Paper 2014-09 (2014).

11. Berkowitz, J. and Depken, C., 'Asymmetric Reactions to Good and Bad News as Market Efficiency: Evidence from Publicly-Traded Soccer Clubs', (2014).

Mon
25

2002: Boots, the UK health and beauty retailer, agrees to sell its Halfords chain to private equity firm CVC Capital Partners for £427m.

FTSE 100	39	0.1	1.1
FTSE 250	38	-0.2	0.7
S&P 500	57	0.1	0.8
NIKKEI	48	-0.2	1.0

Tue
26

Two-day FOMC meeting starts
Golf: PGA, Baltrusol, New Jersey (until 31st)
Horse racing: Glorious Goodwood (untl 30th)

FTSE 100	55	0.1	1.0
FTSE 250	55	-0.1	0.9
S&P 500	63	0.1	0.8
NIKKEI	50	-0.1	1.2

1908: The Federal Bureau of Investigation is established in Washington DC.

Wed
27

FTSE 100	57	0.1	0.9
FTSE 250	35	0.0	0.7
S&P 500	49	0.0	0.8
NIKKEI	48	-0.1	1.3

1900: The H. J. Heinz Company is incorporated.

Thu
28

Golf: Women's British Open, Woburn (until 31st)

FTSE 100	71	0.2	0.6
FTSE 250	57	-0.1	0.7
S&P 500	54	-0.2	0.8
NIKKEI	71	0.4	1.0

1800: The Act of Union 1800 is passed which merges the Kingdom of Great Britain and the Kingdom of Ireland into the United Kingdom of Great Britain and Ireland.

Fri
29

FTSE 100	**77**	**0.4**	**1.3**
FTSE 250	71	0.3	0.8
S&P 500	50	0.1	1.2
NIKKEI	45	-0.2	1.3

1981: A worldwide television audience of over 700 million people watches the wedding of Charles, Prince of Wales and Lady Diana Spencer.

Sat 30   50th anniversary of England winning the FIFA World Cup, beating West Germany 4-2 in the final.

Sun 31   Lammas

COMPANY RESULTS

Interim Acacia Mining, Alent, AstraZeneca, BAE Systems, Barclays, Berendsen, BG Group, Bodycote, BP, British American Tobacco, Capita, Capital & Counties Properties, Centrica, COLT Group SA, Countrywide, Dignity, Domino's Pizza, Drax Group, Elementis, Essentra, Fidelity European Values, Foreign & Colonial Investment Trust, Foxtons, GKN, GlaxoSmithKline, Greggs, Henderson Group, Hiscox, IMI, Inchcape, Indivior, Informa, InterContinental Hotels, International Consolidated Airlines, International Personal Finance, Intu Properties, ITV, Jardine Lloyd Thompson, Jupiter Fund Management, Laird, Lancashire, Lloyds Banking Group, Man Group, Merlin Entertainments, Millennium & Copthorne Hotels, Moneysupermarket. com, National Express, Pace, Pearson, Provident Financial, Rathbone Brothers, Reckitt Benckiser, Rentokil Initial, Rexam, Rightmove, Riverstone Energy, Rolls-Royce Group, Royal Bank of Scotland, Royal Dutch Shell, Schroders, Segro, Shawbrook Group, Smith & Nephew, Spectris, St James's Place, Taylor Wimpey, Telecity Group, Tullett Prebon, Tullow Oil, UBM, Vesuvius, Weir Group
Final Diageo, Renishaw, Sky

AUGUST MARKET

Market performance this month

Not surprisingly, perhaps, during the low-volume summer doldrums, the performance of shares in August is very similar to that in July. Five years ago August was ranked the 5th best month in the year, but now it has slipped to 7th. The average return in the month is 0.5%, while the probability of a positive return in August is 58%. As can be seen in the accompanying chart, there have been some nasty falls in August – most recently in 1998 and 2011.

Internationally, August is not a good month for equities; it has the second lowest average monthly returns for 70 world equity markets. In domestic currency terms, August is the strongest month of the year for the FTSE 100 relative to the S&P 500, but after factoring in the (historically weak) GBPUSD rate much of that outperformance disappears.

In an average month for August the market tends to drift lower for the first couple of weeks and then increase for the final two weeks of the month. The final trading day of the month has historically been strong.

Finally, August is the busiest month for interim results announcements for both the FTSE 100 (43 companies reporting) and FTSE 250 (93 companies).

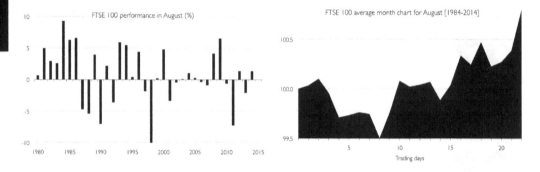

FTSE 100 performance in August (%)

FTSE 100 average month chart for August [1984-2014]

Trading days

August summary

Market performance	Avg return: 0.5%		Positive: 58%		Ranking: 7th
Sector performance	*Strong* Food & Drug Retailers, Gas, Water & Multiutilities, Health Care Equipment & Services, Household Goods, Software & Computer Services		*Weak* Chemicals		
Share performance	*Strong* Bunzl, Fisher (James) & Sons, Keller Group, Melrose Industries, Tullett Prebon		*Weak* Rio Tinto, Standard Chartered, Xaar		
Main features	Busiest month for FTSE 100 and FTSE 250 interim results announcements GBPUSD historically weak this month Weak month for silver First trading day average return: 0.03%; positive: 60% (2nd weakest of the year) Last trading day average return: 0.11%; positive: 61% (3rd strongest of the year) 01 Aug: start of the 5th strongest market week 10 Aug: 5th weakest market day of the year 22 Aug: start of the 2nd strongest market week				
Significant dates	03 Aug: ECB Governing Council Meeting (non-monetary policy) 04 Aug: MPC interest rate announcement at 12 noon (anticipated) 05 Aug: US Nonfarm payroll report (anticipated) 11 Aug: MSCI Quarterly Index Review announcement date 29 Aug: Summer bank holiday, LSE closed 31 Aug: FTSE 100 quarterly review				

Mon
1

Lughnasadh

FTSE 100	57	-0.2	1.3
FTSE 250	43	-0.4	1.4
S&P 500	47	0.0	0.9
NIKKEI	39	-0.1	1.4

'Video Killed the Radio Star' by The Buggles is the first video played on the new channel MTV.

Tue
2

New moon

FTSE 100	73	0.5	1.0
FTSE 250	65	0.1	1.0
S&P 500	57	0.2	1.0
NIKKEI	55	0.4	1.3

1939: Albert Einstein and Leó Szilárd write a letter to Franklin D. Roosevelt, urging him to begin the Manhattan project to develop a nuclear weapon.

Wed
3

ECB Governing Council Meeting (non-monetary policy)

FTSE 100	43	-0.1	1.2
FTSE 250	50	-0.1	1.0
S&P 500	53	0.0	0.9
NIKKEI	33	-0.4	1.1

1978: The British government pumps £54m into John DeLorean's car company, based in Northern Ireland. By 1982 the company is insolvent.

Thu
4

MPC interest rate announcement at 12h00

FTSE 100	**29**	**-0.3**	**0.9**
FTSE 250	50	-0.2	1.1
S&P 500	46	-0.3	1.1
NIKKEI	24	-06	0.7

1870: The British Red Cross Society is founded by Lord Wantage.

Fri
5

Nonfarm payroll report (anticipated)
Olympic Games, Brazil (until 21st)
International Beer Day
50th anniversary of the release of The Beatles' album *Revolver*

FTSE 100	50	-0.2	1.2
FTSE 250	62	-0.1	1.2
S&P 500	42	-0.1	0.9
NIKKEI	32	-0.4	1.2

1960: Burkina Faso (Upper Volta) becomes independent from France.

Sat 6

Sun 7

COMPANY RESULTS

Interim Aggreko, Aviva, BBA Aviation, Cobham, Direct Line Insurance Group, esure Group, Fidessa Group, Fresnillo, HSBC, Inmarsat, Intertek Group, IP Group, JPMorgan American Investment Trust, Keller Group, Kennedy Wilson Europe Real Estate, Legal & General, London Stock Exchange, Meggitt, Mondi, Old Mutual, Randgold Resources, Rio Tinto, RIT Capital Partners, Rotork, RSA Insurance Group, Savills, Senior, Spirax-Sarco Engineering, Standard Chartered, Standard Life, Travis Perkins, Ultra Electronics, UNITE Group, William Hill

OLYMPIC GAMES

Does analysis of the historic behaviour of stock markets around the time of the four-yearly Olympic Games have anything of interest for investors?

The hosts of the Olympic Games are usually announced seven years in advance; for example after Rio de Janeiro this year the next Games will be held in Tokyo in 2020. The Olympic Games are a major event, often requiring much spending to improve infrastructure; such spending can provide a fillip to a nation's economy. If this affects prices on the stock market it is likely to happen soon after the initial announcement of a country winning the competition to host the event – so, long before the Olympics take place.

However, in this analysis we will look at the performance of host country stock markets in the year of the Olympics itself. The following chart shows the performance of stock markets in countries that have recently hosted the Olympics: US (1984, 1996), Australia (2000), Greece (2004), UK (2012). (NB. China was omitted as it hosted the Games in 2008 – a year when stock markets had their focus on other matters. The share price of National Bank of Greece was used as a proxy for the Greek stock market.) The index data has been rebased to start at 100. The Games generally take place in August-September (indicated by the shaded portion in the chart).

There are no easily discernible trends. The following chart plots the average performance for all the markets over three periods:

1. **Before games**: from 1 January to the start of the games
2. **During games**: the two-three week period of the games
3. **After games**: from the end of the games to 31 December

The darker bars are the average performance calculated excluding China and Greece.

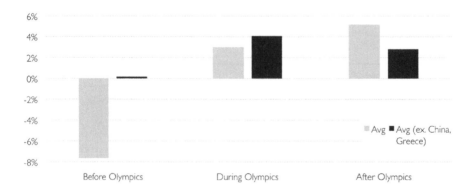

Generally, equities in host country markets appear to be weak in the months leading up to the games, perhaps when the media runs stories of cost overruns and missed timetables. And then there appears to be a relief rally afterwards.

Mon

8

FTSE 100	61	0.1	1.2
FTSE 250	67	0.1	1.2
S&P 500	53	-0.1	1.3
NIKKEI	57	0.0	1.3

1974: Richard Nixon announces he is to step down as president of the United States – the first man ever to do so.

Tue

9

FTSE 100	59	0.1	1.0
FTSE 250	65	0.1	0.9
S&P 500	46	0.0	1.0
NIKKEI	55	-0.1	1.3

1995: Internet browser maker Netscape floats on NASDAQ with an expected opening price of $12. By the time the first trade is made the price has risen to $71. This marks the start of a flurry of internet IPOs.

Wed

10

FTSE 100	**29**	**-0.6**	**1.3**
FTSE 250	40	-0.4	0.9
S&P 500	43	-0.2	1.0
NIKKEI	43	-0.2	1.2

2003: Britain records its hottest-ever day, with temperatures above 100F, leading to jammed roads and packed beaches across the country.

Thu

11

Mountain Day (Japan) – TSE closed
MSCI quarterly index review (announcement date)
Golf: PGA, Baltrusol, New Jersey (until 14th)

FTSE 100	48	0.0	1.3
FTSE 250	52	0.1	1.1
S&P 500	56	0.2	1.1
NIKKEI	67	0.1	1.5

1919: The constitution of the Weimar Republic is adopted.

Fri

12

FTSE 100	64	0.3	1.0
FTSE 250	70	0.3	0.8
S&P 500	43	-0.1	0.7
NIKKEI	41	-0.1	1.0

1923: Enrico Tiraboschi is the first man to swim the English Channel westward.

Sat 13   Tisha B'Av (until 14th)

Sun 14

Interim Balfour Beatty, Centamin, Cineworld Group, CLS, Coca-Cola HBC AG, Derwent London, G4S, Interserve, Just Eat, Ladbrokes, Michael Page International, Murray International Trust, Ophir Energy, Prudential, Serco Group, SIG, Synthomer

COMPANY
RESULTS

US ELECTION PORTFOLIOS

The chart below shows the performance of the UK market (FTSE All-Share index) over the periods the respective US presidents were in office.

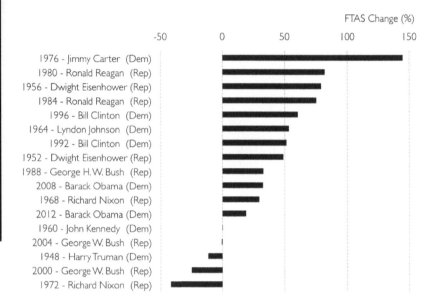

FTAS Change (%)

From the point of view of the UK market, the best president was Jimmy Carter – the market rose 145% during his four years as president. The worst spell was the second term of Richard Nixon, when the market fell 42%.

The chart below plots the values of two portfolios (indexed to 100):

- **Democrat portfolio**: only invests in the UK when there is a Democrat in the White House, and is in cash when the president is a Republican.

- **Republican portfolio**: reverse of the above.

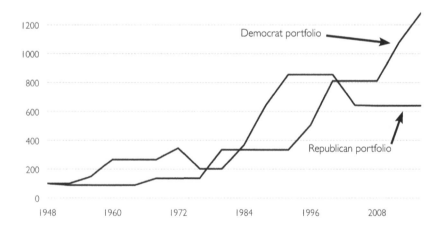

The two portfolios largely tracked each other closely (unlike the equivalent Labour and Conservative portfolios in the UK), until the 2008 election of Barack Obama. From this period, the Democrat portfolio performed strongly, such that by 2015 this portfolio had a value of 1282 compared with 639 for the Republican portfolio.

Mon

15

FTSE 100	57	0.0	1.0
FTSE 250	71	0.1	0.9
S&P 500	53	0.0	0.8
NIKKEI	57	0.3	1.6

1872: Britain introduces secret ballot voting.

Tue

16

FTSE 100	59	-0.1	1.1
FTSE 250	65	-0.1	1.0
S&P 500	59	0.1	0.8
NIKKEI	50	0.2	1.4

1955: Fiat Motors orders the first private atomic reactor.

Wed

17

FTSE 100	62	0.1	1.2
FTSE 250	60	0.0	1.1
S&P 500	76	0.3	1.0
NIKKEI	38	-0.7	1.5

2008: American swimmer Michael Phelps becomes the first person to win eight gold medals in one Olympic Games.

Full moon

Thu

18

FTSE 100	57	0.1	1.4
FTSE 250	62	-0.1	1.2
S&P 500	46	-0.2	1.0
NIKKEI	62	0.0	1.2

1896: Adolph Ochs buys the *NY Times*.

Fri

19

FTSE 100	45	-0.2	1.2
FTSE 250	67	-0.1	1.1
S&P 500	46	-0.2	0.9
NIKKEI	50	-0.1	1.8

1950: The American Broadcasting Company airs the first Saturday morning television shows for children.

Sat 20

Sun 21   25th anniversary of the LSE flotation of Capita Group

Interim Admiral Group, Amlin, BH Macro, Bovis Homes Group, Cairn Energy, Clarkson, Glencore, HellermannTyton Group, Hikma Pharmaceuticals, KAZ Minerals, NMC Health, Persimmon, Phoenix Group, Premier Oil, UK Commercial Property Trust, Wood Group (John)
Final Rank Group

COMPANY

RESULTS

FTSE 100 REVIEWS – COMPANIES LEAVING THE INDEX

The charts below show the share price of nine companies that have recently left the FTSE 100. The time period for each chart is six months, starting from three months before the company left the index. The vertical line in each chart indicates the announcement date of the company leaving the index.

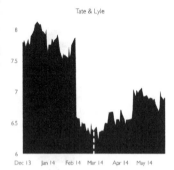

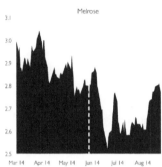

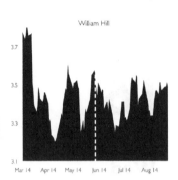

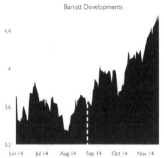

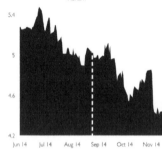

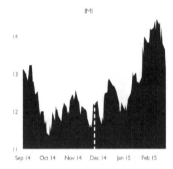

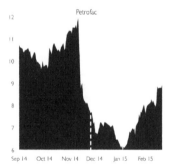

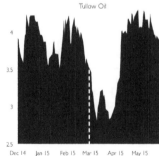

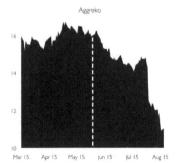

Observation

It can be seen that in most cases the share price falls in the period before the company leaves the FTSE 100. In many cases, after the review announcement the shares rise.

Mon
22

FTSE 100	52	0.2	0.9
FTSE 250	57	0.3	0.9
S&P 500	60	0.0	0.7
NIKKEI	45	0.0	1.5

1851: Gold fields are discovered in Australia.

Tue
23

FTSE 100	55	0.0	0.8
FTSE 250	68	0.0	0.7
S&P 500	41	0.1	1.1
NIKKEI	41	-0.3	1.7

2011: The price of gold hits $1,913.50 – its all-time high.

Wed
24

FTSE 100	75	0.2	0.9
FTSE 250	75	0.2	0.7
S&P 500	50	0.1	1.0
NIKKEI	57	0.2	1.3

1995: Microsoft's Windows 95 computer operating system is released, with much fanfare.

Thu
25

FTSE 100	69	0.0	1.0
FTSE 250	56	0.0	0.8
S&P 500	48	-0.1	0.7
NIKKEI	43	-0.1	1.0

1888: The first successful adding machine is patented in the US by William Seward Burroughs.

Fri
26

FTSE 100	50	-0.1	0.8
FTSE 250	41	-0.1	0.6
S&P 500	50	-0.1	0.8
NIKKEI	55	0.0	1.0

1959: The British Motor Corporation introduces the Morris Mini-Minor. Designed by Alec Issigonis, it is only 10ft long and seats four passengers.

Sat 27

Sun 28

COMPANY RESULTS

Interim Al Noor Hospitals Group, Aldermore Group, Allied Minds, Amec Foster Wheeler, Antofagasta, Bank of Georgia, Bluecrest Allblue Fund, Bunzl, Bwin.Party Digital Entertainment, Carillion, Computacenter, CRH, Evraz, F&C Commercial Property Trust, Fisher (James) & Sons, Grafton Group, Hansteen, Hunting, International Public Partnership, Jimmy Choo, John Laing Group, John Laing Infrastructure Fund, Melrose Industries, NB Global Floating Rate Income Fund, Nostrum Oil & Gas, OneSavings Bank, Petrofac, Playtech, Polymetal International, Regus, Spire Healthcare Group, Tritax Big Box REIT, WPP Group
Final BHP Billiton, Hays

SEPTEMBER MARKET

Market performance this month

September – the worst month of the year for shares! After the summer lull, things can get exciting again for investors in September. Since 1982, the FTSE All-Share index has on average fallen 1.0% in this month – the worst average return of any month in the year. And things haven't improved recently: since 2000 the average return in September has been even worse at -1.9%. The probability of a positive return in September is 45%.

In an average September, the market tends to gently drift lower for the first three weeks before rebounding slightly in the final week – although the final trading day (FTD) has historically been one of the weakest FTDs of all months in the year.

But, however bad the month is for large caps, it is even worse for mid-cap cap stocks. On average the FTSE 100 outperforms the FTSE 250 by 0.7 percentage points in September – making September, along with October, the worst months for mid-cap stocks relative to the large-caps.

By contrast to the weakness in equities, September has often been a strong month for gold and silver.

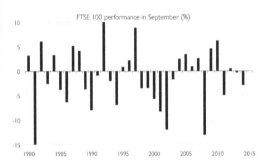

FTSE 100 performance in September (%)

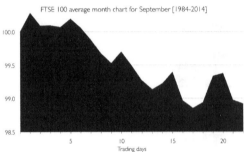

FTSE 100 average month chart for September [1984-2014]

September summary

Market performance	Avg return: -1.0%		Positive: 45%		Ranking: 12th
Sector performance	*Strong* Electricity, Food & Drug Retailers, Mobile Telecommunications, Pharmaceuticals & Biotechnology		*Weak* Aerospace & Defense, Chemicals, Electronic & Electrical Equipment, General Retailers, Media, Real Estate Investment Trusts, Technology Hardware & Equipment		
Share performance	*Strong* Dechra Pharmaceuticals, Diploma, Law Debenture Corporation (The), Polar Capital Technology Trust, United Utilities Group		*Weak* Compass Group, Pace, Premier Farnell, SVG Capital		
Main features	Weakest month in the year The FTSE 250 is particularly weak relative to the FTSE 100 in this month Strong month for gold Strong month for silver First trading day average return: 0.28%; positive: 68% Last trading day average return: -0.08%; positive: 42% (2nd weakest in year) 09 Sep: 3rd weakest market day of the year 11 Sep: 9th weakest market day of the year 19 Sep: start of the 2nd weakest week in the year 23 Sep: 10th weakest market day of the year				
Significant dates	02 Sep: US Nonfarm payroll report (anticipated) 05 Sep: Labor Day (US) – NYSE closed 08 Sep: ECB Governing Council Meeting (monetary policy) 15 Sep: MPC interest rate announcement at 12 noon (anticipated) 16 Sep: Triple Witching 20 Sep: Two-day FOMC meeting starts 21 Sep: ECB Governing Council Meeting (non-monetary policy)				

Mon
29

Summer Bank Holiday – LSE closed
Tennis: US Open, Flushing Meadows (until 11th September)

1885: Gottlieb Daimler patents the world's first internal combustion motorcycle, the Reitwagen.

S&P 500	59	0.1	0.8
NIKKEI	57	0.0	1.4

Tue
30

Waren Buffett's birthday

1974: A powerful bomb explodes at the Mitsubishi Heavy Industries headquarters in Marunouchi, Tokyo, Japan, killing 8 and injuring 378.

FTSE 100	67	0.3	1.0
FTSE 250	56	0.2	1.0
S&P 500	49	-0.1	0.9
NIKKEI	45	0.2	1.1

Wed
31

FTSE 100 quarterly review

1921: Germany pays its first million marks in reparations, causing the value of the mark to plummet 30%. This is the start of the German hyperinflation.

FTSE 100	59	0.2	0.9
FTSE 250	81	0.5	0.8
S&P 500	64	0.1	1.2
NIKKEI	48	-0.2	1.4

Thu
1

MSCI quarterly index review (effective date)
New moon
Annular solar eclipse (Africa and Indian Ocean)

1901: Construction begins on the NY Stock Exchange.

FTSE 100	67	0.3	1.1
FTSE 250	71	0.1	1.2
S&P 500	71	0.2	1.1
NIKKEI	60	0.2	1.2

Fri
2

Nonfarm payroll report (anticipated)

1666: The Great Fire of London breaks out and burns for three days, destroying 10,000 buildings including St. Paul's Cathedral.

FTSE 100	57	0.1	0.9
FTSE 250	57	0.3	0.9
S&P 500	59	0.2	1.0
NIKKEI	57	-0.1	1.0

Sat 3

Sun 4

Interim Restaurant Group, SVG Capital, Witan Investment Trust, Woodford Patient Capital Trust
Final Genus, Go-Ahead Group

COMPANY
RESULTS

SIX-MONTH STRATEGY WITH MACD

We have already looked at the Six-Month Effect (the tendency for the November-April market to outperform the May-October market), and how a portfolio based on this effect can dramatically outperform an index fund. But it is not necessarily the case that the strong half of the year begins every year on exactly 1 November, nor that it ends exactly on 30 April. By tweaking the beginning and end dates it may be possible to enhance the (already impressive) returns of the six-month strategy. An obvious rationale for this is that if investors are queuing up to buy at the end of October and sell at the end of April, it can be advantageous to get a jump on them and buy/sell a little earlier.

This idea of finessing the entry/exit dates was first proposed by Sy Harding in his 1999 book, *Riding the Bear: How to Prosper in the Coming Bear Market*. Harding's system takes the six-month seasonal trading strategy and adds a timing element using the MACD indicator. First, by back-testing, Harding found that the optimal average days to enter and exit the market were in fact 16 October and 20 April. Then, using these dates, his system's rules are:

1. If the MACD already indicates the market is in a bull phase on 16 October the system enters the market, otherwise the system waits until the MACD gives a buy signal.

2. If the MACD already indicates the market is in a bear phase on 20 April the system exits the market, otherwise the system waits until the MACD gives a sell signal.

Following such rules, the entry or exit dates of the strategy can be one or two months later than the standard 1 November and 30 April. Harding calls his system the Seasonal Timing Strategy (or STS). Commenting on the STS, Mark Hulbert of Marketwatch.com said in April 2012 that it produced a 9.0% return (annualised) over the same period (2002-2012), or 2.0 percentage points per year more than a purely mechanical application of this seasonal pattern, and 3.6 percentage points ahead of a buy-and-hold.

Can such a strategy work in the UK market?

It was found difficult to replicate similar results for the UK market using Harding's STS system. One problem was that 1 November is such a good date for entering the market – it was difficult to consistently improve on it with any technical indicator. However, one simple system did emerge that improved on the standard six-month strategy. Briefly, its rules are:

1. The system enters the market at close on 31 October.

2. The system exits the market on the first MACD sell signal after 1 April.

3. The parameters of the MACD indicator were increased from the usual default values to 24, 52, 18.

In effect, the standard entry date is unchanged, but the exit date is determined by the MACD. In some years, this can delay exit to June or later.

To illustrate the performance of this system, the chart to the right shows the returns on three portfolios since 30 October 1999:

1. **Portfolio 1**: a portfolio tracking the FTSE All-Share index

2. **Portfolio 2**: employing the standard Six-Month Strategy

3. **Portfolio 3**: employing the Six-Month Strategy enhanced using MACD

At the end of the 15-year period, Portfolio 1 (the market) was valued at 1295 (from a starting value of 1000), Portfolio 2 was valued at 1784 and Portfolio 3 was valued at 1975. In other words, the addition of the MACD to time exit would appear an effective tool.

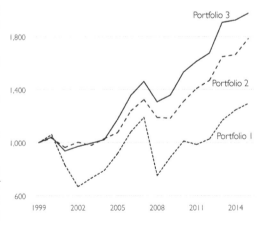

It's quite possible that further tweaking of the parameters and system rules could additionally enhance the strategy's performance.

Labor Day (US) – NYSE closed

Mon

5

FTSE 100	48	-0.3	1.0
FTSE 250	57	-0.3	1.0
NIKKEI	48	-0.4	1.2

1997: Mother Teresa dies at the age of 87.

Tue

6

FTSE 100	68	0.1	1.1
FTSE 250	55	0.1	0.8
S&P 500	65	0.1	0.9
NIKKEI	32	-0.2	1.0

1989: Due to a computer error, 41,000 Parisians receive letters charging them with murder, extortion and organised prostitution instead of traffic violations.

Beige Book published
Paralympic Games, Brazil (until 18th)

Wed

7

FTSE 100	52	0.1	1.4
FTSE 250	50	0.2	1.1
S&P 500	51	-0.1	0.8
NIKKEI	48	0.1	1.7

1979: The Chrysler Corporation asks the United States government for $1bn to avoid bankruptcy.

ECB Governing Council Meeting (monetary policy)

Thu

8

FTSE 100	38	-0.1	1.1
FTSE 250	52	0.1	1.0
S&P 500	52	0.0	1.0
NIKKEI	52	0.3	1.3

1992: The British pound hits a 20-year high of $2.0005 against the US dollar.

Fri

9

FTSE 100	**27**	**-0.3**	**0.8**
FTSE 250	43	-0.2	0.7
S&P 500	57	-0.2	1.0
NIKKEI	50	0.2	1.3

1947: The first actual case of a computer bug is found – a moth becomes lodged in a relay of a Mark II computer at Harvard.

Sat 10 Eid al-Adha (Islam); Horse racing: St Leger, Doncaster racecourse

Sun 11

Interim Morrison (Wm) Supermarkets, Next
Final Ashmore Group, Barratt Developments, Dechra Pharmaceuticals, Dunelm Group, Hargreaves Lansdown, Redrow, Wetherspoon (JD)

COMPANY
RESULTS

MPC MEETINGS AND THE FTSE 100

The Monetary Policy Committee will be meeting on Wednesday and Thursday this week.

The Monetary Policy Committee (MPC) is a committee of the Bank England which was set up in 1997 to decide official interest rates in the UK (referred to as the Bank of England Base Rate). The MPC's primary responsibility is to keep the Consumer Price Index (CPI) close to the government's inflation target (2% as of 2011) and, more recently, it also has a responsibility to support growth and employment.

Monetary policy in the UK is usually effected through the rate at which money is lent (the interest rate), but in March 2009 the MPC announced that it would also start injecting money directly into the economy by purchasing financial assets (*aka* quantitative easing).

The chart on the right plots the BoE base rate since the MPC was established in 1997 (right-hand axis) and the FTSE 100 index. The chart goes to March 2009 – when the base rate was reduced to 0.5% and since when it has not moved.

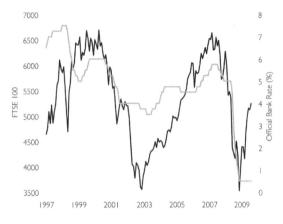

The MPC monthly meetings

The MPC meets once a month to set the bank rate. The meetings take place over two days: on the Wednesday and Thursday following the first Monday of each month. The interest rate decision is announced at noon on the second day of the meeting and the minutes of the meeting are published two weeks later (on the Wednesday of the second week after the meetings take place).

The monthly MPC announcement on interest rates was an important event; the announcement – and the anticipation of the announcement – could move the markets. However, since March 2009 the announcement has generated little interest as the rate has been set at 0.5% with little likelihood of changing in the short term. But this period of abnormally low interest rates may be coming to end, so it could be useful to revisit how the markets behaved around the time of the monthly announcements.

The chart on the right plots the average daily returns of the FTSE 100 for the three days around the MPC announcement: the day before the announcement MPC(-1), the day of the announcement MPC(0), and the day following the announcement MPC(+1). For each day, three values are plotted: the average FTSE 100 return for *all days* (i.e. for all the 144 MPC announcements 1997-2009), the returns on the days for the 18 times the MPC announced an increase in the bank rate, and the returns on the days for the 26 times the MPC announced a decrease in the rate.

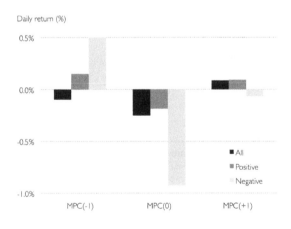

It can be seen that on average for all the MPC announcements equities tend to be weak the day before and on the day of the announcement itself (as shown by the black bars for MPC(-1) and MPC(0)), with a small relief rally on the following day. On those occasions when the rate was increased, equities rose the previous days and then followed the trend for all announcements. In the case of the rate being reduced, equities were significantly strong the day before, and significantly weak on the day of the MPC announcement itself.

Mon
12

30th anniversary of the LSE flotation of Travis Perkins

FTSE 100	48	-0.2	1.1
FTSE 250	52	-0.2	0.9
S&P 500	50	0.0	0.9
NIKKEI	52	-0.2	1.8

2005: England win the Ashes from Australia for the first time since 1987 after the "best ever" Test series.

Tue
13

FTSE 100	50	0.1	0.8
FTSE 250	55	0.0	0.6
S&P 500	69	0.2	0.9
NIKKEI	82	0.5	0.9

1503: Michelangelo begins work on his statue of David.

Wed
14

FTSE 100	57	0.0	1.4
FTSE 250	45	-0.1	1.1
S&P 500	56	0.1	0.8
NIKKEI	62	0.4	1.4

2007: Britain sees its first bank run in more than a century as savers withdraw £1bn in a single day from Northern Rock. The run comes after the BBC reports an unnamed bank has been given emergency support by the Bank of England.

Thu
15

MPC interest rate announcement at 12h00

FTSE 100	48	-0.2	1.3
FTSE 250	57	-0.1	1.0
S&P 500	52	-0.1	1.0
NIKKEI	71	0.8	1.3

2008: Merrill Lynch agrees to be acquired by Bank of America for $50bn.

Fri
16

Triple Witching
HKEX closed
Full moon
Penumbral lunar eclipse (eastern Europe, Africa, Asia and Australia)

FTSE 100	59	-0.1	1.1
FTSE 250	48	-0.2	1.1
S&P 500	67	0.4	0.7
NIKKEI	35	-0.9	2.1

1956: Play-Doh is introduced to the world.

Sat 17

Sun 18

Interim Card Factory, JD Sports Fashion, Kingfisher, Premier Farnell
Final City of London Investment Trust, Galliford Try, Just Retirement Group, Kier Group

COMPANY
RESULTS

AN AVERAGE MONTH

What does an average month for the FTSE 100 look like?

The summary pages for each month in the diary section carry charts that show the average cumulative behaviour of the market day-by-day. These charts are produced by calculating the daily mean return for each day in the trading year over a specific period (in this case from 1984). These charts then show the average behaviour of the market for the 12 calendar months for each day of the month. But we can also combine those 12 month charts into one, to show the average behaviour of the market on each day in any month.

The following chart plots the average daily returns for each day in the month for the FTSE 100 over the period 1984-2015. For example, since 1984 the market has traded 236 times on the first calendar day of all the months, and the average return of the FTSE 100 on those 236 days has been 0.25% (the first data point plotted in the chart).

Note: the chart here plots the average returns on the *calendar days* of the months, whereas elsewhere in the Almanac we usually look at just the trading days.

From this data we can calculate the average cumulative performance of the FTSE 100 in a month based on each day's average gain/loss (see following chart).

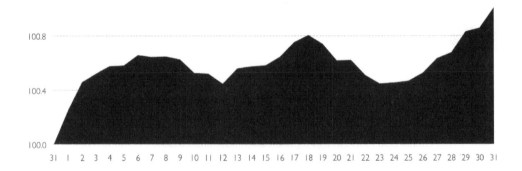

So, in an average month the FTSE 100 rises to the 5th of the month, then falls back until the 12th. It then increases again briefly to the 18th, before falling back and then finally bottoming on the 23rd, before rising quite strongly from there to the end of the month.

In conclusion, we have the rather remarkable fact that 76% of all the index gains in a month come from the first and last six days of the month.

Mon
19

Respect for the Aged Day (Japan) – TSE closed

FTSE 100	57	0.3	2.1
FTSE 250	33	0.2	2.0
S&P 500	46	0.0	1.2

2012: The Bank of Japan extends its asset purchasing programme by ¥10trn (£78bn), following similar moves by the Federal Reserve and the European Central Bank.

Tue
20

Two-day FOMC meeting starts

FTSE 100	45	-0.1	1.3
FTSE 250	45	-0.3	1.1
S&P 500	46	-0.1	0.8
NIKKEI	32	-0.3	1.2

1946: The first Cannes Film Festival is held.

Wed
21

ECB Governing Council Meeting (non-monetary policy)

FTSE 100	33	-0.4	0.9
FTSE 250	45	-0.3	1.1
S&P 500	37	-0.2	0.9
NIKKEI	55	-0.1	1.1

1915: Stonehenge is sold at auction to Mr CH Chubb for £6,600. Mr Chubb presents it to the nation three years later.

Thu
22

TSE closed
ECB General Council Meeting
September equinox
55th anniversary of the LSE flotation of Lonmin

FTSE 100	48	-0.3	1.3
FTSE 250	24	-0.5	1.0
S&P 500	47	-0.1	1.0

1991: Dutch banks ABN and AMRO merge

Fri
23

FTSE 100	**32**	**-0.3**	**1.0**
FTSE 250	33	-0.5	0.9
S&P 500	42	-0.1	0.9

1998: 14 Wall Street banks stump up $3.65bn to prevent the collapse of Long-Term Capital Management, the hedge fund run by John Meriwether.

Sat 24

Sun 25

Interim AA, Barr (AG)
Final Close Brothers Group, Genesis Emerging Markets Fund, Petra Diamonds, Smiths Group

COMPANY
RESULTS

OCTOBER MARKET

Market performance this month

October is a puzzling month for investors. On the one hand it has a reputation for volatility – and this is well deserved. Since 1984, seven of the ten largest one-day falls in the market have occurred in October! The largest fall occurred on 20 October 1987, when the FTSE 100 fell 12.2%. And, additional bad news for investors, is that since 1970 the average return in the month has been just 0.3%, ranking it 9th of the 12 months. However, things have changed in recent years.

Although the market occasionally suffers large falls in this month (as can be seen in the accompanying chart), for the most part the market posts a positive return. In fact, in the last 22 years the market has only fallen five times in October – this is a performance only bettered by December. In recent years the market has posted an average return of 0.7% in this month (albeit with a very high standard deviation) – ranking it 5th for monthly performance.

In an average October, the market tends to rise in the first two weeks, then fall back, before a surge in prices in the last few days of the month – with the last trading day (LTD) being the strongest of the year.

October marks the end of the weak six-month period of the year, so many investors are looking to increase their exposure to equities towards the end of the month.

Aside from equities, October has been a weak month for gold, silver and oil.

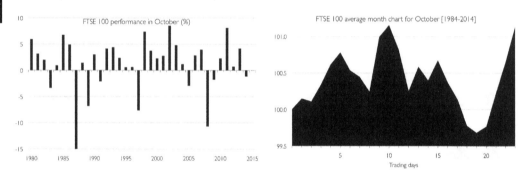

October summary

Market performance	Avg return: 0.7%		Positive: 74%	Ranking: 5th
Sector performance	**Strong**		**Weak** Automobiles & Parts, Construction & Materials, Equity Investment Instruments, Food & Drug Retailers, Health Care Equipment & Services, Household Goods, Life Insurance, Pharmaceuticals & Biotechnology	
Share performance	**Strong** Diageo, Marks & Spencer Group, Restaurant Group (The), Tate & Lyle		**Weak** Centrica, Tullett Prebon, William Hill	
Main features	Sell in May effect: end of the weak six months of the year The FTSE 100 is particularly strong relative to the FTSE 250 in this month Weak month for gold Weak month for silver Weak month for oil GBPUSD historically strong this month First trading day average return: 0.15%; positive: 58% Last trading day average return: 0.49%; positive: 71% (year's strongest)			
Significant dates	05 Oct: ECB Governing Council Meeting (non-monetary policy) 07 Oct: US Nonfarm payroll report (anticipated) 13 Oct: MPC interest rate announcement at 12 noon (anticipated) 20 Oct: ECB Governing Council Meeting (monetary policy)			

Mon
26

1889: The first General Conference on Weights and Measures (CGPM) defines the length of a meter as the distance between two lines on a standard bar of an alloy of platinum with 10% iridium, measured at the melting point of ice.

FTSE 100	57	0.2	1.4
FTSE 250	57	-0.1	0.9
S&P 500	57	-0.2	1.3
NIKKEI	43	-0.2	1.5

Golf: Ryder Cup, Hazeltine, Minnesota (until 2nd October)

Tue
27

1989: Sony buys Columbia for $3.4bn (and Columbia's string of Hollywood successes abruptly come to an end).

FTSE 100	73	0.6	1.1
FTSE 250	63	0.3	0.8
S&P 500	53	0.0	0.9
NIKKEI	55	0.3	1.4

Wed
28

FTSE 100	52	0.1	1.1
FTSE 250	55	0.1	0.7
S&P 500	64	0.3	0.9
NIKKEI	57	0.0	1.6

1894: Simon Marks and Tom Spencer open Penny Bazaar in Manchester.

Thu
29

FTSE 100	43	-0.3	1.3
FTSE 250	62	-0.2	1.3
S&P 500	43	-0.3	1.4
NIKKEI	48	0.1	0.7

1885: The first practical public electric tramway in the world is opened in Blackpool, England.

Fri
30

FTSE 100	41	-0.2	1.2
FTSE 250	38	-0.2	0.8
S&P 500	41	-0.1	1.2
NIKKEI	36	-0.7	1.3

1955: Hollywood actor James Dean is killed when his sports car is involved in a head-on collision with another vehicle.

Sat 1   Navratri (until 9th); New moon; 20th anniversary of the LSE flotation of Imperial Tobacco Group

Sun 2   Rosh Hashanah (at sundown, until 4th); Al-Hijra (until 30th)

Interim Johnson Matthey, Mercantile Investment Trust, Saga
Final JPMorgan Emerging Markets Inv Trust, Wolseley

COMPANY
RESULTS

NONFARM PAYROLLS

There are many statistics released every month by governments that investors follow to assess the strength of economies, but one of the most important and widely followed announcements is the Nonfarm payroll (NFP). This data is released every month by the US Bureau of Labor Statistics; it gives an overview of the employment situation in the US, not including – as the name suggests – farm employees and also a few others such as employees of the government and non-profit organisations.

The specific release of interest is the *Commissioner's Statement on The Employment Situation* and the key figure is usually in the first line. For example, the statement of 7 August 2015 starts:

> Nonfarm payroll employment rose by 215,000 in July.

It is the monthly change in employment (rather than the overall employment number) – and the deviation from the expected figure – that is watched closely.

The monthly Nonfarm payroll statistic can have a large impact on financial markets, primarily the US dollar, but also equities and gold. Regarding foreign exchange, there has been a small negative correlation between the NFP data and the US dollar index. Below we will look at the impact on equities.

The Nonfarm payroll statistic is reported monthly, usually on the first Friday of the month. The following chart shows the average daily returns of the S&P 500 index on the three days around the announcement date:

1. **NFP(-1)**: the average daily return on the day before the announcement

2. **NFP(0)**: on the day of the announcement

3. **NFP(+1)**: one day after the announcement

The results of analysis for two periods are shown:

1. **black bars**: 1990-2015

2. **grey bars**: 2006-2015

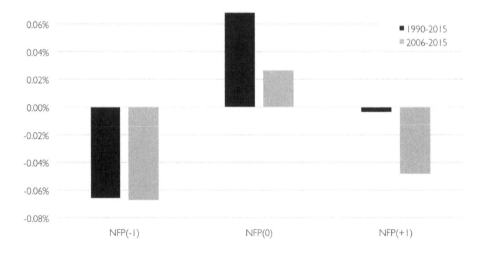

The analysis shows that since 1990 the S&P 500 index on average experiences a negative return (-0.066%) on the day before the Nonfarm payroll announcement, a positive return (+0.068%) on the day of the release, and again a negative return (-0.004%) the day afterwards.

In the last ten years, 2006-2015, the behaviour profile has largely been the same, except the average positive return has been less on NFP day, and the negative return greater the day after.

For reference, the average daily return on the S&P 500 index for all days since 1990 has been 0.03%.

Mon
3

1836: At the end of a five-year voyage, explorer Charles Darwin returns to Britain having completed a survey of the coast of South America.

FTSE 100	61	0.3	1.0
FTSE 250	48	0.0	0.7
S&P 500	46	-0.1	1.0
NIKKEI	43	-0.1	1.1

Tue
4

1976: British Rail begins its new 125mph Intercity High Speed Train service.

FTSE 100	64	0.1	1.0
FTSE 250	60	0.0	1.1
S&P 500	61	0.1	0.8
NIKKEI	50	0.1	1.2

Wed
5

ECB Governing Council Meeting (non-monetary policy)

2010: Jérôme Kerviel is found guilty of breach of trust, forgery and unauthorised use of Société Générale's computers, after his illicit trading loses the bank €4.9bn.

FTSE 100	76	0.3	1.6
FTSE 250	65	0.1	1.0
S&P 500	61	0.2	0.8
NIKKEI	62	0.2	1.0

Thu
6

1889: The Moulin Rouge in Paris opens its doors to the public.

FTSE 100	57	0.3	2.3
FTSE 250	62	0.1	1.8
S&P 500	54	0.2	1.2
NIKKEI	67	0.2	1.4

Fri
7

Nonfarm payroll report (anticipated)

1806: The first carbon paper is patented by English inventor Ralph Wedgwood.

FTSE 100	45	0.0	0.7
FTSE 250	52	0.0	1.6
S&P 500	38	-0.1	1.3
NIKKEI	45	-0.1	1.9

Sat 8   30th anniversary of the LSE flotation of Lloyds Banking Group

Sun 9

Interim Brown (N) Group, Ted Baker, Tesco

COMPANY
RESULTS

QUARTERLY SECTOR STRATEGY

The 2013 edition of the Almanac proposed a simple quarterly trading strategy for FTSE 350 sectors. This page brings the results of the strategy's performance up to date.

To recap, in the Statistics section the performance of the FTSE 350 sectors in each quarter can be found. From this data can be identified the sectors that have been consistently strong in each quarter over the past ten years. The four strongest sectors for each quarter selected with this analysis can be seen in the table to the right.

Quarter	Strong
1st	Industrial Engineering
2nd	Electricity
3rd	Software & Comp Srvs
4th	Beverages

The strategy cycles a portfolio through the four strong sectors throughout the year. In other words, the portfolio is 100% invested in the Industrial Engineering sector from 31 December to 31 March, then switches into Electricity to 31 June, then switches into Software and Computing Services to 30 September, then switches into Beverages to 31 December, and then switches back into Industrial Engineering and starts the cycle again.

Obviously, a more sophisticated strategy would be to run the analysis again each year to see if the strongest sectors in each quarter have changed. Another variation would be to hold the top three strongest sectors for each quarter – which would likely reduce the portfolio volatility. However, the purpose of this strategy is to keep things as simple as possible and to see how far such a simple strategy can go without any further calculation.

The accompanying chart illustrates the performance of such a strategy for the period Q3 2007 to Q2 2015, with a comparison of the FTSE All-Share index (the data series have been rebased to start at 100).

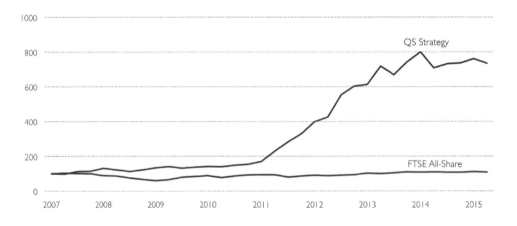

Over the eight years from 2007 the strategy would have grown £1000 into £7350; while a £1000 investment in the FTSE All-Share would have become just £1090.

Overall the strategy has greatly outperformed the market, although it has not been so strong in the last year.

Mon 10

Heath and Sports Day (Japan) – TSE closed
The day following the Chung Yeung Festival (China) – HKSE closed

FTSE 100	43	-0.3	2.1
FTSE 250	55	-0.3	1.6
S&P 500	45	0.1	1.3

1999: Thousands gather to watch giant Ferris wheel The Millennium Eye become the latest landmark on the London skyline.

Tue 11

Yom Kippur

FTSE 100	67	0.4	1.2
FTSE 250	65	0.4	0.9
S&P 500	54	0.2	1.0
NIKKEI	56	0.2	1.7

1982: The Mary Rose, flagship of King Henry VIII, is brought to the surface after 437 years at the bottom of the Solent.

Wed 12

FTSE 100	48	0.2	1.2
FTSE 250	45	0.2	0.8
S&P 500	42	0.0	0.9
NIKKEI	35	0.1	1.6

1983: Kakuei Tanaka, the former Prime Minister of Japan, is found guilty of taking a $2m bribe from Lockheed and sentenced to four years in jail.

Thu 13

MPC interest rate announcement at 12h00

FTSE 100	62	0.7	1.9
FTSE 250	57	0.2	1.1
S&P 500	49	0.3	2.1
NIKKEI	44	-0.2	1.0

1989: A failed leveraged buyout of United Airlines causes a mini-crash in the stock market.

Fri 14

FTSE 100	50	0.1	1.0
FTSE 250	52	0.2	0.5
S&P 500	54	0.1	1.0
NIKKEI	50	0.6	3.2

1920: University of Oxford degrees are conferred on women for the first time.

Sat 15

Sun 16   Full moon; Supermoon

Interim Booker Group
Final Bellway, WH Smith

COMPANY
RESULTS

VERY LARGE ONE-DAY MARKET FALLS

Analysis of the behaviour of the FTSE 100 for very large one-day falls.

26 years ago this week, on 20 October 1987, the FTSE 100 fell 12.2% in one day. This is the largest one-day fall in the index since its inception in 1984. The accompanying table shows the ten largest one-day falls in the index since 1984.

Judging by the table, it would seem that many of the largest one-day falls have occurred in recent years.

Is the FTSE 100 becoming increasingly volatile?

Since 1984 there have been 212 very large one-day falls, where 'very large' is defined as a move more than two standard deviations beyond the average daily change in the index. In other words, a very large fall is any decrease over -2.17%. These falls are plotted on the following chart.

Date	Change(%)
20 Oct 87	-12.2
10 Oct 08	-8.8
06 Oct 08	-7.9
15 Oct 08	-7.2
26 Oct 87	-6.2
19 Oct 87	-5.7
06 Nov 08	-5.7
22 Oct 87	-5.7
21 Jan 08	-5.5
15 Jul 02	-5.4

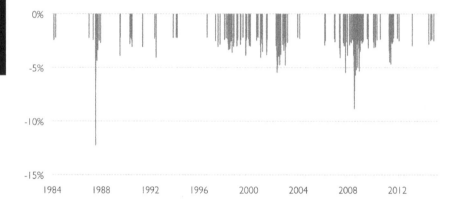

As can be seen in the chart, the periods 1997-2003 and 2007-2010 saw an increased frequency of large one-day falls.

After the fall

The following chart shows how on average the index behaves in the days immediately following a very large fall. The Y-axis is the percentage move from the close of the index on the day of the large fall. For example, by day five the index has risen 0.8% above the index close on the day of the large fall.

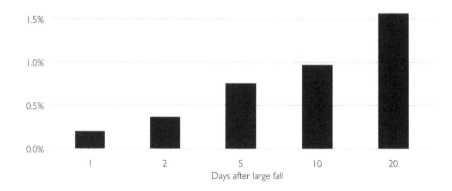

Days after large fall

As can be seen, the index rises steadily in the days following a very large fall, such that by the 20th day the index has bounced back 1.6%.

Mon
17

FTSE 100	70	0.5	1.5
FTSE 250	57	0.2	0.8
S&P 500	45	-0.1	0.9
NIKKEI	48	0.2	1.0

1980: Queen Elizabeth II makes the first state visit to the Vatican by a British monarch.

Tue
18

FTSE 100	55	-0.1	0.8
FTSE 250	60	0.0	0.8
S&P 500	65	0.3	0.9
NIKKEI	45	-0.1	1.3

1985: Nintendo releases the Nintendo Entertainment System in the US.

Wed
19

Beige Book published
World Economic Forum Special Meeting (until 22nd)

FTSE 100	48	-0.2	1.7
FTSE 250	50	-0.4	2.1
S&P 500	46	-0.6	3.2
NIKKEI	52	-0.1	1.1

1985: The first Blockbuster video store is opened in Dallas, Texas.

Thu
20

ECB Governing Council Meeting (monetary policy)

FTSE 100	48	-0.3	3.1
FTSE 250	57	-0.4	2.5
S&P 500	63	0.4	1.3
NIKKEI	71	-0.1	3.6

1997: The Chancellor officially launches the Stock Exchange Electronic Trading System (SETS), which introduces electronic order-driven trading for the FTSE 100.

Fri
21

FTSE 100	64	0.5	1.8
FTSE 250	70	0.5	1.2
S&P 500	50	0.2	1.6
NIKKEI	43	0.0	1.3

1805: Battle of Trafalgar.

Sat 22   20th anniversary of the LSE flotation of JD Sports Fashion

Sun 23   Shemini Atzeret (until 24th)

Interim Home Retail Group, Whitbread
Final Debenhams

COMPANY
RESULTS

DAYLIGHT SAVING EFFECT

British Summer Time will end this Sunday, 30 October.

Although Benjamin Franklin first suggested the idea of daylight saving time in 1784, it was William Willett, a builder living in Petts Wood, Kent, who first took the idea seriously enough to circulate a pamphlet to Members of Parliament in 1907. Willett's argument was that advancing the clocks in spring and returning to GMT in the autumn would lead to an increase in health and happiness, and it would also save the country £2.5m (after taking account of the loss of earnings to the producers of artificial light).

British Summer Time (BST) was finally introduced in April 1916, as an economy measure during wartime – a move quickly followed by many other countries in the following few weeks. During the second world war, double summer time (two hours advance on GMT) was introduced for the summer, while winter clocks stayed one hour ahead of GMT. For three years from 1968, Britain kept on BST throughout the whole year. But the experiment was abandoned in 1972, since when Britain has used GMT in winter and BST in summer.

In 1996 all clocks in Europe changed on the same day for the first time. The European Union has now adopted The Ninth European Parliament and Council Directive on Summer Time Arrangements in which summer (or daylight saving) time will be kept between the last Sunday in March to the last Sunday in October. The changes take place at 01h00 GMT.

And the relevance to shares is…?

Research has shown that even minor sleep disruptions can cause profound changes in cognition, leading to anxiety, inattention and impaired judgment.

An academic paper[1] looked at the potential effect the switches to and from daylight saving time might have on stock markets in the US, UK, Canada and Germany. The authors investigated the possibility that investors prefer safer investments and shun risk on the trading day following daylight saving time changes.

Some of the results they found were:

*   In all cases, it was found that stock returns were significantly lower following a daylight saving time change than they were on other trading days, even after controlling for other known seasonalities like the Monday effect. This is consistent with anxiety-prone investors selling risky assets on the trading day following the sleep disruption caused by daylight saving time changes.

*   The daylight saving effect was found to be extremely significant for the UK and US markets, strongly significant in Canada, and relatively insignificant in Germany (likely due to the relatively shorter period of data available for Germany since there were no daylight saving time changes in that country between 1950 and 1979).

*   The autumn daylight saving change had a greater impact than that in spring.

*   In the US, the financial impact of this phenomenon amounts to an average of roughly $30bn each time the clocks have been shifted over the past 30 years.

The following chart shows the FTSE 100 returns for the day following the end of BST for the period 1985-2014.

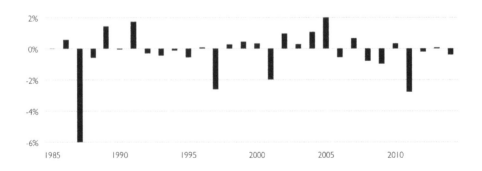

1. Mark J. Kamstra, Lisa A. Kramer, Maurice D. Levi, 'Losing Sleep at the Market: The Daylight-Savings Anomaly' (2000).

Mon
24

Simchat Torah (until 25th)

FTSE 100	48	-0.2	1.4
FTSE 250	43	-0.2	1.4
S&P 500	49	-0.1	1.0
NIKKEI	39	-0.4	2.1

1945: Allies of World War II ratify the UN Charter at a ceremony in Washington DC.

Tue
25

FTSE 100	41	-0.3	0.7
FTSE 250	47	0.1	0.6
S&P 500	37	-0.2	0.9
NIKKEI	36	-0.2	1.2

1861: The Toronto Stock Exchange is formed.

Wed
26

FTSE 100	43	-0.3	1.8
FTSE 250	45	-0.5	2.1
S&P 500	50	-0.2	1.5
NIKKEI	52	-0.4	1.3

1529: Sir Thomas More is appointed Lord Chancellor of England.

Thu
27

FTSE 100	52	0.0	1.2
FTSE 250	48	-0.2	1.1
S&P 500	53	-0.1	1.5
NIKKEI	48	-0.5	1.8

1987: Andrew Krieger, a currency trader at Bankers Trust, allegedly sells short more kiwi dollars than the entire money supply of New Zealand.

Fri
28

35th anniversary of the LSE flotation of Cable & Wireless Communications

FTSE 100	68	0.1	1.2
FTSE 250	67	-0.3	1.4
S&P 500	70	0.5	1.9
NIKKEI	55	0.2	2.0

1938: DuPont announces the launch of a new material made out of coal, air and water. Developed over eight years, it is marketed as 'nylon'.

Sat 29

Sun 30   Diwali (until 3rd November); BST ends (clocks go back); New moon

Interim BT Group
Final Redefine International

COMPANY
RESULTS

NOVEMBER MARKET

Market performance this month

Since 1984, the FTSE 100 has risen in 58% of years in November, with an average return over the period of 0.7%. This gives it a rank of 6th place for monthly performance. From 1980 its relative performance had been steadily improving, but that trend has reversed since 2006 – the market has risen only three times in November in the last nine years.

Although the longer-term performance of November is only average, the significant feature of November is that it marks the start of the strong six-month period of the year (November to April). In other words, investors should be increasing exposure to the market this month (if they haven't already done so in October).

On average the market tends to rise for the first three days of the month, then to give up those gains over the following few days, rise again and fall back, until finally increasing quite strongly over the final seven trading days of the month.

This is a busy month for interim results: 63 companies from the FTSE 350 make their announcements this month.

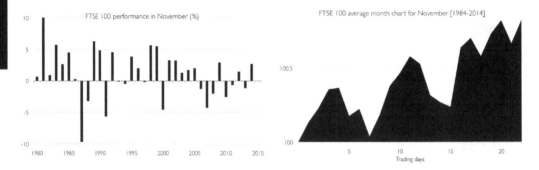

FTSE 100 performance in November (%)

FTSE 100 average month chart for November [1984-2014]

November summary

Market performance	Avg return: 0.7%		Positive: 58%	Ranking: 6th
Sector performance	*Strong* Beverages, Electronic & Electrical Equipment, Fixed Line Telecommunications, Food Producers, Life Insurance, Media, Mining, Technology Hardware & Equipment, Travel & Leisure		*Weak* Aerospace & Defense, Banks, General Industrials, Oil & Gas Producers, Real Estate Investment Trusts	
Share performance	*Strong* Babcock International Group, Compass Group, Greene King, Shire		*Weak* CSR, Lloyds Banking Group, Tullett Prebon	
Main features of the month	Busy month for FTSE 350 interim results Strong month for gold Weak month for oil GBPUSD historically weak this month First trading day average return: 0.13%; positive: 65% Last trading day average return: -0.12%; positive: 42% (year's weakest) 19 Nov: 7th weakest market day of the year			
Significant dates	01 Nov: Two-day FOMC meeting starts 02 Nov: ECB Governing Council Meeting (non-monetary policy) 03 Nov: MPC interest rate announcement at 12 noon (anticipated) 04 Nov: US Nonfarm payroll report (anticipated) 08 Nov: US Presidential Election 11 Nov: MSCI semi-annual index review (announcement date) 16 Nov: ECB Governing Council Meeting (non-monetary policy) 24 Nov: Thanksgiving Day (US) – NYSE closed 30 Nov: FTSE 100 quarterly review			

Mon

31

Reformation Day
Samhain
Halloween

FTSE 100	74	0.4	1.0
FTSE 250	81	0.4	1.0
S&P 500	51	0.1	0.9
NIKKEI	61	0.1	1.7

2011: 7 Billion Day. According to the United Nations, the world population has now reached 7bn.

Tue

1

Two-day FOMC meeting starts
All Saints' Day

FTSE 100	59	-0.1	0.9
FTSE 250	55	0.0	0.9
S&P 500	59	0.2	1.2
NIKKEI	41	-0.3	1.2

1848: The first W. H. Smith railway bookstall opens, at Euston Station, London.

Wed

2

All Souls' Day
ECB Governing Council Meeting (non-monetary policy)

FTSE 100	57	0.2	0.8
FTSE 250	60	0.3	0.6
S&P 500	67	0.4	0.7
NIKKEI	48	0.2	1.5

2000: The first crew arrives at the International Space Station.

Thu

3

Culture Day (Japan) – TSE closed
MPC interest rate announcement at 12h00

FTSE 100	52	0.1	1.2
FTSE 250	62	0.2	1.1
S&P 500	67	0.4	1.1

1975: The Queen formally begins the operation of the UK's first oil pipeline, at a £500,000 ceremony in Scotland.

Fri

4

Nonfarm payroll report (anticipated)

FTSE 100	41	0.4	1.5
FTSE 250	52	0.4	1.8
S&P 500	53	0.1	1.0
NIKKEI	76	1.3	2.0

1880: The first cash register is patented by James and John Ritty of Dayton, Ohio.

Sat 5   Guy Fawkes Night/Bonfire Night

Sun 6

Interim 3i Infrastructure, Cable & Wireless Communications, Dairy Crest Group, Experian, FirstGroup, Marks & Spencer Group, RPC Group, Synergy Health, Tate & Lyle, Vedanta Resources, Worldwide Healthcare Trust
Final Associated British Foods, Imperial Tobacco Group, Shaftesbury

COMPANY

RESULTS

TRADING DAYS AROUND US ELECTIONS

How does the UK market trade in the days around US presidential elections?

US presidential elections are held every fours years on the Tuesday following the first Monday in November (hence they are always between 2 and 8 November). The newly elected president takes office at midday on Inauguration Day (20 January the following year).

In 2016 the US presidential election will take place on 8 November.

The table below shows the result of analysing the FTSE All-Share index for the nine days around each US election since 1972. The day numbers are as follows:

- **Days 1-4**: the four trading days leading up to the election

- **Day 5**: the election day

- **Days 6-9**: the four trading days following the election

Day	1	2	3	4	5	6	7	8	9
Proportion of days up (%)	45	73	64	55	64	55	45	55	45
Average change for the day (%)	0.56	0.33	0.39	0.36	0.64	-0.18	-0.49	0.29	-0.39
Standard deviation	2.45	0.66	1.11	1.05	1.35	0.95	2.09	1.17	1.28

The average change for each day is shown in the chart below.

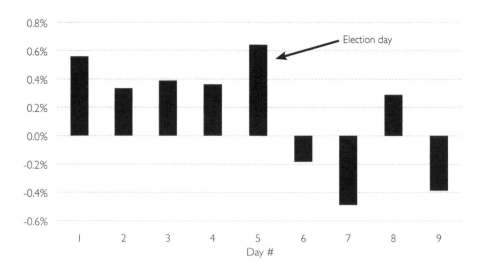

As can be seen, the UK market tends to trade stronger as the election day approaches, and then tails off in the few days following the election. The strongest day of the period has been the election day itself.

Mon

7

FTSE 100	48	-0.2	0.9
FTSE 250	43	-0.1	0.7
S&P 500	49	-0.2	1.0
NIKKEI	17	-0.8	1.3

2001: SABENA, the national airline of Belgium, goes bankrupt.

Tue

8

US Presidential Election

FTSE 100	59	0.1	0.6
FTSE 250	45	0.1	0.8
S&P 500	51	0.1	0.7
NIKKEI	38	-0.3	1.2

2001: Enron revises its financial statements for the past five years. Instead of the massive profits claimed previously, the company says it has actually lost $586m.

Wed

9

FTSE 100	43	-0.2	1.1
FTSE 250	40	-0.2	1.0
S&P 500	54	0.0	1.1
NIKKEI	38	-0.5	1.1

1989: The Berlin Wall is breached after nearly three decades of keeping East and West Berliners apart.

Thu

10

FTSE 100	52	0.0	0.5
FTSE 250	62	-0.1	0.8
S&P 500	59	0.0	0.8
NIKKEI	48	0.0	1.7

1970: The Great Wall of China is opened to visitors.

Fri

11

Armistice Day
MSCI semi-annual index review (announcement date)

FTSE 100	59	0.2	1.4
FTSE 250	48	0.1	1.5
S&P 500	72	0.2	0.9
NIKKEI	55	-0.3	1.6

1994: Bill Gates buys Leonardo da Vinci's *Codex* for $30.8m.

Sat 12   65th anniversary of the LSE flotation of Invensys

Sun 13   Remembrance Sunday

COMPANY RESULTS

Interim 3i Group, Atkins (WS), Auto Trader Group, Aveva Group, B&M European Value Retail SA, British Land Co, BTG, Burberry Group, DCC, Edinburgh Investment Trust, Electrocomponents, Entertainment One Group, Great Portland Estates, Halfords Group, Halma, Homeserve, Intermediate Capital Group, Land Securities Group, National Grid, SABMiller, Sainsbury (J), Scottish Mortgage Investment Trust, SSE, TalkTalk Telecom Group, Vectura Group, Vodafone Group, Workspace Group
Final British Empire Securities & General Trust, Lonmin

OIL

The following chart shows the monthly seasonality of the oil price (West Texas Intermediate) since 1986.

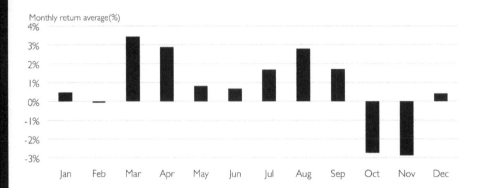

Monthly return average(%)

As can be seen, the oil price has historically had relatively strong returns in the months of March and April, and weak returns in October and November. The recent behaviour, since year 2000, has seen a similar trend.

Oil and the stock market

What is the connection between the oil price and the stock market?

The chart on the right plots the monthly returns of oil and the FTSE All-Share index. As can be seen, there is very little correlation ($R^2 = 0.001$).

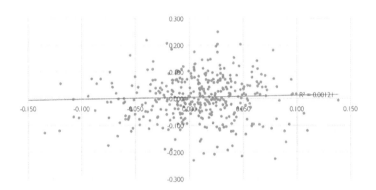

The following chart shows the ratio of the FTSE All-Share index to oil since 1971. (One can regard the chart as the UK equity market priced in oil.)

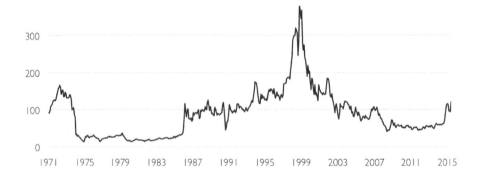

The ratio had a minimum value of 13.6 in March 1980 and maximum of 380.9 in November 1998. Since 1971, the average value is 88.6, and the chart does suggest a certain reversion to the mean over time. At the time of writing the ratio is 121.2.

Mon
14

Full moon
Supermoon

FTSE 100	57	0.2	0.7
FTSE 250	57	0.1	0.6
S&P 500	51	0.0	1.1
NIKKEI	57	0.2	1.2

1922: The BBC begins radio service in the UK.

Tue
15

FTSE 100	59	0.1	0.7
FTSE 250	65	0.2	0.7
S&P 500	46	-0.1	0.9
NIKKEI	50	0.5	1.5

2001: Microsoft releases the Xbox in North America – the company's first video game console.

Wed
16

ECB Governing Council Meeting (non-monetary policy)

FTSE 100	62	0.1	0.9
FTSE 250	65	0.1	0.8
S&P 500	54	0.0	0.8
NIKKEI	48	0.0	1.0

1849: A Russian court sentences Fyodor Dostoevsky to death for anti-government activities. The sentence is later commuted to hard labour.

Thu
17

World Philosophy Day

FTSE 100	43	-0.2	1.1
FTSE 250	48	-0.3	0.9
S&P 500	64	0.0	0.8
NIKKEI	48	0.0	2.1

2011: Virgin Money announces it will buy Northern Rock for £747m.

Fri
18

FTSE 100	64	0.1	0.8
FTSE 250	57	0.1	0.7
S&P 500	48	0.0	1.0
NIKKEI	55	0.4	1.8

1996: A fire breaks out in the Channel Tunnel just six months after it officially opened.

Sat 19

Sun 20

Interim Big Yellow Group, Caledonia Investments, Fidelity China Special Situation, HICL Infrastructure Company, ICAP, Investec, Perpetual Income & Growth Investment Trust, QinetiQ Group, Royal Mail Group, Telecom plus
Final Diploma, easyJet, Enterprise Inns, Euromoney Institutional Investor, Grainger

COMPANY
RESULTS

QUARTERLY SECTOR (HEDGE) STRATEGY

On page 84 we saw the performance of a strategy cycling investment in historically strong sectors through the calendar quarters. On this page we look at enhancing that strategy by, in each quarter, going long of the strong sector and hedging that by also going short of the quarter's weak sector.

First, the weak sectors for each quarter are shown in the table to the right (with a recap of the strong sectors).

As before, the strategy trades just four times a year. For example, in Q1 the strategy would be long the Industrial Engineering sector and short the Pharmaceuticals & Biotech sector.

Quarter	Strong	Weak
1st	Industrial Engineering	Pharma & Biotech
2nd	Electricity	Construction & Materials
3rd	Software & Comp Srvs	Oil & Gas Producers
4th	Beverages	Banks

The following chart shows the outperformance of the strong sector over the weak sector for each respective quarter for the period 2007-2014.

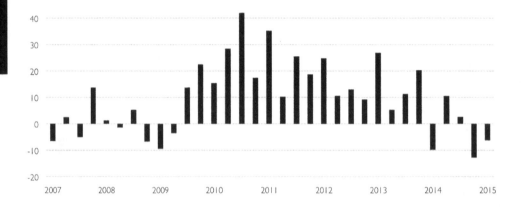

The following chart shows the cumulative performance of the Hedged Quarterly Sector (HQS) Strategy compared to the simple Quarterly Sector (QS) Strategy (from page 84), and the FTSE All-Share – with all series rebased to start at 100.

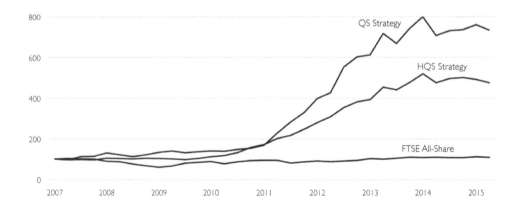

Although the hedge strategy underperforms the simple long strategy, the volatility of the former is much less than that of the latter (the standard deviation of the hedge strategy is 0.10 compared to 0.15 for the simple long strategy).

Again, a more sophisticated variation would be to re-analyse the data annually to identify any changes in the strongest/weakest sectors, but this strategy keeps things simple and sticks with the same sectors each year.

52, -0.1, 3.0

Mon
21

FTSE 100	57	0.0	1.2
FTSE 250	33	-0.3	1.0
S&P 500	57	0.2	1.2
NIKKEI	59	0.3	1.2

1990: Michael Milken, the Junk Bond King, is sentenced to a ten-year prison term for securities law infractions.

Tue
22

FTSE 100	45	-0.1	0.9
FTSE 250	60	-0.1	0.6
S&P 500	56	0.0	0.9
NIKKEI	64	0.1	1.2

2003: England's rugby team wins the World Cup, beating Australia 20-17 in a nailbiting final in Sydney.

Labor Thanksgiving Day (Japan) – TSE closed

Wed
23

FTSE 100	57	0.3	1.2
FTSE 250	70	0.2	1.0
S&P 500	59	0.2	0.9

1954: For the first time, the Dow Jones Industrial Average closes above the peak it reached just before the 1929 crash.

Thanksgiving (US) – NYSE closed

Thu
24

FTSE 100	52	0.6	2.2
FTSE 250	57	0.4	1.3
NIKKEI	50	-0.2	1.1

2005: Round-the-clock drinking in England and Wales is now a reality, as new licensing laws come into force.

NYSE closes at 13h00

Fri
25

FTSE 100	64	0.0	0.9
FTSE 250	62	0.1	0.7
S&P 500	64	0.1	0.6
NIKKEI	73	0.4	1.7

1994: Sony founder, Akio Morita, announces he is to step down as CEO of the company.

Sat 26

Sun 27

COMPANY RESULTS

Interim AO World, Babcock International Group, Daejan, Londonmetric Property, Mitie Group, PayPoint, Pennon Group, Pets at Home Group, Poundland Group, Severn Trent, Templeton Emerging Markets Investment Trust, TR Property Investment Trust, United Utilities Group

Final Britvic, Compass Group, Electra Private Equity, Greencore Group, Marston's, Mitchells & Butlers, Paragon Group of Companies, SSP Group, Thomas Cook Group, UDG Healthcare, Zoopla Property Group

DECEMBER MARKET

Market performance this month

December is the best month for shares. Since 1984 (when the FTSE 100 was created), the index has increased on average by 2.3% in December. In fact, in the 28 years since 1984 the market has only fallen five times in December – a quite remarkable record. It hasn't always been like this, as for many years April was the strongest month, but for the moment December is top dog.

And this stellar share strength in December is seen across the world: the average monthly returns across 70 world equity markets are highest in December.

As can be seen in the accompanying chart, the market tends to increase gently in the first two weeks of the month, but then goes into overdrive and rises strongly in the final two weeks. Indeed, this is the strongest two-week period in the whole year, with the three strongest days of the year all occurring in this two-week period.

Continuing the everything-is-awesome theme of the month, the FTSE 100 also tends to outperform the S&P 500 in December.

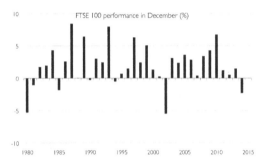
FTSE 100 performance in December (%)

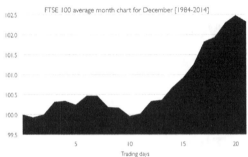
FTSE 100 average month chart for December [1984-2014]

Trading days

December summary

Market performance	Avg return: 2.3%	Positive: 84%	Ranking: 1st
Sector performance	*Strong* Construction & Materials, Life Insurance, Support Services, Travel & Leisure	*Weak* Banks, General Retailers, Pharmaceuticals & Biotechnology	
Share performance	*Strong* Ashtead Group, Balfour Beatty, G4S, William Hill, Witan Investment Trust	*Weak* Randgold Resources Ltd, Rank Group (The)	
Main features	Strongest month of the year FTSE 100 often outperforms the S&P 500 First trading day average return: -0.07%; positive: 45% (year's weakest) Last trading day average return: 0.05%; positive: 52% 04 Dec: 8th weakest market day of the year 16 Dec: 9th strongest market day of the year 19 Dec: start of the strongest market week of the year 23 Dec: 3rd strongest market day of the year 24 Dec: 2nd strongest market day of the year 26 Dec: Start of the 3rd strongest market week of the year 27 Dec: Strongest market day of the year		
Significant dates	02 Dec: US Nonfarm payroll report (anticipated) 08: ECB Governing Council Meeting (monetary policy) 13 Dec: Two-day FOMC meeting starts 15 Dec: MPC interest rate announcement at 12 noon (anticipated) 16 Dec: Triple Witching 25 Dec: Christmas Day – LSE, NYSE, HKSE closed 26 Dec: Boxing Day – LSE, HKSE closed 30 Dec: LSE closed		

NOV/DEC

Mon
28

FTSE 100	48	0.1	1.1
FTSE 250	57	0.3	1.1
S&P 500	53	0.1	1.1
NIKKEI	55	0.1	1.5

1717: Blackbeard attacks and captures the French merchant vessel La Concorde, which he renames Queen Anne's Revenge.

Tue
29

New moon

FTSE 100	66	0.1	0.7
FTSE 250	58	0.1	0.7
S&P 500	48	0.0	0.6
NIKKEI	59	0.2	1.3

1956: Panic-buying breaks out at garages across the UK as the government reveals details of petrol rationing plans.

Wed
30

St Andrew's Day
FTSE 100 quarterly review
Beige Book published

FTSE 100	43	-0.2	1.4
FTSE 250	65	-0.1	1.2
S&P 500	48	0.0	1.3
NIKKEI	62	0.2	1.3

1998: The London International Financial Futures and Options Exchange (LIFFE) launches an electronic trading system: Liffe Connect.

Thu
1

MSCI semi-annual index review (effective date)

FTSE 100	55	0.0	1.8
FTSE 250	67	0.0	1.4
S&P 500	59	0.1	1.6
NIKKEI	62	0.7	1.5

1998: Exxon announces a $73.7bn deal to buy Mobil, thus creating Exxon-Mobil, the largest company on the planet.

Fri
2

Nonfarm payroll report (anticipated)

FTSE 100	50	0.1	0.9
FTSE 250	71	0.3	0.8
S&P 500	48	0.1	1.0
NIKKEI	59	-0.1	1.8

1939: New York's La Guardia airport opens.

Sat 3

Sun 4

Interim Berkeley Group, Betfair Group, Cranswick, DS Smith, Greene King, Monks Investment Trust, Northgate, Polar Capital Technology Trust, Wizz Air
Final Aberdeen Asset Management, Brewin Dolphin, Finsbury Growth & Income Trust, Sage Group, TUI AG

COMPANY
RESULTS

BOUNCEBACK PORTFOLIO

There is a theory that stocks that have fallen greatly in a year tend to bounce back in the first three months of the following year.

Is this true?

To analyse this, the ten worst performing stocks in the FTSE 350 in a year were put into an equally-weighted portfolio, the performance of which is measured for January-March of the following year.

The chart below shows the results for the years from 2003 to 2014: the charts plot the Bounceback Portfolio and FTSE 350 returns for the period January-March each year.

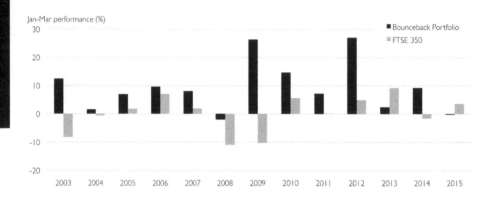

We can observe:

1. The Bounceback Portfolio has outperformed the FTSE350 every year since 2003, except in 2013 and 2015.

2. The FTSE 350 has fallen in four years in the Jan-Mar period since 2003; whereas the Bounceback Portfolio has fallen just twice (by relatively small amounts).

3. The Bounceback Portfolio has outperformed the FTSE 350 by an average of 9.3 percentage points each year since 2003.

The following chart plots the cumulative performance of two portfolios that invested in the market only over the January-March period for the years 2003-2015; one portfolio invests in the FTSE 350, the other in that year's Bounceback Portfolio.

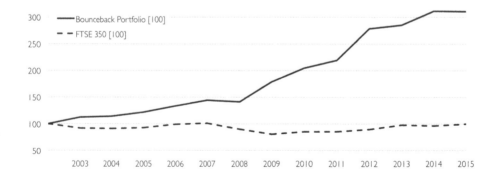

By 2015 the FTSE 350 portfolio value had fallen 0.3%, while the Bounceback Portfolio would have risen 210.7%.

Mon
5

250th anniversary of the first sale at Christie's auction house in London

FTSE 100	57	0.3	1.1
FTSE 250	67	0.3	1.0
S&P 500	49	0.2	1.1
NIKKEI	61	0.2	1.0

1766: The world-famous auction house Christie's is founded by James Christie.

Tue
6

St Nicholas' Day

FTSE 100	55	0.0	0.7
FTSE 250	50	0.1	0.8
S&P 500	60	0.2	0.8
NIKKEI	59	0.0	1.3

2000: French Internet service provider Wanadoo agrees to buy Britain's Freeserve for £1.65bn.

Wed
7

FTSE 100	45	0.0	0.7
FTSE 250	55	0.1	0.6
S&P 500	48	0.1	0.7
NIKKEI	57	0.4	1.2

1703: The Great Storm of 1703, the greatest windstorm ever recorded in the southern part of Great Britain, makes landfall. Winds gust up to 120mph and 9,000 people are killed

Thu
8

Feast of the Immaculate Conception
Bodhi Day
ECB Governing Council Meeting (monetary policy)

FTSE 100	57	0.4	1.5
FTSE 250	52	0.1	1.3
S&P 500	48	0.0	1.0
NIKKEI	43	-0.2	1.6

1864: The Clifton Suspension Bridge over the River Avon officially opens.

Fri
9

FTSE 100	50	0.0	1.0
FTSE 250	62	0.1	1.0
S&P 500	57	0.0	0.8
NIKKEI	55	0.3	1.4

1960: The first episode of the world's longest-running television soap opera *Coronation Street* is broadcast.

Sat 10

Sun 11

Interim Ashtead Group, Micro Focus International, Sports Direct International, Stagecoach, SuperGroup
Final Victrex

COMPANY
RESULTS

DAYS OF THE MONTH

On page 78 we looked at the behaviour of the UK stock market in an average month; here we will look in some detail at the historic behaviour of the market on each day of the month.

The following chart plots the average daily returns for the 31 calendar days in a month for the FTSE 100 over the period 1984-2015. For example, since 1984, the FTSE 100 has on average increased 0.27% on the 1st day of each month.

Note: the chart here plots the average returns on the *calendar days* of the months, whereas elsewhere in the Almanac we usually look at just the trading days.

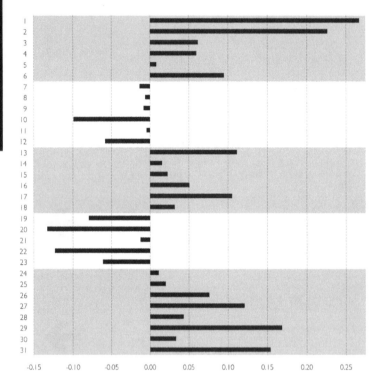

Some observations:

1. The first day of each month has the highest average daily return for the FTSE 100, followed closely by the second day.

2. The worst average daily return has been on the 20th of the month.

3. As can be seen in the chart, the periods of strongest daily returns occur in the first and final weeks of months.

4. The pattern of daily returns in months divides into five (rather surprisingly precise) phases:

    *   **Phase 1** (1st-6th): the index sees positive daily returns

    *   **Phase 2** (7th-12th): the index sees negative daily returns

    *   **Phase 3** (13th-18th): the index sees positive daily returns

    *   **Phase 4** (19th-23rd): the index sees negative daily returns

    *   **Phase 5** (24th-31st): the index sees positive daily returns

NB. The chart above highlights the positive daily return phases of a month.

Mon

12

1980: Apple goes public, with an initial offering of $22 per share. It generates more capital than any IPO since Ford Motor Company in 1956 and instantly creates more millionaires (about 300) than any company in history.

FTSE 100	43	-0.4	1.0
FTSE 250	43	-0.5	0.9
S&P 500	51	-0.1	0.7
NIKKEI	65	0.2	1.5

Tue

13

Two-day FOMC meeting starts

1642: Abel Tasman becomes first European to sight New Zealand, on the north-west coast of the South Island.

FTSE 100	64	0.0	0.9
FTSE 250	65	0.0	0.8
S&P 500	52	0.0	0.6
NIKKEI	55	0.1	1.7

Wed

14

ECB Governing Council Meeting (non-monetary policy)
Full moon
Supermoon

1960: The charter of the new Organisation for Economic Co-operation and Development (OECD) is signed by the US, Canada and 18 European countries.

FTSE 100	52	-0.1	0.8
FTSE 250	55	0.0	0.7
S&P 500	39	-0.2	0.9
NIKKEI	43	-0.2	0.9

Thu

15

MPC interest rate announcement at 12h00
ECB General Council Meeting
50th anniversary of the death of Walt Disney

1906: The London Underground's Great Northern, Piccadilly and Brompton Railway opens.

FTSE 100	48	-0.1	0.8
FTSE 250	62	0.1	0.6
S&P 500	44	-0.1	0.7
NIKKEI	43	0.1	1.6

Fri

16

Triple Witching

1994: The web browser Netscape Navigator 1.0 is released.

FTSE 100	**77**	**0.7**	**0.8**
FTSE 250	76	0.4	0.6
S&P 500	67	0.4	1.0
NIKKEI	50	-0.2	0.9

Sat 17

Sun 18

Interim Dixons Carphone

COMPANY
RESULTS

TRADING AROUND CHRISTMAS & NEW YEAR – FTSE 100

This page updates the analysis of the historical behaviour of the FTSE 100 since 1984 for the nine days around Christmas and New Year. The days studied were:

- **Days 1-3**: the three trading days leading up to Christmas
- **Days 4-6**: the three trading days between Christmas and New Year
- **Days 7-9**: the first three trading days of the year

The following table shows the results of the analysis, where:

1. *Positive(%)*: the percentage of all days that the market has risen on this day
2. *Average daily return(%)*: the average return of the market for this day
3. *Standard Deviation*: the standard deviation of the average returns for this day

	1	2	3	4	5	6	7	8	9
Positive (%)	59	69	79	83	62	56	55	62	45
Average daily return (%)	0.16%	0.40%	0.25%	0.47%	0.17%	0.10%	0.33%	0.10%	0.08%
Standard Deviation	0.0082	0.0070	0.0054	0.0120	0.0087	0.0091	0.0134	0.0113	0.0101

The following chart plots the average daily returns from the above table.

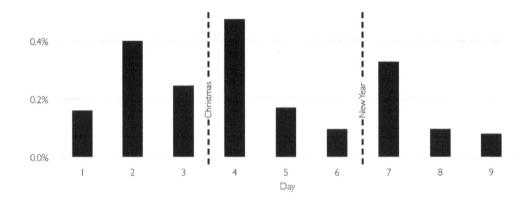

Analysis

1. The average daily change of the FTSE 100 from 1984 for all days is 0.03%, so it can be seen that all nine days around Christmas and New Year are stronger than the average daily returns for the rest of the year.

2. Generally, the market strength increases to the fourth day (the trading day immediately after Christmas) – this is the strongest day of the whole period, when the market has increased in 83% of years since 1984, with an average daily return of 0.47%. However, it should be noted that the standard deviation is the second highest on this day, meaning that the volatility of returns is greatest (the index actually fell 3% on this day in 1987 and 2002).

3. The weakest day in the period is the third day of the new year.

4. The new year generally starts strongly on the first day, with performance trailing off in the following two days.

Mon
19

1843: Charles Dickens' *A Christmas Carol* goes on sale. It is priced at five shillings (equal to £20 today) and the first run of 6,000 copies sells out by Christmas Eve.

FTSE 100	61	0.0	0.9
FTSE 250	57	0.1	0.7
S&P 500	43	0.0	0.7
NIKKEI	52	-0.2	1.9

Tue
20

1955: The United Nations General Assembly elects Yugoslavia to a hotly-contested temporary seat on the Security Council.

FTSE 100	64	0.2	0.9
FTSE 250	70	0.2	0.6
S&P 500	38	-0.1	0.9
NIKKEI	59	-0.1	1.2

December solstice

Wed
21

1898: Scientists Pierre Curie and Marie Curie announce their discovery of the radioactive element, radium.

FTSE 100	57	0.4	0.9
FTSE 250	74	0.4	0.7
S&P 500	67	0.3	0.7
NIKKEI	48	0.0	1.2

Thu
22

1882: The first Christmas tree lights are revealed by Thomas Edison.

FTSE 100	71	0.3	0.6
FTSE 250	90	0.4	0.4
S&P 500	61	0.1	0.7
NIKKEI	62	0.1	1.3

Emporer's Birthday (Japan)
LSE closes at 12h30, TSE closed

Fri
23

1922: The BBC begins daily news broadcasts.

FTSE 100	**82**	**0.5**	**0.5**
FTSE 250	90	0.4	0.4
S&P 500	51	0.0	0.6

Sat 24	Christmas Eve; Hanukkah (until 1st January)
Sun 25	Christmas Day

Final Carnival, GCP Infrastructure Investments

COMPANY
RESULTS

MSCI INDEX REVIEWS

When it comes to stock market indices, FTSE isn't the only player; a big competitor is MSCI, which has been calculating global equity indices since 1969. As with FTSE, the MSCI indices are used as benchmarks for many funds, and as the basis for index funds and ETFs. When companies are added to, or deleted from, their indices this can have a significant impact on the share prices as funds rebalance their portfolios. The MSCI indices are reviewed quarterly, in February, May, August and November (details at: www.msci.com/index-review).

The charts below show the share price of the last nine companies that have joined the MSCI United Kingdom Index in the last couple of years. The time period for each chart is 12 weeks, starting from six weeks before the company joined the index. The dashed line in each chart indicates the announcement date of the company joining the index.

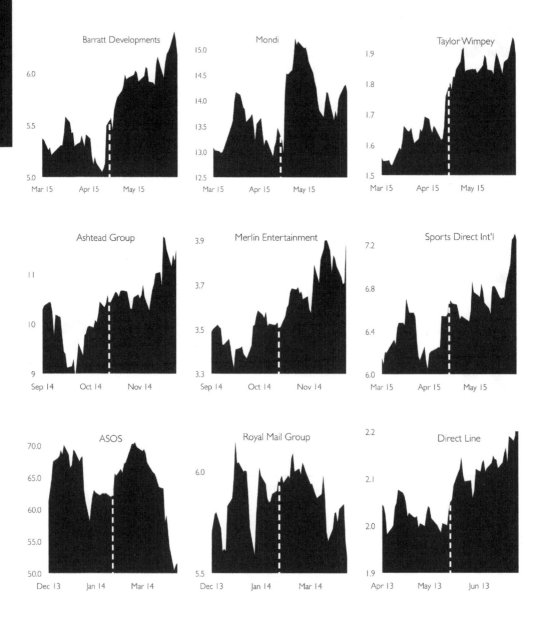

As with companies joining the FTSE 100, it can be seen that addition to the MSCI index can result in a spike in the share price.

Mon
26

Boxing Day
LSE, HKEX closed

S&P 500	84	0.4	0.6
NIKKEI	81	0.6	1.4

1933: The Nissan Motor Company is incorporated in Tokyo under the name Dat Jidosha Seizo Co.

Tue
27

LSE, HKEX closed

S&P 500	56	0.1	0.8
NIKKEI	59	0.2	0.8

1945: The International Monetary Fund and World Bank are established.

Wed
28

→

FTSE 100	62	0.2	0.5
FTSE 250	85	0.3	0.3
S&P 500	58	0.0	0.6
NIKKEI	52	-0.1	1.3

1895: The world's first cinema opens in Paris, France.

Thu
29

New moon

↑

FTSE 100	76	0.4	1.1
FTSE 250	81	0.3	0.9
S&P 500	54	0.2	0.7
NIKKEI	67	0.2	0.5

1989: Canada becomes the first country in the world to ban smoking on domestic airlines.

Fri
30

LSE closed

S&P 500	62	0.2	0.7
NIKKEI	50	0.2	1.4

1960: The farthing ceases to be legal tender in the UK.

Sat 31   New Year's Eve

Sun 1   New Year's Day

COMPANY
RESULTS

2.
STATISTICS

CONTENTS

MARKET INDICES

PRICE HISTORY PROFILE OF THE FTSE ALL-SHARE INDEX

The FTSE All-Share index is the aggregation of the FTSE 100, FTSE 250 and FTSE SmallCap indices. Effectively, all those LSE listed companies with a market capitalisation above the lower limit for inclusion in the FTSE SmallCap (in 2015 this was around £80m) are included. The FTSE All-Share is the standard benchmark for measuring the performance of the broad UK market.

The following tables list some statistical data on the yearly, monthly and daily performance of the index.

Yearly data

Data starts	1899 (116 years)
Largest one year rise	136.3% (1975)
Largest one year fall	-55.3% (1974)
Average annual return (standard deviation)	5.78% (20.36)
Number of times the index has risen 5 years in a row (last time)	15 (2003-2007)
Number of times the index has risen 8 years in a row (last time)	6 (1983-1989)
Number of times the index has risen 10 years in a row (last time)	4 (1980-1989)
Most number of consecutive years risen	13 (1977-1989)
Number of times the index has fallen 3 years in a row (last time)	8 (2000-2002)
Number of times the index has fallen 4 years in a row (last time)	2 (1912-1915)
Number of times the index has fallen 5 years in a row	0

Monthly data

Data starts	1946 (811 months)
Largest one month rise	52.7% (Jan 1975)
Largest one month fall	-26.6% (Oct 1987)
Average monthly change (standard deviation)	0.66% (5.08)
Number of times the index has risen 6 months in a row (last time)	59 (Dec 12 – May 13)
Number of times the index has risen 8 months in a row (last time)	21 (Oct 12 – May 13)
Number of times the index has risen 10 months in a row (last time)	9 (Sep 12 – May 13)
Most number of consecutive months risen (last time)	12 (Jun 12 – May 13)
Number of times the index has fallen 4 months in a row (last time)	20 (Jun 11 – Sep 11)
Number of times the index has fallen 6 months in a row (last time)	3 (Apr 02 – Sep 02)
Number of times the index has fallen 7 months in a row	0

Daily data

Data starts	2 Jan 1969 (11,744 days)
Largest one day rise	9.4% (24 Jan 75)
Largest one day fall	-11.2% (20 Oct 87)
Average daily change (standard deviation)	0.03% (1.06)
Number of times the index has risen 5 days in a row	607
Number of times the index has risen 8 days in a row (last time)	105 (15 Jan 15 – 26 Jan 15)
Number of times the index has risen 10 days in a row (last time)	34 (9 May 12 – 2 May 12)
Most number of consecutive days risen	18 (19 Dec 86 – 16 Jan 87)
Number of times the index has fallen 5 days in a row	306
Number of times the index has fallen 8 days in a row (last time)	25 (15 Nov 11 – 24 Nov 11)
Number of times the index has fallen 10 days in a row (last time)	7 (14 Jan 03 – 27 Jan 03)
Most number of consecutive days fallen	13 (6 Jun 74 – 24 Jun 74)

DAY OF THE WEEK PERFORMANCE

Is the performance of the FTSE 100 affected by the day of the week?

The following two charts show the performance of the FTSE 100 on the five days of the week since the index began in 1984. The chart on the left displays the proportion of days when the return was positive on each of the five days; the chart on the right shows the average return for each day.

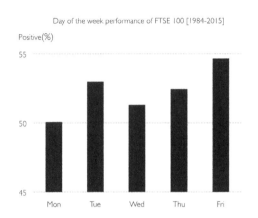

Day of the week performance of FTSE 100 [1984-2015]

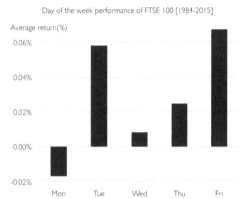

Day of the week performance of FTSE 100 [1984-2015]

Since 1984 the strongest day of the week has been Friday; the FTSE 100 has had a positive return on 55% of all Fridays. The weakest day has been Monday; the FTSE 100 has had a positive return on 50% of Mondays. This profile is reflected in the average returns: Friday being strongest with an average return of 0.07% and Monday being the only day of the week with a negative return (-0.02%).

But market behaviour changes over time, so what has been the situation recently?

The two following charts are similar to those above except they are for the period from the beginning of 2012 to mid-2015.

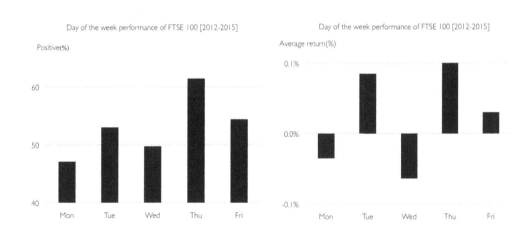

We can see that the daily market behaviour has changed over time.

In recent years the weakest day could be considered Wednesday, which has had an average return of -0.06% since 2012. Thursday has recently been the strongest day of the week, with 61% of Thursdays having positive returns and an average Thursday return of 0.1%. The biggest change in the last year has the relative weakening of Tuesdays – still strong, but much less so in the last 12 months.

FTSE 100 MONTH-END VALUES

The following table shows the month-end and year-end values of the FTSE 100.

NB. The FTSE 100 was launched on the first trading day of January 1984, but was given a starting value of 1000 assigned for the last trading day of 1983.

	Jan	Feb	Mar	Apr	May	Jun	Jul	Aug	Sep	Oct	Nov	Dec
1984	1063.0	1040.3	1112.5	1138.3	1021.0	1041.4	1010.1	1103.9	1140.3	1151.0	1181.3	1232.2
1985	1280.8	1259.7	1277.0	1291.0	1313.0	1234.9	1261.7	1341.1	1290.0	1377.2	1439.1	1412.6
1986	1435.0	1543.9	1668.8	1660.5	1602.8	1649.8	1558.1	1661.2	1555.8	1632.1	1636.7	1679.0
1987	1808.3	1979.2	1997.6	2050.5	2203.0	2284.1	2360.9	2249.7	2366.0	1749.8	1579.9	1712.7
1988	1790.8	1768.8	1742.5	1802.2	1784.4	1857.6	1853.6	1753.6	1826.5	1852.4	1792.4	1793.1
1989	2051.8	2002.4	2075.0	2118.0	2114.4	2151.0	2297.0	2387.9	2299.4	2142.6	2276.8	2422.7
1990	2337.3	2255.4	2247.9	2103.4	2345.1	2374.6	2326.2	2162.8	1990.2	2050.3	2149.4	2143.5
1991	2170.3	2380.9	2456.5	2486.2	2499.5	2414.8	2588.8	2645.7	2621.7	2566.0	2420.2	2493.1
1992	2571.2	2562.1	2440.1	2654.1	2707.6	2521.2	2399.6	2312.6	2553.0	2658.3	2778.8	2846.5
1993	2807.2	2868.0	2878.7	2813.1	2840.7	2900.0	2926.5	3100.0	3037.5	3171.0	3166.9	3418.4
1994	3491.8	3328.1	3086.4	3125.3	2970.5	2919.2	3082.6	3251.3	3026.3	3097.4	3081.4	3065.5
1995	2991.6	3009.3	3137.9	3216.7	3319.4	3314.6	3463.3	3477.8	3508.2	3529.1	3664.3	3689.3
1996	3759.3	3727.6	3699.7	3817.9	3747.8	3711.0	3703.2	3867.6	3953.7	3979.1	4058.0	4118.5
1997	4275.8	4308.3	4312.9	4436.0	4621.3	4604.6	4907.5	4817.5	5244.2	4842.3	4831.8	5135.5
1998	5458.5	5767.3	5932.2	5928.3	5870.7	5832.5	5837.0	5249.4	5064.4	5438.4	5743.9	5882.6
1999	5896.0	6175.1	6295.3	6552.2	6226.2	6318.5	6231.9	6246.4	6029.8	6255.7	6597.2	6930.2
2000	6268.5	6232.6	6540.2	6327.4	6359.3	6312.7	6365.3	6672.7	6294.2	6438.4	6142.2	6222.5
2001	6297.5	5917.9	5633.7	5966.9	5796.1	5642.5	5529.1	5345.0	4903.4	5039.7	5203.6	5217.4
2002	5164.8	5101.0	5271.8	5165.6	5085.1	4656.4	4246.2	4227.3	3721.8	4039.7	4169.4	3940.4
2003	3567.4	3655.6	3613.3	3926.0	4048.1	4031.2	4157.0	4161.1	4091.3	4287.6	4342.6	4476.9
2004	4390.7	4492.2	4385.7	4489.7	4430.7	4464.1	4413.1	4459.3	4570.8	4624.2	4703.2	4814.3
2005	4852.3	4968.5	4894.4	4801.7	4964.0	5113.2	5282.3	5296.9	5477.7	5317.3	5423.2	5618.8
2006	5760.3	5791.5	5964.6	6023.1	5723.8	5833.4	5928.3	5906.1	5960.8	6129.2	6048.8	6220.8
2007	6203.1	6171.5	6308.0	6449.2	6621.4	6607.9	6360.1	6303.3	6466.8	6721.6	6432.5	6456.9
2008	5879.8	5884.3	5702.1	6087.3	6053.5	5625.9	5411.9	5636.6	4902.5	4377.3	4288.0	4434.2
2009	4149.6	3830.1	3926.1	4243.7	4417.9	4249.2	4608.4	4908.9	5133.9	5044.5	5190.7	5412.9
2010	5188.5	5354.5	5679.6	5553.3	5188.4	4916.9	5258.0	5225.2	5548.6	5675.2	5528.3	5899.9
2011	5862.9	5994.0	5908.8	6069.9	5990.0	5945.7	5815.2	5394.5	5128.5	5544.2	5505.4	5572.3
2012	5681.6	5871.5	5768.5	5737.8	5320.9	5571.1	5635.3	5711.5	5742.1	5782.7	5866.8	5897.8
2013	6276.9	6360.8	6411.7	6430.1	6583.1	6215.5	6621.1	6483.0	6462.2	6731.4	6650.6	6749.1
2014	6510.4	6809.7	6598.4	6780.0	6844.5	6743.9	6730.1	6819.8	6622.7	6546.5	6722.6	6566.1
2015	6749.4	6946.7	6773.0	6960.6	6984.4	6521.0	6738.0					

MONTHLY PERFORMANCE OF THE FTSE 100

The table below shows the percentage performance of the FTSE 100 for every month since 1986. The months where the index fell are highlighted. By scanning the columns it is possible to get a feel for how the market moves in certain months.

	Jan	Feb	Mar	Apr	May	Jun	Jul	Aug	Sep	Oct	Nov	Dec
1980	9.2	4.9	-9.2	3.4	-2.3	11.2	3.7	0.7	3.2	5.9	0.6	-5.3
1981	-1.5	4.3	0.4	6.9	-5.0	1.9	0.4	5.0	-16.6	3.2	10.5	-1.1
1982	4.5	-4.9	3.5	1.1	3.4	-4.3	3.6	2.9	6.1	2.0	0.9	1.7
1983	3.1	0.6	1.8	8.1	0.2	2.8	-2.1	2.6	-2.6	-3.4	5.7	1.9
1984	6.3	-2.1	6.9	2.3	-10.3	2.0	-3.0	9.3	3.3	0.9	2.6	4.3
1985	3.9	-1.6	1.4	1.1	1.7	-5.9	2.2	6.3	-3.8	6.8	4.5	-1.8
1986	1.6	7.6	8.1	-0.5	-3.5	2.9	-5.6	6.6	-6.3	4.9	0.3	2.6
1987	7.7	9.5	0.9	2.6	7.4	3.7	3.4	-4.7	5.2	-26.0	-9.7	8.4
1988	4.6	-1.2	-1.5	3.4	-1.0	4.1	-0.2	-5.4	4.2	1.4	-3.2	0.0
1989	14.4	-2.4	3.6	2.1	-0.2	1.7	6.8	4.0	-3.7	-6.8	6.3	6.4
1990	-3.5	-3.5	-0.3	-6.4	11.5	1.3	-2.0	-7.0	-8.0	3.0	4.8	-0.3
1991	1.3	9.7	3.2	1.2	0.5	-3.4	7.2	2.2	-0.9	-2.1	-5.7	3.0
1992	3.1	-0.4	-4.8	8.8	2.0	-6.9	-4.8	-3.6	10.4	4.1	4.5	2.4
1993	-1.4	2.2	0.4	-2.3	1.0	2.1	0.9	5.9	-2.0	4.4	-0.1	7.9
1994	2.1	-4.7	-7.3	1.3	-5.0	-1.7	5.6	5.5	-6.9	2.3	-0.5	-0.5
1995	-2.4	0.6	4.3	2.5	3.2	-0.1	4.5	0.4	0.9	0.6	3.8	0.7
1996	1.9	-0.8	-0.7	3.2	-1.8	-1.0	-0.2	4.4	2.2	0.6	2.0	1.5
1997	3.8	0.8	0.1	2.9	4.2	-0.4	6.6	-1.8	8.9	-7.7	-0.2	6.3
1998	6.3	5.7	2.9	-0.1	-1.0	-0.7	0.1	-10.1	-3.5	7.4	5.6	2.4
1999	0.2	4.7	1.9	4.1	-5.0	1.5	-1.4	0.2	-3.5	3.7	5.5	5.0
2000	-9.5	-0.6	4.9	-3.3	0.5	-0.7	0.8	4.8	-5.7	2.3	-4.6	1.3
2001	1.2	-6.0	-4.8	5.9	-2.9	-2.7	-2.0	-3.3	-8.3	2.8	3.3	0.3
2002	-1.0	-1.2	3.3	-2.0	-1.6	-8.4	-8.8	-0.4	-12.0	8.5	3.2	-5.5
2003	-9.5	2.5	-1.2	8.7	3.1	-0.4	3.1	0.1	-1.7	4.8	1.3	3.1
2004	-1.9	2.3	-2.4	2.4	-1.3	0.8	-1.1	1.0	2.5	1.2	1.7	2.4
2005	0.8	2.4	-1.5	-1.9	3.4	3.0	3.3	0.3	3.4	-2.9	2.0	3.6
2006	2.5	0.5	3.0	1.0	-5.0	1.9	1.6	-0.4	0.9	2.8	-1.3	2.8
2007	-0.3	-0.5	2.2	2.2	2.7	-0.2	-3.8	-0.9	2.6	3.9	-4.3	0.4
2008	-8.9	0.1	-3.1	6.8	-0.6	-7.1	-3.8	4.2	-13.0	-10.7	-2.0	3.4
2009	-6.4	-7.7	2.5	8.1	4.1	-3.8	8.5	6.5	4.6	-1.7	2.9	4.3
2010	-4.1	3.2	6.1	-2.2	-6.6	-5.2	6.9	-0.6	6.2	2.3	-2.6	6.7
2011	-0.6	2.2	-1.4	2.7	-1.3	-0.7	-2.2	-7.2	-4.9	8.1	-0.7	1.2
2012	2.0	3.3	-1.8	-0.5	-7.3	4.7	1.2	1.4	0.5	0.7	1.5	0.5
2013	6.4	1.3	0.8	0.3	2.4	-5.6	6.5	-2.1	-0.3	4.2	-1.2	1.5
2014	-3.5	4.6	-3.1	2.8	1.0	-1.5	-0.2	1.3	-2.9	-1.2	2.7	-2.3
2015	2.8	2.9	-2.5	2.8	0.3	-6.6	3.3					

Observations

1. In recent years (i.e. since 2000) the index has been weak in January and June; and strong in April, October and December.

2. In the last 20 years it can clearly be seen that the strongest month has been December (only down seven times in 31 years). However, in the 70s and 80s the strongest month was April (which increased every year from 1971 to 1985).

3. Looking across the table, it can be seen that the longest period of consecutive down months was April 2002-September 2002. While the longest periods of consecutive up months were July 1982-June 1983 and June 2012-May 2013 (the only times the FTSE 100 has risen for 12 months without a break).

FTSE 250 MONTH-END VALUES

The following table shows the month-end and year-end values of the FTSE 250.

NB. The FTSE 250 was launched on 12 October 1992, but the base date for the index is 31 December 1985.

	Jan	Feb	Mar	Apr	May	Jun	Jul	Aug	Sep	Oct	Nov	Dec
1986	1449.5	1575.1	1695.8	1755.2	1696.5	1771.0	1690.2	1763.1	1665.5	1751.9	1798.0	1817.9
1987	1990.6	2126.4	2190.2	2219.9	2357.2	2556.2	2710.1	2585.8	2753.7	1964.2	1754.0	1974.0
1988	2103.9	2100.1	2075.3	2156.1	2164.7	2266.2	2291.5	2147.9	2227.1	2303.1	2220.8	2176.1
1989	2461.7	2491.7	2545.5	2526.7	2555.5	2533.1	2701.9	2723.4	2679.3	2438.4	2528.7	2645.8
1990	2578.6	2451.9	2425.4	2276.2	2474.5	2524.8	2465.4	2174.9	1960.4	2052.2	2092.8	2112.9
1991	2082.0	2383.6	2492.9	2483.7	2441.5	2359.7	2482.7	2584.0	2608.6	2543.5	2388.6	2364.6
1992	2476.4	2523.5	2408.2	2712.4	2779.2	2548.7	2302.3	2192.5	2397.4	2521.6	2637.5	2862.9
1993	2954.8	3036.1	3107.8	3132.1	3165.4	3235.7	3306.5	3511.9	3433.2	3528.1	3484.9	3791.3
1994	4084.3	3960.0	3752.9	3781.1	3564.3	3414.1	3640.2	3816.6	3494.8	3516.9	3497.3	3501.8
1995	3370.4	3384.1	3434.7	3530.2	3653.8	3592.6	3826.0	3913.4	3948.8	3894.3	3959.1	4021.3
1996	4125.0	4215.0	4326.7	4551.8	4510.0	4353.2	4230.6	4416.2	4391.1	4422.5	4428.5	4490.4
1997	4595.4	4654.4	4576.2	4498.7	4495.8	4431.3	4492.0	4603.4	4829.9	4643.2	4656.7	4787.6
1998	4861.5	5201.0	5525.4	5610.8	5901.4	5503.8	5482.7	4786.2	4544.2	4811.4	4901.7	4854.7
1999	5024.2	5248.3	5475.2	5849.6	5639.1	5858.2	5969.5	6017.9	5687.1	5622.3	6194.8	6444.9
2000	6181.0	6451.2	6475.1	6194.6	6227.8	6601.0	6779.1	7057.8	6676.9	6629.3	6419.9	6547.5
2001	6735.9	6649.5	6094.7	6409.2	6571.1	6298.9	6082.2	6116.3	5118.6	5364.8	5849.5	5939.1
2002	5849.2	5834.0	6175.5	6123.7	6049.0	5496.6	4783.6	4858.8	4287.1	4417.7	4558.2	4319.3
2003	4016.4	4037.6	3959.8	4389.3	4815.6	4963.4	5325.6	5593.2	5457.8	5724.4	5712.6	5802.3
2004	6023.9	6269.9	6259.4	6210.7	6053.6	6277.9	6023.5	6087.3	6269.1	6321.8	6577.4	6936.8
2005	7166.2	7254.0	7130.5	6728.9	7114.3	7368.7	7605.1	7749.2	7951.1	7711.1	8327.9	8794.3
2006	9172.6	9448.3	9850.3	9878.7	9298.2	9422.7	9355.6	9601.2	9996.8	10372.2	10673.9	11177.8
2007	11100.3	11082.9	11689.3	11929.4	12111.1	11527.6	11337.5	11309.2	11037.4	11666.0	10748.8	10657.8
2008	9881.8	10067.9	10013.2	10122.3	10049.3	9145.8	8856.7	9381.8	7888.2	6282.6	6093.3	6360.9
2009	6250.8	6049.1	6373.9	7529.0	7572.0	7414.6	8000.0	8817.5	9142.3	8885.8	8918.4	9306.9
2010	9237.3	9344.4	10165.3	10366.0	9637.1	9366.1	9948.7	9825.1	10531.8	10843.5	10607.8	11558.8
2011	11471.5	11621.3	11592.0	12013.9	12060.8	11934.0	11552.1	10525.9	9819.4	10479.7	10315.3	10102.9
2012	10769.4	11449.5	11538.9	11417.6	10558.2	10932.1	11136.7	11410.2	11734.1	11935.0	12034.2	12375.0
2013	13030.5	13704.0	13923.0	13949.9	14350.9	13798.2	14872.9	14625.2	14908.2	15480.0	15466.6	15935.4
2014	15674.4	16726.0	16273.7	15817.2	16010.2	15723.6	15495.6	15885.7	15379.7	15501.4	15851.8	16085.4
2015	16305.8	17273.8	17090.6	17474.6	17468.3	17531.5	17677.4					

MONTHLY PERFORMANCE OF THE FTSE 250

The table below shows the percentage performance of the FTSE 250 for every month since 1986. The months where the index fell are highlighted. By scanning the columns it is possible to get a feel for how the market moves in certain months.

	Jan	Feb	Mar	Apr	May	Jun	Jul	Aug	Sep	Oct	Nov	Dec
1986	6.8	2.6	8.7	7.7	3.5	-3.3	4.4	-4.6	4.3	-5.5	5.2	2.6
1987	1.1	9.5	6.8	3.0	1.4	6.2	8.4	6.0	-4.6	6.5	-28.7	-10.7
1988	12.5	6.6	-0.2	-1.2	3.9	0.4	4.7	1.1	-6.3	3.7	3.4	-3.6
1989	-2.0	13.1	1.2	2.2	-0.7	1.1	-0.9	6.7	0.8	-1.6	-9.0	3.7
1990	4.6	-2.5	-4.9	-1.1	-6.2	8.7	2.0	-2.4	-11.8	-9.9	4.7	2.0
1991	1.0	-1.5	14.5	4.6	-0.4	-1.7	-3.4	5.2	4.1	0.9	-2.5	-6.1
1992	-1.0	4.7	1.9	-4.6	12.6	2.5	-8.3	-9.7	-4.8	9.3	5.2	4.6
1993	8.5	3.2	2.8	2.4	0.8	1.1	2.2	2.2	6.2	-2.2	2.8	-1.2
1994	8.8	7.7	-3.0	-5.2	0.8	-5.7	-4.2	6.6	4.8	-8.4	0.6	-0.6
1995	0.1	-3.8	0.4	1.5	2.8	3.5	-1.7	6.5	2.3	0.9	-1.4	1.7
1996	1.6	2.6	2.2	2.7	5.2	-0.9	-3.5	-2.8	4.4	-0.6	0.7	0.1
1997	1.4	2.3	1.3	-1.7	-1.7	-0.1	-1.4	1.4	2.5	4.9	-3.9	0.3
1998	2.8	1.5	7.0	6.2	1.5	5.2	-6.7	-0.4	-12.7	-5.1	5.9	1.9
1999	-1.0	3.5	4.5	4.3	6.8	-3.6	3.9	1.9	0.8	-5.5	-1.1	10.2
2000	4.0	-4.1	4.4	0.4	-4.3	0.5	6.0	2.7	4.1	-5.4	-0.7	-3.2
2001	2.0	2.9	-1.3	-8.3	5.2	2.5	-4.1	-3.4	0.6	-16.3	4.8	9.0
2002	1.5	-1.5	-0.3	5.9	-0.8	-1.2	-9.1	-13.0	1.6	-11.8	3.0	3.2
2003	-5.2	-7.0	0.5	-1.9	10.8	9.7	3.1	7.3	5.0	-2.4	4.9	-0.2
2004	1.6	3.8	4.1	-0.2	-0.8	-2.5	3.7	-4.1	1.1	3.0	0.8	4.0
2005	5.5	3.3	1.2	-1.7	-5.6	5.7	3.6	3.2	1.9	2.6	-3.0	8.0
2006	5.6	4.3	3.0	4.3	0.3	-5.9	1.3	-0.7	2.6	4.1	3.8	2.9
2007	4.7	-0.7	-0.2	5.5	2.1	1.5	-4.8	-1.6	-0.2	-2.4	5.7	-7.9
2008	-0.8	-7.3	1.9	-0.5	1.1	-0.7	-9.0	-3.2	5.9	-15.9	-20.4	-3.0
2009	4.4	-1.7	-3.2	5.4	18.1	0.6	-2.1	7.9	10.2	3.7	-2.8	0.4
2010	4.4	-0.7	1.2	8.8	2.0	-7.0	-2.8	6.2	-1.2	7.2	3.0	-2.2
2011	9.0	-0.8	1.3	-0.3	3.6	0.4	-1.1	-3.2	-8.9	-6.7	6.7	-1.6
2012	-2.1	6.6	6.3	0.8	-1.1	-7.5	3.5	1.9	2.5	2.8	1.7	0.8
2013	2.8	5.3	5.2	1.6	0.2	2.9	-3.9	7.8	-1.7	1.9	3.8	-0.1
2014	3.0	-1.6	6.7	-2.7	-2.8	1.2	-1.8	-1.5	2.5	-3.2	0.8	2.3
2015	1.5	1.4	5.9	-1.1	2.2	0.0	0.4	0.8				

Observations

1. Historically the strongest months for the FTSE 250 have been January and March, and the weakest July and October.

2. In recent years (i.e. since 2000) the index has also been strong in September and November.

COMPARATIVE PERFORMANCE OF FTSE 100 & FTSE 250

The table below shows the monthly outperformance of the FTSE 100 over the mid-cap FTSE 250. For example, in January 1986, the FTSE 100 increased 1.6%, while the FTSE 250 increased 2.6%, so the outperformance of the former over the latter was therefore -1.0. The cells are highlighted if the number is negative (i.e. the FTSE 250 outperformed the FTSE 100).

	Jan	Feb	Mar	Apr	May	Jun	Jul	Aug	Sep	Oct	Nov	Dec
1986	-1.0	-1.1	0.4	-4.0	-0.1	-1.5	-1.0	2.3	-0.8	-0.3	-2.3	1.5
1987	-1.8	2.6	-2.1	1.3	1.3	-4.8	-2.7	-0.1	-1.3	2.6	1.0	-4.1
1988	-2.0	-1.0	-0.3	-0.5	-1.4	-0.6	-1.3	0.9	0.5	-2.0	0.3	2.0
1989	1.3	-3.6	1.5	2.8	-1.3	2.6	0.1	3.2	-2.1	2.2	2.6	1.8
1990	-1.0	1.4	0.7	-0.3	2.8	-0.8	0.3	4.8	1.9	-1.7	2.9	-1.2
1991	2.7	-4.8	-1.4	1.6	2.2	0.0	2.0	-1.9	-1.9	0.4	0.4	4.0
1992	-1.6	-2.3	-0.2	-3.9	-0.4	1.4	4.8	1.1	1.0	-1.1	-0.1	-6.1
1993	-4.6	-0.6	-2.0	-3.1	-0.1	-0.1	-1.3	-0.3	0.2	1.6	1.1	-0.9
1994	-5.6	-1.6	-2.0	0.5	0.8	2.5	-1.0	0.6	1.5	1.7	0.0	-0.6
1995	1.3	0.2	2.8	-0.3	-0.3	1.5	-2.0	-1.9	0.0	2.0	2.2	-0.9
1996	-0.7	-3.0	-3.4	-2.0	-0.9	2.5	2.6	0.1	2.8	-0.1	1.8	0.1
1997	1.5	-0.5	1.8	4.5	4.2	1.1	5.2	-4.3	3.9	-3.8	-0.5	3.5
1998	4.7	-1.3	-3.4	-1.6	-6.2	6.1	0.5	2.6	1.5	1.5	3.7	3.4
1999	-3.3	0.3	-2.4	-2.8	-1.4	-2.4	-3.3	-0.6	2.0	4.9	-4.7	1.0
2000	-5.5	-4.9	4.6	1.1	0.0	-6.7	-1.9	0.7	-0.3	3.0	-1.4	-0.7
2001	-1.7	-4.7	3.5	0.8	-5.4	1.5	1.4	-3.9	8.1	-2.0	-5.8	-1.3
2002	0.5	-1.0	-2.5	-1.2	-0.3	0.7	4.2	-2.0	-0.2	5.5	0.0	-0.3
2003	-2.5	1.9	0.8	-2.2	-6.6	-3.5	-4.2	-4.9	0.7	-0.1	1.5	1.5
2004	-5.7	-1.8	-2.2	3.1	1.2	-3.0	2.9	0.0	-0.5	0.3	-2.3	-3.1
2005	-2.5	1.2	0.2	3.7	-2.3	-0.6	0.1	-1.6	0.8	0.1	-6.0	-2.0
2006	-1.8	-2.5	-1.3	0.7	0.9	0.6	2.3	-3.0	-3.2	-0.9	-4.2	-1.9
2007	0.4	-0.4	-3.3	0.2	1.1	4.6	-2.1	-0.6	5.0	-1.8	3.6	1.2
2008	-1.7	-1.8	-2.6	5.7	0.2	1.9	-0.6	-1.8	2.9	9.6	1.0	-1.0
2009	-4.7	-4.5	-2.9	-10.0	3.5	-1.7	0.6	-3.7	0.9	1.1	2.5	-0.1
2010	-3.4	2.0	-2.7	-4.2	0.5	-2.4	0.7	0.6	-1.0	-0.7	-0.4	-2.2
2011	0.1	0.9	-1.2	-0.9	-1.7	0.3	1.0	1.6	1.8	1.4	0.9	3.3
2012	-4.6	-3.0	-2.5	0.5	0.3	1.2	-0.7	-1.1	-2.3	-1.0	0.6	-2.3
2013	1.1	-3.8	-0.8	0.1	-0.5	-1.7	-1.3	-0.4	-2.3	0.3	-1.1	-1.5
2014	-1.9	-2.1	-0.4	5.6	-0.3	0.3	1.2	-1.2	0.3	-1.9	0.4	-3.8
2015	1.4	-3.0	-1.4	0.5	0.4	-7.0	2.5					

The proportion of years that the FTSE 100 has outperformed the FTSE 250 for each month since 1986 is shown in the chart.

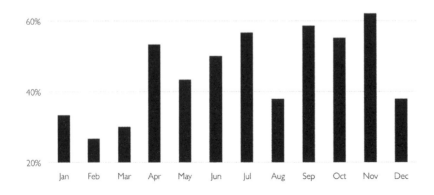

1. The FTSE 250 tends to outperform the FTSE 100 in the first three months of the year and in August and December. For example, as can be seen in the table, the mid-cap index has outperformed the large-cap index in every March since 2006.

2. The FTSE 100 is strong relative to the FTSE 250 in September and November.

3. In recent years (since 2000) the above characteristics have if anything been even stronger, suggesting a certain degree of persistency.

See also: The FTSE 100/250 monthly switching strategy on page 16.

FIRST TRADING DAYS OF THE MONTH

Does the market display any special effect on the first trading day of each month?

FTSE 100 daily data was analysed from 1984 to discover if the UK equity market displayed abnormal returns on the first trading day (FTD) of each month. The results are shown in the table below.

	Number of days	Positive	Positive (%)	Average (%)
All days	7917	4142	52.3	0.03%
First trading day of each month	376	225	59.8	0.22%
First trading day of each month (from 2000)	188	118	62.8	0.28%

Of the 376 months since 1984, the market has risen 225 times (59.8%) on the FTD of each month, with an average rise of 0.22%. These figures have declined slightly in the last year, but they are still significantly greater than the average for all days, where the market has risen 52.3% of the time with an average return of 0.03%.

The FTD effect seems to be even stronger in recent years. Since 2000, the market has increased on 62.8% of months' FTDs, with an average rise of 0.28% (nine times greater than the average return for all days in the period).

The following charts break down the performance of the market on the first trading days by month since 1984.

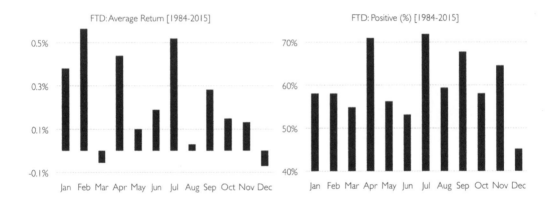

FTD: Average Return [1984-2015]

FTD: Positive (%) [1984-2015]

The average returns on the FTDs have been strongest for the months of February, April and July. The average return on the FTD of February has been 0.56% (19 times greater than the average return for all days of the month). While returns have been positive for 72% of all July FTDs.

The weakest month FTD is December – the only month when the market has fallen more often than risen on the first trading day. This is an unexpected result as December as a whole is one of the strongest months for the market.

LAST TRADING DAYS OF THE MONTH

On the previous page we looked at the first trading day of each month; here we will look at the last trading days.

The following table shows the results of analysing the performance of the FTSE 100 on the last trading day (LTD) of each month for the periods 1984-2015 and 2000-2015, and compares this to the average performance on all days in the month.

	Number of days	Positive	Positive (%)	Average (%)
All days	7917	4142	52.3	0.03%
Last trading day of each month	376	197	52.4	0.08%
Last trading day of each month (from 2000)	187	81	43.3	0.02%

Overall, since 1984 the market has a tendency to increase above the average on the LTD of each month. On average, the market has risen 0.08% on months' last trading days, against 0.03% for all days in the month; and the market has had a positive return on 52.4% of all LTDs since 1984. However, since 2000 the effect has somewhat reversed, with the majority of last trading days seeing falls in the market (when the market only rises on 43.3% of month LTDs).

This behaviour is very different from that of the first trading days in the month, which strongly outperform the average for all days, and where the effect has strengthened in recent years.

The following charts break down the performance of the market on the last trading days by month since 1984.

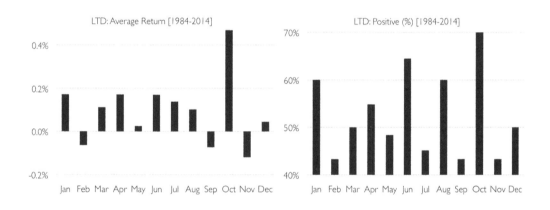

The difference in performance between the months is quite striking. The last trading days in January, June, August and October are all abnormally strong. By contrast, the last trading days of February, September and November are very weak.

FTSE 100 INDEX QUARTERLY REVIEWS

To keep the FTSE 100 in accordance with its purpose, the constituents of the index are periodically reviewed. The reviews take place and are announced on the Wednesday before the first Friday of the month in March, June, September and December.

NB. The reviews used to take place on the Wednesday after the first Friday of the month, but this was changed starting from March 2014.

If any changes are to be made (i.e. companies ejected or introduced), these are announced sometime after the market has closed on the day of the review.

The review dates for 2016 are: 2 March, 1 June, 31 August and 30 November.

Changes to the index following the review are implemented on the third Friday of the month.

Since the index's inception in 1984, the company that has danced in and out of the index the most is Tate & Lyle; it has been added six times and ejected six times.

The accompanying table lists the companies entering and exiting the FTSE 100 in the last few years, as a result of the FTSE quarterly reviews.

Date	Company added	TIDM	Company deleted	TIDM
08 Sep 10	Tomkins		Home Retail Group	HOME
08 Sep 10	Weir Group	WEIR	Segro	SGRO
08 Dec 10	IMI	IMI	Cobham	COB
09 Mar 11	Wood Group (John)	WG.	Bunzl	BNZL
09 Mar 11	ITV	ITV	Alliance Trust	ATST
09 Mar 11	Hargreaves Lansdown	HL.	African Barrick Gold	ABG
25 May 11	Glencore	GLEN	Invensys	ISYS
08 Jun 11	Tate & Lyle	TATE	TUI Travel	TT.
07 Sep 11	Ashmore Group	ASHM	Wood Group (John)	WG.
07 Sep 11	Bunzl	BNZL	3i Group	III
07 Dec 11	CRH	CRH	Inmarsat	ISAT
07 Dec 11	Evraz	EVR	Investec	INVP
07 Dec 11	Polymetal International	POLY	Lonmin	LMI
07 Mar 12	Croda International	CRDA	Cairn Energy	CNE
07 Mar 12	Aberdeen Asset Management	AND	Essar Energy	ESSR
06 Jun 12	Babcock International Group	BAB	Man Group	EMG
29 Jun 12	Pennon Group	PNN	International Power	
12 Sep 12	Melrose	MRO	ICAP	IAP
12 Sep 12	Wood Group (John)	WG.	Ashmore Group	ASHM
12 Dec 12	TUI Travel	TT.	Pennon Group	PNN
06 Mar 13	Easyjet	EZJ	Intu Properties	INTU
06 Mar 13	London Stock Exchange	LSE	Kazakhmys	KAZ
11 Sep 13	Coca-Cola HBC AG	CCH	Wood Group (John)	WG.
11 Sep 13	Sports Direct International	SPD	Eurasian Natural Resources Corporation	ENRC
11 Sep 13	Mondi	MNDI	Serco Group	SRP
11 Dec 13	Royal Mail Group	RMG	Croda International	CRDA
11 Dec 13	Ashtead Group	AHT	Vedanta Resources	VED
05 Mar 14	Barratt Developments	BDEV	Amec	AMEC
05 Mar 14	St. James's Place	STJ	Tate & Lyle	TATE
04 Jun 14	3i Group	III	Melrose	MRO
04 Jun 14	Intu Properties	INTU	William Hill	WMH
03 Sep 14	Direct Line Insurance Group	DLG	Barratt Developments	BDEV
03 Sep 14	Dixons Carphone	DC.	Rexam	REX
03 Dec 14	Barratt Developments	BDEV	IMI	IMI
03 Dec 14	Taylor Wimpey	TW.	Petrofac	PFC
04 Mar 15	Hikma Pharmaceuticals	HIK	Tullow Oil	TLW
03 Jun 15	Inmarsat	ISAT	Aggreko	AGK

COMPARATIVE PERFORMANCE OF UK INDICES

The table below gives the year-end closing values for eight UK stock indices.

Year-end closing values of UK indices

Index	TIDM	2005	2006	2007	2008	2009	2010	2011	2012	2013	2014
FTSE 100	UKX	5,618.80	6,220.80	6,456.90	4,434.17	5,412.88	5,899.94	5,572.28	5,897.81	6,749.09	6,566.09
FTSE 250	MCX	8,794.30	11,177.80	10,657.80	6,360.85	9,306.89	11,558.80	10,102.90	12,375.00	15,935.35	16,085.44
FTSE All-Share	ASX	2,847.02	3,221.42	3,286.67	2,209.29	2,760.80	3,062.85	2,857.88	3,093.41	3,609.63	3,532.74
FTSE Fledgling	NSX	3,748.80	4,389.40	4,022.30	2,321.76	4,035.39	4,789.69	4,081.64	4,751.92	6,453.65	6,849.46
FTSE SmallCap	SMX	3,305.50	3,905.60	3,420.30	1,854.20	2,780.20	3,228.60	2,748.80	3,419.07	4,431.11	4,365.92
FTSE TechMARK 100	TIX	1,431.72	1,512.38	1,641.10	1,217.00	1,704.80	2,040.00	2,064.10	2,479.80	3,197.32	3,522.00
FTSE 4Good UK 50	4UK5	4,802.23	5,267.43	5,428.60	3,787.40	4,577.90	4,852.90	4,529.80	4,864.74	5,636.57	5,496.77
FTSE AIM	AXX	1,046.10	1,054.00	1,049.10	394.32	653.24	933.63	693.18	707.21	850.68	702.00

The table below gives the annual percentage performance of the eight indices. The light grey cells highlight the best performing index in each respective year; the dark grey cells the worst performing.

Annual performance (%) of UK indices

Index	TIDM	2005	2006	2007	2008	2009	2010	2011	2012	2013	2014
FTSE 100	UKX	16.7	10.7	3.8	-31.3	22.1	9.0	-5.6	5.8	14.4	-2.7
FTSE 250	MCX	26.8	27.1	-4.7	-40.3	46.3	24.2	-12.6	22.5	28.8	0.9
FTSE All-Share	AXX	18.1	13.2	2.0	-32.8	25.0	10.9	-6.7	8.2	16.7	-2.1
FTSE Fledgling	NSX	18.2	17.1	-8.4	-42.3	73.8	18.7	-14.8	16.4	35.8	6.1
FTSE SmallCap	SMX	19.8	18.2	-12.4	-45.8	49.9	16.1	-14.9	24.4	29.6	-1.5
FTSE TechMARK 100	TIX	19.7	5.6	8.5	-25.8	40.1	19.7	1.2	20.1	28.9	10.2
FTSE 4Good UK 50	4UK5	14.4	9.7	3.1	-30.2	20.9	6.0	-6.7	7.4	15.9	-2.5
FTSE AIM	AXX	4.0	0.8	-0.5	-62.4	65.7	42.9	-25.8	2.0	20.3	-17.5

The FTSE Fledgling and FTSE TechMARK 100 have been the best performing indices in the year the most number of times, while the FTSE AIM and FTSE 4Good UK 50 are at the bottom of the class, having been the worst performing indices in the year the most number of times.

The following chart shows the relative performance of the FTSE 100, FTSE 250, FTSE AIM and FTSE Fledgling.

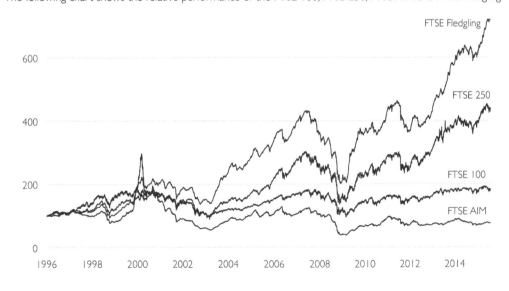

125

MARKET MOMENTUM (UP) ANALYSIS

The table below displays the results of analysis on market momentum – the tendency of the market to increase in one period, having also risen in the previous period(s). Notes on the analysis:

1. The index analysed was the FTSE All-Share. The number of observations to August 2015 (for each frequency) is indicated in column 0. For example, 11,744 days to August 2015 (from January 1969) was the sample data for the 'Daily' analysis.

2. The first rows of the columns ('Total') display the number of consecutive periods the index rose for that frequency. For example, the market rose 6213 days (out of the total 11,744); 3486 times it rose on two consecutive days; and 335 times it rose six days in a row. The second rows ('% Total') express the first row as a percentage of the total sample. For example, the market rose six days in a row 2.9% of the whole period (11,744 days).

3. The rows '% 1 up' express the proportion of times that the market rose for n consecutive periods following the market rising for 1 period (expressed as a percentage of the number of times the market rose once). For example: after the market had risen for one day, the market rose for a second day in 56.1% of all cases; after the market had risen for one day, the market went on to rise six days consecutively in 5.4% of all cases.

4. The subsequent rows display the tendency of the market to rise following n consecutive increases. For example: after the market has risen four days consecutively, the market rose for a 5th day in 56.2% of all cases; after the market had risen three years in a row, the market rose again the following year in 72.4% of all cases.

Frequency		0	1	2	3	4	5	6
Daily	Total	11744	6213	3486	1927	1081	607	335
	% Total		52.9	29.7	16.4	9.2	5.2	2.9
	% 1 up			56.1	31.0	17.4	9.8	5.4
	% 2 up				55.3	31.0	17.4	9.6
	% 3 up					56.1	31.5	17.4
	% 4 up						56.2	31.0
	% 5 up							55.2
Weekly	Total	2638	1457	804	456	259	150	81
	% Total		55.2	30.5	17.3	9.8	5.7	3.1
	% 1 up			55.2	31.3	17.8	10.3	5.6
	% 2 up				56.7	32.2	18.7	10.1
	% 3 up					56.8	32.9	17.8
	% 4 up						57.9	31.3
	% 5 up							54.0
Monthly	Total	834	508	315	196	127	87	59
	% Total		60.9	37.8	23.5	15.2	10.4	7.1
	% 1 up			62.0	38.6	25.0	17.1	11.6
	% 2 up				62.2	40.3	27.6	18.7
	% 3 up					64.8	44.4	30.1
	% 4 up						68.5	46.5
	% 5 up							67.8
Yearly	Total	115	70	46	29	21	15	10
	% Total		60.9	40.0	25.2	18.3	13.0	8.7
	% 1 up			65.7	41.4	30.0	21.4	14.3
	% 2 up				63.0	45.7	32.6	21.7
	% 3 up					72.4	51.7	34.5
	% 4 up						71.4	47.6
	% 5 up							66.7

Observations

The market would appear to display a degree of fractal behaviour – where its properties are similar whatever time-frame one looks at. Trends do seem to become more established the longer they last. For example, the probability of the market rising in a week increases the longer the period of previous consecutive up weeks. Although this trend falls off after five consecutive up periods.

The market displays greater momentum for longer frequencies. For example, the market only rose six days consecutively 2.9% of the time, whereas it rose six years consecutively 8.7% of the time. In addition, the market rose for a 6th year (after five years of consecutive increases) 66.7% of the time, against just 55.2% for daily increases.

MARKET MOMENTUM (DOWN) ANALYSIS

The table on the previous page looked at market momentum for the market going up. The table below shows the equivalent results for when the market falls.

The structure of the table is similar to that on the previous page (where an explanation of the figures is given).

Frequency		0	1	2	3	4	5	6
Daily	Total	11744	5514	2787	1379	656	306	140
	% Total		47.0	23.7	11.7	5.6	2.6	1.2
	% 1 down			50.5	25.0	11.9	5.5	2.5
	% 2 down				49.5	23.5	11.0	5.0
	% 3 down					47.6	22.2	10.2
	% 4 down						46.6	21.3
	% 5 down							45.8
Weekly	Total	2638	1178	524	254	130	61	33
	% Total		44.7	19.9	9.6	4.9	2.3	1.3
	% 1 down			44.5	21.6	11.0	5.2	2.8
	% 2 down				48.5	24.8	11.6	6.3
	% 3 down					51.2	24.0	13.0
	% 4 down						46.9	25.4
	% 5 down							54.1
Monthly	Total	834	324	133	54	20	10	3
	% Total		38.8	15.9	6.5	2.4	1.2	0.4
	% 1 down			41.0	16.7	6.2	3.1	0.9
	% 2 down				40.6	15.0	7.5	2.3
	% 3 down					37.0	18.5	5.6
	% 4 down						50.0	15.0
	% 5 down							30.0
Yearly	Total	115	45	20	8	2	0	0
	% Total		39.1	17.4	7.0	1.7	0.0	0.0
	% 1 down			44.4	17.8	4.4	0.0	0.0
	% 2 down				40.0	10.0	0.0	0.0
	% 3 down					25.0	0.0	0.0
	% 4 down						0.0	0.0
	% 5 down							0.0

Observations

1. Since 1969, the market has fallen on six consecutive days on 139 occasions (the last time was March 2014). The most consecutive days the market has fallen is 13, which it has done once (in June 1974).

2. Since 1946 the market has only fallen four consecutive months on 20 occasions (2.4%). Random chance would suggest 6.3%.

3. Since 1900, the market has never fallen for five consecutive years. The market has fallen for three consecutive years on eight occasions, but having done so the market continued to fall for a 4th year only twice.

4. As with up markets (previous page), down markets appear to display a degree of fractal behaviour, where the properties are similar whatever time-frame one looks at.

5. Down markets displays far less momentum tendency than that seen for up markets. For example, if the market rises for three consecutive months, there's a 63.1% probability that the market will continue to rise for a 4th month as well. However, if the market falls three consecutive months, there's only a 37.0% probability that the market will fall for a 4th month as well.

INTRA-DAY VOLATILITY

Since 1985, the average daily Hi-Lo range of the FTSE 100 has been 1.23% (expressing the Hi-Lo difference as a percentage of the close). This means that when the index is at, say, 6000, the average daily difference between the high and low levels is 74 points. The standard deviation of this daily range is 0.9. We could define a very volatile day as one where the day's Hi-Lo range is 2 standard deviations above the average (i.e. above 3.03%).

The chart below plots the Hi-Lo range for the 308 days since 1985 when the range has been over 3.03%.

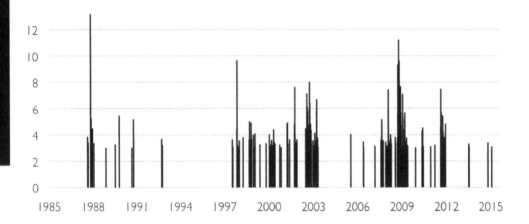

As can be seen, the index has experienced periods of heightened intra-day volatility, notably 1997-2003 and 2007-2009. The record for the greatest Hi-Lo range in a day is still 13.1%, seen on 20 October 1987.

After a greater than 2SD daily movement, the average return on the following day is 0.11%, and the average return over the following five-day period is 0.44%.

Hi-Lo-Close

The table below shows the frequency with which the index closes within a certain percentage of the high (or low) of the day. For example, since 1985 the FTSE 100 has closed within 10% of its daily high on 21.0% of all days, and it has closed within 1% of its low on 5.6% of all days.

	10%	5%	1%
Top (%)	21.0	15.3	9.9
Bottom (%)	14.6	9.6	5.6

It's interesting to note that for one in ten days the index closes within 1% of its high for the day.

Continuing this analysis of where the index closes relative to the Hi-Lo range of the day, the next table shows the performance of the FTSE 100 on the following day. For example, on the days when the index closes within 10% of its low for the day, on average the index return is 0.004% the following day; and when the index closes within 1% of its high for the day, on average the index return is 0.172% the following day.

	10%	5%	1%
Top (%)	0.111	0.134	0.172
Bottom (%)	0.004	0.008	0.028

TURN OF THE MONTH

This study analyses the behaviour of the market on the ten days around each turn of the month (ToM). The days studied are the five last trading days of the month, from ToM(-5) to ToM(-1) (the latter being the last trading day of the month), and the first five trading days of the following month, from ToM(+1) to ToM(+5). The index analysed is the FTSE All-Share.

From 1970

The charts below analyse the 548 ToMs since 1970. The left chart shows the percentage of positive days, and the right chart is the average return on the day. For example, on ToM(-5) the market has on average risen 49.8% of the time with an average return of -0.03%.

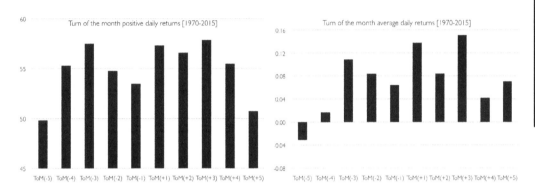

We can see that there is a definite trend for the market to be weak at the beginning of the ten-day period, to then strengthen on the third day before the end of the month, then weaken in the final two days, before starting strongly in the new month.

Does this behaviour persist in more recent years?

From 2000

The charts below are the same configuration as above, except they look at a shorter time period: the 188 ToMs since the year 2000 to mid-2015.

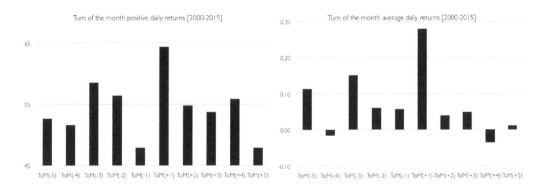

Broadly, the behaviour has been the same for the last few years as that from 1970. The main observation is that the strength of the first trading day of the month, ToM(1), has become even more pronounced. On average since 2000 the market has risen on 64% of all ToM(1) days, with an average change of 0.28% (which is nine times the average change on all trading days).

COMPANY PROFILE OF THE FTSE 100

Rank 2015	Company	TIDM	Turnover (£m)	Profit (£m)	Profit margin (%)	Capital (£m)	Weighting (%)	Cumulative weighting (%)
1	Royal Dutch Shell	RDSB	270,550	18,191	6.3	110,206	6.2	6.2
2	HSBC Holdings	HSBA		12,002		105,645	6.0	12.2
3	British American Tobacco	BATS	13,971	4,848	36.4	68,174	3.9	16.1
4	BP	BP.	227,160	3,180	4.2	67,181	3.8	19.9
5	GlaxoSmithKline	GSK	23,006	2,968	22.8	67,085	3.8	23.7
6	Vodafone Group	VOD	42,227	1,095	5.3	62,386	3.5	27.2
7	Lloyds Banking Group	LLOY		1,475		56,385	3.2	30.4
8	AstraZeneca	AZN	16,766	801	12.7	53,579	3.0	33.5
9	SABMiller	SAB	14,945	3,262	20.0	52,111	3.0	36.4
10	Barclays	BARC		2,256		44,946	2.5	39.0
11	Diageo	DGE	10,813	2,933	24.4	43,891	2.5	41.5
12	Reckitt Benckiser Group	RB.	8,836	2,126	24.0	41,867	2.4	43.8
13	Prudential	PRU		2,614		38,939	2.2	46.0
14	BT Group	BT.A	17,979	2,645	21.0	37,284	2.1	48.2
15	BG Group	BG.	12,393	-1,497	34.3	35,709	2.0	50.2
16	Unilever	ULVR	37,847	5,974	14.3	34,984	2.0	52.2
17	National Grid	NG.	15,201	2,628	25.7	32,791	1.9	54.0
18	Rio Tinto	RIO	30,623	6,137	26.1	32,418	1.8	55.9
19	Imperial Tobacco Group	IMT	26,625	78	9.4	30,857	1.7	57.6
20	Shire	SHP	3,869	2,144	33.1	30,043	1.7	59.3
21	Associated British Foods	ABF	12,943	1,020	8.2	25,508	1.4	60.8
22	BHP Billiton	BLT	39,459	13,056	28.9	22,631	1.3	62.0
23	Royal Bank of Scotland Group	RBS		2,643		21,492	1.2	63.3
24	Standard Chartered	STAN		2,721		21,037	1.2	64.4
25	Glencore	GLEN	142,040	2,733	2.4	20,787	1.2	65.6
26	Aviva	AV.		2,281		20,083	1.1	66.8
27	Sky	SKY	9,989	1,516		18,531	1.1	67.8
28	WPP Group	WPP	11,529	1,452	12.7	18,144	1.0	68.8
29	Compass Group	CPG	17,058	1,147	7.1	16,921	1.0	69.8
30	Tesco	TSCO	62,284	-6,376	0.4	15,847	0.9	70.7
31	CRH	CRH	14,777	595	5.9	15,759	0.9	71.6
32	Legal & General Group	LGEN		1,238		15,549	0.9	72.5
33	SSE	SSE	31,654	735	4.2	15,016	0.9	73.3
34	BAE Systems	BA.	15,430	882	8.5	14,540	0.8	74.1
35	Rolls-Royce Group	RR.	13,736	67	9.4	14,011	0.8	74.9
36	Centrica	CNA	29,408	-1,403	0.0	13,312	0.8	75.7
37	ARM Holdings	ARM	795	317	38.1	12,579	0.7	76.4
38	Next	NXT	4,000	795	20.1	12,100	0.7	77.1
39	RELX	REL	3,054	493	18.4	11,962	0.7	77.8
40	Wolseley	WOS	13,130	698	5.2	11,390	0.6	78.4
41	Experian	EXPN	3,248	679	24.1	11,001	0.6	79.0
42	International Consolidated Airlines Group	IAG	15,760	647	6.5	10,954	0.6	79.7
43	Smith & Nephew	SN.	2,966	459	18.6	10,448	0.6	80.3
44	Land Securities Group	LAND	770	2,417	304.2	10,340	0.6	80.8
45	ITV	ITV	2,590	605	25.4	10,333	0.6	81.4
46	Old Mutual	OML		1,364		10,271	0.6	82.0
47	Anglo American	AAL	17,394	-166	18.1	9,945	0.6	82.6
48	Schroders	SDR	1,915	517	24.3	9,472	0.5	83.1
49	Pearson	PSON	4,874	305	10.4	9,388	0.5	83.6
50	Whitbread	WTB	2,608	464	19.3	9,224	0.5	84.2
51	London Stock Exchange Group	LSE	971	191	27.3	9,040	0.5	84.7
52	British Land Co	BLND	464	1,789	261.9	8,788	0.5	85.2
53	Standard Life	SL.		422		8,704	0.5	85.7
54	Marks & Spencer Group	MKS	10,311	600	7.7	8,616	0.5	86.2
55	Kingfisher	KGF	10,966	644	5.9	8,547	0.5	86.6
56	Capita	CPI	4,378	292	9.0	8,506	0.5	87.1
57	Carnival	CCL	10,104	792	11.1	7,457	0.4	87.5
58	Mondi	MNDI	5,002	484	12.3	7,448	0.4	88.0
59	TUI AG	TUI	14,623	395	4.3	6,799	0.4	88.3
60	easyJet	EZJ	4,527	581	12.9	6,745	0.4	88.7
61	Taylor Wimpey	TW.	2,686	469	18.6	6,637	0.4	89.1
62	Persimmon	PSN	2,574	467	18.2	6,545	0.4	89.5
63	Burberry Group	BRBY	2,523	445	17.8	6,410	0.4	89.8
64	Barratt Developments	BDEV	3,157	391	13.0	6,373	0.4	90.2
65	United Utilities Group	UU.	1,720	342	38.9	6,134	0.3	90.6

Rank 2015	Company	TIDM	Turnover (£m)	Profit (£m)	Profit margin (%)	Capital (£m)	Weighting (%)	Cumulative weighting (%)
66	Bunzl	BNZL	6,157	300	5.6	6,115	0.3	90.9
67	InterContinental Hotels Group	IHG	1,194	385	33.8	5,816	0.3	91.2
68	Sage Group (The)	SGE	1,307	278	26.3	5,605	0.3	91.5
69	Johnson Matthey	JMAT	10,060	496	4.6	5,557	0.3	91.9
70	Hargreaves Lansdown	HL.	358	210	58.0	5,483	0.3	92.2
71	Antofagasta	ANTO	3,399	1,011	31.3	5,442	0.3	92.5
72	Hammerson	HMSO	207	703	202.9	5,248	0.3	92.8
73	Severn Trent	SVT	1,801	148	30.3	5,191	0.3	93.1
74	Coca-Cola HBC AG	CCH	5,087	275	6.9	5,189	0.3	93.4
75	RSA Insurance Group	RSA		60		5,146	0.3	93.7
76	Travis Perkins	TPK	5,581	321	5.8	5,124	0.3	93.9
77	Direct Line Insurance Group	DLG		457		5,000	0.3	94.2
78	Dixons Carphone	DC.	8,255	287	4.4	4,999	0.3	94.5
79	St James's Place	STJ		183		4,976	0.3	94.8
80	3i Group	III				4,965	0.3	95.1
81	GKN	GKN	6,982	221	4.9	4,959	0.3	95.4
82	Hikma Pharmaceuticals	HIK	957	233	27.0	4,907	0.3	95.6
83	Babcock International Group	BAB	3,997	313	8.5	4,850	0.3	95.9
84	Sports Direct International	SPD	2,833	313	9.8	4,833	0.3	96.2
85	Fresnillo	FRES	908	161	18.8	4,775	0.3	96.5
86	Sainsbury (J)	SBRY	23,775	-72	2.8	4,734	0.3	96.7
87	Royal Mail Group	RMG	9,328	400	4.1	4,650	0.3	97.0
88	Ashtead Group	AHT	2,039	474	25.2	4,588	0.3	97.2
89	Intu Properties	INTU	536	-1,354	165.2	4,520	0.3	97.5
90	Smiths Group	SMIN	2,952	302	13.6	4,474	0.3	97.8
91	Inmarsat	ISAT	826	220	31.8	4,444	0.3	98.0
92	Aberdeen Asset Management	ADN	1,289	355	30.3	4,357	0.2	98.3
93	Admiral Group	ADM		351		4,248	0.2	98.5
94	Intertek Group	ITRK	2,093	252	14.4	4,199	0.2	98.7
95	Merlin Entertainments	MERL	1,249	226	24.9	4,020	0.2	99.0
96	G4S	GFS	6,848	148	4.1	3,952	0.2	99.2
97	Morrison (Wm) Supermarkets	MRW	16,816	-792	1.7	3,944	0.2	99.4
98	Meggitt	MGGT	1,554	209	14.6	3,787	0.2	99.6
99	Randgold Resources Ltd	RRS	698	227	25.9	3,750	0.2	99.8
100	Weir Group	WEIR	2,438	149	15.6	2,895	0.2	100.0

Notes to the table

1. The Weighting column expresses a company's market capitalisation as a percentage of the total capitalisation of all companies in the FTSE 100. The table is ranked (in descending order) by this column.

2. Figures accurate as of August 2015.

Observations

1. The five largest companies in the FTSE 100 account for 24% of the total market capitalisation. This figure has fallen quite considerably in the last few years; in 2004 the top five companies accounted for 36% of the FTSE 100, in 2013 it had decreased to 29% and last year it was 27%.

2. The 15 largest companies in the index account for just over half of total capitalisation (2004: 10 companies).

3. The 21 smallest companies in the index account for only 5% of total capitalisation. In other words, the individual movements of these 25 companies have very little impact on the level of the index.

4. The aggregate capitalisation of all 100 companies in the index is £1,764bn (2014: £1,827bn; 2012: £1,640bn; 2006: £1,397bn). When the index started in 1984, the aggregate capitalisation was £100bn.

INDEX PROFILES – SHARE PRICES

The table below presents a range of share price related characteristics for six stock market indices in the UK.

	FTSE 100	FTSE 250	SmallCap	Fledgling	AIM	techMARK Focus
Number of companies in index	100	250	288	110	1,073	43
Market capitalisation, mean (£m)	17,645	1,597	294	45	73	2,776
Market capitalisation, standard deviation	20,663	913	156	33	173	5,427
Market capitalisation, median (£m)	9,132	1,287	253	39	20	832
Market capitalisation, largest company (£m)	110,206	4,728	900	139	2,712	30,043
Market capitalisation, smallest company (£m)	2,895	168	20			75
Share price, average (£)	14.21	7.69	5.20	6.20	1.17	8.43
Number of companies paying a dividend	94	210	230	63	296	34
Number of companies paying a dividend (%)	94	84	80	57	28	79
Dividend yield, average (%)	3.1	2.7	4.1	4.7	4.2	2.2
Dividend yield, standard deviation	1.7	1.4	15.0	7.9	21.2	1.2
PE ratio, average	21.9	30.0	46.2	55.4	34.1	37.9
PE ratio, standard deviation	17.6	46.5	84.8	87.9	69.7	45.1
PEG, average	1.7	1.8	1.5	1.3	1.3	2.1
Correlation (FTSE 100), average	0.5	0.3	0.3	0.2	0.1	0.3
Correlation (FTSE 100), standard deviation	0.1	0.2	0.2	0.1	0.1	0.1
Beta (FTSE 100), average	0.8	0.5	0.4	0.2	0.2	0.5
Beta (FTSE 100), standard deviation	0.3	0.3	0.2	0.2	0.5	0.3

Notes and observations

1. As for the company financials table on the opposite page, care should be taken with some of the figures above – especially those of indices with few companies (such as the FTSE Fledgling and techMARK).

2. Just 28% of AIM companies pay a dividend. The figures for all the indices have changed very little from 2007. (NB. The average dividend yield only includes those companies that pay a dividend – not all the companies in the index.)

3. The average PE for the FTSE 100 companies is 21.9, with the PE values fairly tightly clustered around this average level; but the PEs for companies in the other indices have a very wide range around the average (i.e. a high standard deviation).

4. Correlation is calculated relative to the FTSE 100. (Note: the averages calculated here are equally weighted, not market capitalisation weighted.)

5. Beta is calculated relative to the FTSE 100.

Data compiled August 2015.

INDEX PROFILES – COMPANY FINANCIALS

The table below presents a range of company financials characteristics for six UK stock market indices. For example, the average turnover for the 288 companies in the FTSE SmallCap is £189m.

	FTSE 100	FTSE 250	SmallCap	Fledgling	AIM	techMARK Focus
Number of companies in index	100	250	288	110	1,073	43
Turnover, average (£m)	14,518	1,011	189	48	47	1,073
Turnover growth last five years, average (%)	44	56	48	32	362	49
Turnover growth last five years, median (%)	30	39	25	8	45	35
Turnover to capitalisation ratio, average	1.2	1.4	2.1	2.0	11.3	0.4
Number of companies making a profit	92	190	122	34	439	33
Number of companies making a profit (%)	92	76	42	31	41	77
Profit, average (£m)	1,255.1	57.7	6.2	-2.0	-0.4	134.1
Profit, median (£m)	471.3	69.1	0.0	0.0	-0.3	24.3
Profit growth last five years, average (%)	289	217	274	120	306	105
Profit growth last five years, median (%)	45	63	57	14	66	46
Profit / turnover, average (%)	56	56	52	46		59
Current ratio, average	1.2	1.8	5.4	3.9	6.3	1.7
Net cash, average (£m)	5,332	186	27	7	10	174
Net cash, median (£m)	497	75	9	3	3	54
Net cash, sum total (£m)	527,877	45,551	7,427	753	10,385	6,772
Net borrowings, average (£m)	51,545	692	64	13	6	139
Net borrowings, sum total (£m)	5,102,995	169,590	17,754	1,286	5,625	5,436
Net gearing, average	361	138	80	62	-57	25
Interest cover, average	14	24	41	14	17	28
Dividend cover, average	2	3	2	2	3	3
ROCE, average (%)	22	-11	4	4	-295	2
ROCE, standard deviation	89	305	140	18	12,193	70

Notes and observations

1. Care should be taken with some of the figures – especially those of indices with few companies (such as the FTSE Fledgling and techMARK Focus) – as the averages can be significantly affected by one or two outlier numbers. In addition, the techMARK is very non-homogenous, combining very large and very small companies in the same index. In such cases, a median figure can be more useful to look at than an average.

2. Only 31% of Fledgling and 41% of AIM companies reported a profit for 2014.

3. On average, FTSE 100 companies have £5,332m net cash (2007: £1,647m), while FTSE 250 companies have net cash of £186m (2007: £114m).

Data compiled August 2015.

SECTORS

SECTOR QUARTERLY PERFORMANCE

The following four tables show the performance of FTSE 350 sectors in the four quarters of the year for the past ten years.

Notes:

1. The tables are ranked by the *Avg* column – the average performance for each sector over the ten years.

2. For each year the top five performing sectors are highlighted in light grey, the bottom five in dark grey.

The general clustering of light grey highlights at the top of the tables, and dark grey at the bottom, suggests that certain sectors consistently perform well (or badly) in certain quarters. This effect is the strongest in the first quarter and weakest in the third.

The table on the right gives a subjective listing of the three strongest and three weakest sectors in each quarter (sectors with just one or two constituents have been left out).

Quarter	Strong	Weak
1	Industrial Engineering	Oil & Gas Producers
	Chemicals	Banks
	Technology Hard & Equip	Mobile Telecoms
2	Personal Goods	Construction & Materials
	Electricity	Media
	Fixed Line Telecoms	Food & Drug Retailers
3	Technology Hard & Equip	Oil & Gas Producers
	Industrial Engineering	Industrial Transportation
	Life Insurance	Food Producers
4	Chemicals	Banks
	Food Producers	General Industrials
	Health Care Equip & Servs	Oil Equip, Servs & Dist

First quarter

Sector	Avg	2006	2007	2008	2009	2010	2011	2012	2013	2014	2015
Industrial Metals	18.8	49.2	14.4	21.0	80.7	39.5	0.1	5.1	-18.5	-24.7	21.5
Forestry & Paper	14.2			-1.6	-27.4	38.5	16.7	29.6	33.5	0.3	23.6
Oil Equip; Srvs & Dist	9.2		4.0	-0.3	19.6	11.1	2.5	20.1	3.1	11.1	11.6
Industrial Engineering	9.1	14.1	9.6	3.2	10.2	21.0	1.6	7.8	17.3	2.5	3.3
Chemicals	7.5	13.9	10.0	7.4	-3.0	14.0	-4.1	25.5	6.7	2.2	2.7
Technology Hard & Equip	9.2	12.5	5.2	-28.1	27.1	19.7	22.9	8.2	19.4	-4.0	9.5
Construction & Materials	6.5	15.1	5.2	-2.7	-2.3	10.8	5.8	1.5	11	7.4	12.7
Automobiles & Parts	7.6	15.5	37.2	7.9	-29.6	17.9	-9.6	12.6	15.6	4.6	4.2
Real Estate Inv & Srvs	6.6					-0.6	2.8	5.9	11.9	7.8	11.5
Household Goods	6.5		5.8	-4.4	3.6	5.6	-5.0	14.2	23.9	4.1	10.8
Electronic & Elect Equip	4.9	10.0	8.6	-2.0	-20.8	12.3	3.8	25.6	12.3	-6.1	5.3
Support Services	5.4	12.3	5.7	-4.8	-6.9	8.7	1.5	14.7	15.8	1.8	5.2
Industrial Transportation	5.5	20.1	-3.2	-12.6	3.2	19.7	3.0	15.8	7.5	1.7	-0.3
Financial Services	5.3	22.5	4.6	-15.6	-2.9	-1.2	-4.0	17.5	18.2	2.2	11.4
Media	4.1	4.8	7.5	-13.5	-4.2	11.3	3.8	9.4	13.7	-5.9	13.8
Aerospace & Defense	3.3	5.8	8.2	-9.4	-12.2	10.1	0.1	9.9	22.5	-9.3	7.6
Personal Goods	4.1	6.6	2.7	-18.6	6.7	11.7	1.8	21.2	8.3	-6.2	7
Health Care Equip & Srvs	4.8	-3.7	22.6	6.9	-2.3	2.1	3.1	1.2	9.9	7.1	0.8
Software & Comp Srvs	5.1	1.0	2.2	-11.7	10.8	15.8	0.9	14.5	11.5	2.2	4
Mining	3.6	16.5	9.5	-0.9	13.4	11.5	-4.2	2.7	-10.1	1.4	-4.2
General Industrials	3.6		5.9	-4.7	-20.6	12.6	5.9	21.1	9.6	-8.8	11.6
General Retailers	4.1	7.4	3.4	-19.1	20.6	-3.8	-9.0	19.9	7.3	11.2	3.3
Equity Inv Instruments	3.3	9.1	3.1	-5.8	-2.4	6.7	-0.1	7.7	9.6	0.3	4.3
Travel & Leisure	2.6	2.5	4.2	-16.5	-6.5	17.8	-8.3	8.5	14.4	0.5	9
Nonlife Insurance	2.4	7.9	1.5	-10.4	-8.2	7.5	2.3	7.7	6.3	1.2	7.7
Tobacco	1.8	2.6	9.7	-7.9	-12.1	9.3	0.5	3.4	8.5	3.2	1.1
Life Insurance	1.6	16.2	-2.8	-10.7	-28.5	-4.6	9.5	15.3	11.3	-1.9	12.6
Real Estate Inv Trusts	1.2	19.7	-5.0	1.8	-31.5	-2.1	4.8	9.6	0.5	5.3	8.7
Beverages	1.0	7.4	1.2	-9.2	-15.5	3.9	-1.2	8.6	18.4	-5.7	2.5
Electricity	0.0	12.9	1.3	-7.0	-10.5	-3.3	2.1	2.5	5.7	5.0	-9.1
Food Producers	-0.6	1.6	6.7	-9.7	-15.6	2.6	-3.3	-2.0	17.5	3.4	-6.9
Gas; Water & Multiutilities	-0.9	4.0	5.3	-13.6	-18.6	1.0	1.5	5.1	8.6	3.0	-5.4
Oil & Gas Producers	-1.5	6.0	-3.4	-14.4	-7.2	2.6	5.7	-2.7	4.3	-2.6	-3.1
Food & Drug Retailers	-1.0	0.4	16.3	-19.3	-7.2	2.3	-7.6	-12.5	12.5	-11.0	16.1
Fixed Line Telecoms	-1.0	-0.5	1.8	-19.9	-32.5	-4.6	-0.5	17.1	19.7	0.2	8.8
Pharm & Biotech	-0.7	2.9	2.3	-15.3	-14.3	-0.7	-1.7	-5.5	14	2.5	9.1
Mobile Telecom	-1.8		-4.1	-19.6	-11.2	5.9	5.9	-3.4	20.8	-10.3	-0.1
Banks	-1.6	6.2	-3.1	-10.1	-27.4	6.7	-2.3	17.0	7.5	-8.8	-1.7

Second quarter

Sector	Avg	2006	2007	2008	2009	2010	2011	2012	2013	2014	2015
Personal Goods	4.7	-6.9	5.0	-1.1	35.2	7.0	17.1	-11.5	0.8	0.9	-3.4
Electricity	4.5	1.7	-0.8	6.8	2.8	-0.7	12.3	4.4	1.5	2.5	1.9
Fixed Line Telecoms	3.5	6.4	10.0	-6.5	16.9	2.8	5.4	-2.9	8.7	0.1	4
Automobiles & Parts	3.4	-17.9	4.4	-26.7	81.7	-15.7	15.4	-12.4	13.9	-7.0	-6.7
Pharm & Biotech	2.6	4.2	-3.9	6.0	2.3	-2.8	10.4	2.2	2.5	9.8	-11.8
Beverages	2.2	-4.2	5.1	-5.2	13.9	-3.1	5.2	5.7	-8.9	4.4	-2.9
Electronic & Elect Equip	1.8	-7.3	13.2	9.1	23.6	12.1	13.7	-4.6	-14.3	-8.4	0.5
Software & Comp Srvs	1.5	-14.4	-3.5	7.1	20.8	-8.2	5.1	-0.5	4.4	-4.0	12.9
Tobacco	1.5	-1.9	5.0	-7.8	2.8	-6.1	8.7	1.1	-3.6	5.4	-0.4
Oil & Gas Producers	1.5	-1.4	15.1	16.4	1.4	-25.9	-3.2	-5.0	-2.2	9.1	-4.3
Industrial Engineering	0.8	-0.7	6.2	14.7	4.8	-1.2	8.7	-11.4	-5.4	-2.7	-6
Oil Equip; Srvs & Dist	0.7	-7.8	8.4	21.0	21.8	-3.8	-1.3	-17.8	-10.7	-0.2	-2.4
Real Estate Inv & Srvs	0.5					-14.5	8.6	1.2	11.8	-9.3	5.3
Gas; Water & Multiutilities	0.5	0.6	-3.8	-2.1	2.4	-5.4	2.7	5.4	-2.2	1.4	-2.6
Chemicals	0.4	0.8	15.2	-6.5	7.6	-4.6	9.4	-3.4	-3.0	-8.1	-5.1
Industrial Transportation	0.0	10.0	-4.0	-19.0	14.6	-7.0	3.8	-6.8	5.5	-9.3	8.6
Food Producers	0.0	-6.5	3.9	-13.1	7.2	-6.2	5.0	2.7	-4.7	4.5	0.1
Mobile Telecom	-0.3	-4.5	23.4	-0.7	-4.0	-8.3	-6.4	4.2	0.5	-10.8	3.9
Equity Inv Instruments	-0.3	-7.1	2.5	-2.7	10.7	-6.3	1.7	-4.7	-2.3	1.0	-1.3
Travel & Leisure	-0.5	-0.9	-3.9	-7.6	6.3	-11.7	3.1	1.3	3.3	-1.0	-4.9
General Retailers	-0.5	-0.5	-8.8	-15.9	14.5	-10.3	9.8	-5.8	9.2	-7.6	3.1
Nonlife Insurance	-0.6	-6.6	-6.5	-7.8	-3.3	0.4	5.8	3.8	1.7	4.1	-0.7
Aerospace & Defense	-0.6	-10.3	-1.5	-9.6	8.2	-9.5	1.7	0.4	0.6	2.1	-10.1
General Industrials	-0.8	-8.9	-1.7	-1.8	13.1	-6.6	0.9	-6.2	1.0	0.4	1.9
Financial Services	-0.9	-4.4	1.3	-3.6	21.7	-8.1	-1.5	-8.7	-0.1	0.8	-1.6
Mining	-1.3	0.5	18.5	16.9	17.2	-21.6	-2.0	-13.2	-18.3	-0.8	-7.8
Life Insurance	-1.3	-9.2	-0.7	-18.5	31.8	-13.1	0.9	-6.5	0.6	4.2	-8.5
Banks	-1.4	-4.2	-1.0	-21.2	34.9	-11.9	-4.7	-7.6	-2.2	-3.2	2.2
Support Services	-1.4	-8.2	2.3	-9.4	11.0	-5.0	3.1	-4.8	-2.9	-5.1	3.6
Health Care Equip & Srvs	-1.5	-17.7	-0.5	-22.0	6.8	-2.6	-4.3	0.9	-2.6	12.3	-6.4
Technology Hard & Equip	-1.6	-6.4	14.5	-4.8	31.5	4.4	0.4	-15.2	-13.1	-12.0	-4
Forestry & Paper	-2.3			-29.1	39.9	-17.2	3.5	-7.5	-8.5	1.2	5.6
Food & Drug Retailers	-2.4	2.1	-1.2	-3.4	2.9	-10.7	4.5	-6.3	-8.9	-6.5	-5.1
Media	-2.4	-3.9	3.2	-14.5	1.0	-5.8	3.1	-3.2	0.2	0.5	-4
Real Estate Inv Trusts	-2.5	-5.0	-15.3	-21.7	15.9	-13.9	9.0	3.1	3.8	3.0	-4
Household Goods	-3.5	-4.8	-6.3	-24.9	5.3	-15.3	7.1	-3.8	1.7	0.4	5.4
Construction & Materials	-4.3	-8.2	14.4	-16.5	0.0	-17.8	-9.8	-1.7	-5.1	-11.3	2.8
Industrial Metals	-7.9	3.7		-2.9	79.2	-25.0	-8.1	-29.4	-48.9	4.5	-34.4

Third quarter

Sector	Avg	2005	2006	2007	2008	2009	2010	2011	2012	2013	2014
Technology Hard & Equip	9.7	15.2	-7.4	-6.0	6.5	23.2	29.8	-6.9	12.4	18.9	3.3
Life Insurance	6.2	2.9	5.4	-2.2	-3.5	35.8	26.2	-21.4	10.7	8.9	1.7
Automobiles & Parts	6.0	12.9	5.2	-11.1	-12.2	35.9	45.7	-24.1	18.9	13.5	-12.1
Industrial Engineering	5.8	12.0	-0.4	-1.7	-20.5	47.6	25.1	-20.4	11.5	13.7	-5.6
Mining	4.9	31.1	-5.1	12.8	-44.1	26.5	19.1	-30.9	3.2	14.4	-3.6
Mobile Telecom	4.8		6.3	5.3	-17.4	18.9	12.0	0.2	-1.4	14.7	4.2
Software & Comp Srvs	4.5	1.7	2.3	3.6	-5.4	23.8	14.0	-7.1	9.3	3.0	-2.2
Aerospace & Defense	4.4	17.3	5.9	8.2	-5.8	15.6	6.7	-12.4	3.5	6.2	-3.1
Personal Goods	4.3	4.7	18.9	-3.4	-7.9	20.3	35.8	-16.4	-21.2	21.5	2.8
Household Goods	4.3		10.4	-6.9	6.7	14.3	11.1	-6.4	8.2	2.2	3.4
Chemicals	3.8	14.8	6.7	2.1	-21.4	23.0	25.4	-20.3	9.8	6.6	-6.1
Gas; Water & Multiutilities	3.8	0.8	13.9	1.6	3.8	6.7	9.1	-0.3	1.9	0.7	1.6
Banks	3.6	1.4	4.8	-8.5	-1.4	39.2	10.7	-24.1	7.8	2.7	4.5
Forestry & Paper	3.3	3.6		-45.0	-13.0	49.2	33.9	-23.7	15.6	27.5	-4.8
Real Estate Inv Trusts	3.3		6.0	-9.4	4.4	27.8	13.2	-21.9	3.7	4.3	1.2
Oil Equip; Srvs & Dist	3.2		4.6	7.1	-26.9	24.5	26.1	-22.3	14.5	8.7	-7.7
Nonlife Insurance	3.0	13.3	13.9	3.8	18.3	16.5	8.5	-16.1	5.7	-1.1	-1.8
Electronic & Elect Equip	2.9	22.6	4.0	-8.8	-18.1	24.4	22.0	-26.9	7.1	11.5	-8.6
Beverages	2.9	6.3	4.4	4.1	-1.0	15.2	5.4	-5.3	6.2	2.9	-2.3
Electricity	2.8	10.6	8.1	1.4	-1.0	7.7	8.3	-6.7	-1.2	-0.4	-1
Pharm & Biotech	2.7	9.0	-2.4	-3.4	10.4	11.9	6.2	-2.7	0.2	-0.6	-0.7
Equity Inv Instruments	2.5	12.1	4.0	2.5	-14.4	16.5	8.5	-13.6	3.8	3.6	2.1
Food & Drug Retailers	2.4	-2.7	9.3	1.9	4.0	12.3	12.7	-7.2	7.6	9.1	-27.7
General Industrials	2.4		-1.4	-3.8	-6.1	24.8	20.0	-21.2	5.7	8.2	-4.8
Construction & Materials	2.3	4.9	16.8	-0.6	-24.2	10.9	13.1	-15.7	-1.3	12.7	-6.4
Tobacco	2.3	9.1	5.8	0.9	1.5	16.4	8.0	1.3	-3.2	-1.9	0.4
Fixed Line Telecoms	2.3	6.9	11.4	-7.0	-14.1	21.5	2.9	-14.6	8.5	10.0	-1.8
Media	1.8	1.5	1.6	-5.2	-8.2	24.7	9.2	-16.1	7.5	11.3	2.4
Travel & Leisure	1.6	2.6	7.8	-9.2	-11.2	22.1	8.5	-16.8	5.6	3.9	-0.6
Health Care Equip & Srvs	1.6	-11.8	15.3	-5.8	5.6	24.6	-7.3	-12.0	6.6	4.3	0.1
Food Producers	1.5	6.1	9.4	-11.3	-0.1	30.2	2.4	0.0	4.2	-5.7	-9
General Retailers	1.4	-4.0	6.5	-10.7	-12.1	16.2	10.8	-10.8	5.1	14.6	-2.2
Financial Services	1.3	13.9	6.5	-4.0	-21.9	21.6	12.4	-21.8	7.2	8.8	-5.3
Support Services	1.2	2.5	5.9	-10.9	-10.5	19.4	8.8	-13.7	9.0	6.8	-1.8
Real Estate Inv & Srvs	-0.2						7.9	-18.8	6.7	6.0	-3
Oil & Gas Producers	-0.3	12.7	-6.0	-2.5	-21.9	13.0	19.2	-12.2	0.1	-1.8	-7.2
Industrial Metals	-0.3	22.6	-15.0	-65.5	-60.8	10.9	30.6	-44.7	-7.5	32.7	29.2
Industrial Transportation	-0.5	7.6	3.0	-9.9	-19.1	26.9	7.1	-19.3	-1.3	8.3	-12.1

Fourth quarter

Sector	Avg	2005	2006	2007	2008	2009	2010	2011	2012	2013	2014
Chemicals	7.6	9.2	9.1	9.2	-21.3	12.0	16.3	10.3	1.8	10.2	18.2
Health Care Equip & Srvs	7.6	13.3	6.3	3.2	-27.6	13.1	16.7	6.7	0.8	12.0	15.6
Food Producers	7.5	-1.0	5.6	14.9	2.2	6.1	7.9	6.2	7.8	7.6	14.1
Real Estate Inv & Srvs	6.9						6.8	8.8	7.8	6.6	4.6
Beverages	6.9	1.5	8.5	3.4	3.8	16.3	9.0	11.0	3.3	0.7	0.7
Travel & Leisure	6.9	11.5	16.6	-7.6	-13.6	0.9	10.0	6.9	7.9	12.4	11.1
Tobacco	6.8	7.0	7.7	15.4	-0.9	4.5	3.7	12.0	-0.4	-0.3	2.2
Mobile Telecom	6.6		15.3	6.7	12.8	3.3	5.4	9.3	-11.8	9.6	9.2
Industrial Metals	6.3	14.6	36.7	10.0	-65.0	13.5	26.3	-9.6	2.8	-6.9	6.3
Technology Hard & Equip	6.3	13.9	-8.1	-12.6	-22.2	12.5	5.0	5.9	22.0	9.6	8.4
Personal Goods	6.0	11.3	19.2	-1.8	-23.0	18.7	8.6	-1.3	22.3	-4.9	2.3
Mining	5.4	11.2	10.6	2.7	-31.5	24.1	22.8	8.5	8.8	-0.5	-10.2
Financial Services	4.8	10.2	10.6	0.3	-29.9	-2.7	19.0	-3.2	7.4	10.8	11.9
Electronic & Elect Equip	4.6	17.4	16.3	-15.7	-21.6	1.1	18.0	8.2	10.5	13.1	13
Media	4.6	3.5	1.7	-4.7	-2.9	6.4	6.2	9.3	4.7	6.3	4.7
Construction & Materials	4.5	13.7	4.5	-12.6	4.3	-8.4	16.3	8.0	1.9	4.0	7.5
Fixed Line Telecoms	4.3	-8.2	12.6	-9.2	-13.7	2.5	18.7	5.9	0.9	13.0	5.3
Food & Drug Retailers	4.1	7.6	10.2	2.7	-4.3	4.9	-1.1	7.5	-0.3	-4.8	6.9
Oil & Gas Producers	3.9	-5.6	-0.3	10.1	8.1	6.5	11.0	16.6	-4.6	7.9	-12.2
Gas; Water & Multiutilities	3.9	6.2	9.9	4.3	-6.4	11.8	3.5	-1.1	0.3	1.0	2
Aerospace & Defense	3.8	11.5	5.4	4.4	-6.2	5.4	1.3	13.3	2.3	5.2	-1.7
Support Services	3.8	8.0	10.3	-6.3	-5.7	4.3	6.5	8.0	1.1	5.4	4.2
Life Insurance	3.8	9.8	6.6	-4.8	-19.2	-1.1	-2.5	9.7	11.3	11.6	4.9
Household Goods	3.4		11.9	-7.9	-6.8	5.0	1.6	-0.5	11	9.6	6.4
Equity Inv Instruments	3.3	8.5	6.6	-1.7	-18.6	4.3	9.3	1.5	3.3	3.4	3.5
Nonlife Insurance	3.1	17.0	12.0	-4.8	3.5	-5.0	0.4	-3.4	4.8	4.2	2.2
Industrial Engineering	2.6	10.9	6.3	-18.8	-26.8	7.3	19.2	17.5	7.8	0.9	-9.6
Industrial Transportation	2.6	9.6	10.2	-5.3	-32.2	1.5	5.3	1.7	6.4	6.3	7.7
Software & Comp Srvs	2.4	10.3	9.7	-9.5	-17.5	-1.1	2.0	3.6	3.3	4.8	11.1
General Retailers	2.3	14.1	2.6	-12.1	-12.9	9.2	2.0	-1.0	11.5	-1.3	11.9
Electricity	1.9	-1.7	13.7	4.6	-14.8	-0.1	9.6	1.4	2.6	-3.1	-0.1
Automobiles & Parts	1.3	4.2	-3.2	-20.3	-50.4	2.9	31.2	4.0	6.5	9.2	7.8
Pharm & Biotech	0.9	3.7	-9.3	-4.7	8.9	6.2	-3.6	8.4	-3.9	7.4	-2.6
General Industrials	0.8		1.4	-13.2	-20.4	10.0	9.0	4.1	7.4	11.7	-3.2
Forestry & Paper	-0.2	9.8		-8.6	-21.0	8.4	-0.2	-3.9	6.3	0.3	3.9
Real Estate Inv Trusts	-0.3		11.0	-12.8	-33.6	4.7	7.6	-2.1	7.2	5.8	9.5
Oil Equip; Srvs & Dist	-0.7		23.8	14.5	-38.3	3.6	15.9	14.0	-6.1	-6.4	-27.3
Banks	-2.0	6.5	3.2	-10.3	-38.2	-9.2	-4.0	-0.3	15.4	-0.2	-1.9

SECTOR ANNUAL PERFORMANCE

The table below shows the year-on-year percentage performance of the FTSE 350 sectors. The three best [worst] performing sectors in each year are highlighted in light grey [dark grey]. The table is ranked by the final column – the average annual return for the sector for the period 2005-2014.

Sector performance 2005-2014 (percentage change YoY)

EPIC	Sector	2005	2006	2007	2008	2009	2010	2011	2012	2013	2014	Avg
NMX3760	Personal Goods	20.9	40.7	2.2	-42.9	105.8	76.1	-1.6	3.4	26.2	-0.5	23.0
NMX9570	Tech Hardware & Equipment	5.5	-10.4	-1.2	-43.3	131.6	70.4	21.6	25.7	35.1	-5.4	23.0
NMX1350	Chemicals	32.1	33.6	41.3	-37.8	43.8	58.5	-7.8	35.5	21.5	4.2	22.5
NMX1750	Industrial Metals	16.8	79.8	-56.6	-83.9	307.3	72.4	-54.0	-29.4	-48.6	8.0	21.2
NMX2750	Industrial Engineering	27.6	19.8	-7.2	-31.1	83.1	78.2	3.2	14.7	27.5	-14.9	20.1
NMX3350	Automobiles & Parts	25.0	-3.5	1.4	-65.6	78.7	89.9	-17.6	25.0	63.2	-7.8	18.9
NMX2730	Electronic & Electrical Equip	35.7	23.4	-5.5	-31.4	23.0	81.2	-6.6	41.8	21.3	-11.1	17.2
NMX1770	Mining	63.0	22.9	50.4	-55.7	108.5	27.8	-29.7	0.2	-16.3	-13.0	15.8
NMX9530	Software & Computer Services	16.7	-2.9	-7.5	-26.2	63.9	23.7	2.1	28.8	25.6	6.6	13.1
NMX3780	Tobacco	31.0	14.8	34.0	-14.6	9.9	15.0	23.9	0.8	2.3	11.7	12.9
NMX1730	Forestry & Paper	6.6		-49.7	-52.1	64.4	53.3	-11.4	47.1	56.2	0.4	12.8
NMX3530	Beverages	19.7	16.5	14.4	-11.6	28.9	15.6	9.3	25.8	11.7	-3.1	12.7
NMX0570	Oil Equipment, Services & Dist			38.1	-45.7	87.8	56.3	-10.4	6.2	-6.3	-25.7	12.5
NMX8630	Real Estate Inv & Services						-2.0	-1.3	23.4	41.4	-0.8	12.1
NMX2710	Aerospace & Defense	54.3	6.0	20.4	-27.6	15.8	7.7	1.1	16.9	37.6	-11.8	12.0
NMX8770	Financial Services	25.9	37.9	2.0	-55.4	39.7	21.5	-28.5	23.5	42.3	9.1	11.8
NMX8530	Nonlife Insurance	44.6	28.6	-6.2	1.2	-1.7	17.6	-12.3	23.8	11.4	5.7	11.3
NMX7530	Electricity	33.4	41.2	6.5	-16.2	-1.0	14.0	8.5	8.4	3.6	6.4	10.5
NMX4530	Health Care Equip & Services	4.0	-2.9	18.6	-36.3	47.0	7.5	-7.2	9.7	25.0	39.3	10.5
NMX5750	Travel & Leisure	18.5	27.6	-15.9	-40.8	22.5	24.2	-15.9	25.2	38.1	9.9	9.3
NMX3570	Food Producers	12.1	9.8	12.9	-19.9	25.1	6.3	7.8	13.2	13.7	12.1	9.3
NMX2790	Support Services	17.5	20.4	-9.7	-27.2	28.7	19.7	-2.4	20.2	26.6	-1.1	9.3
NMX2770	Industrial Transportation	25.7	49.9	-20.8	-61.2	52.3	25.7	-12.2	13.4	30.7	-12.6	9.1
NMX5370	General Retailers	3.3	16.6	-25.9	-47.8	75.2	-2.5	-11.7	32.4	32.6	12.4	8.5
NMX6530	Fixed Line Telecommunications	-1.1	32.9	-5.4	-44.5	-1.7	19.8	-5.2	24.4	61.8	3.6	8.5
NMX8980	Equity Investment Instruments	30.8	12.4	6.5	-36.1	31.3	18.5	-10.9	10.1	14.6	7.0	8.4
NMX8570	Life Insurance	17.1	18.5	-10.1	-43.3	26.5	2.0	-4.6	32.8	36.0	9.1	8.4
NMX6570	Mobile Telecommunications			32.9	-25.7	4.6	14.7	8.6	-12.5	52.7	-8.9	8.3
NMX3720	Household Goods			-15.0	-28.6	30.9	1.0	-5.2	31.9	35.1	14.9	8.1
NMX5550	Media	6.0	4.0	0.2	-34.1	28.3	21.5	-1.9	19.2	34.9	1.4	8.0
NMX7570	Gas; Water & Multiutilities	13.9	31.0	7.3	-17.8	-0.6	7.9	2.8	13.2	8.0	8.2	7.4
NMX4570	Pharma & Biotech	28.7	-5.1	-9.5	8.0	4.2	-1.2	14.5	-7.0	24.8	8.7	6.6
NMX2720	General Industrials			-13.1	-30.0	23.2	37.6	-12.3	28.9	33.9	-15.7	6.6
NMX2350	Construction & Materials	35.1	29.0	4.5	-35.7	-0.7	19.6	-13.1	0.3	23.4	-4.1	5.8
NMX0530	Oil & Gas Producers	25.6	-2.0	19.3	-16.0	13.3	0.5	4.8	-11.8	8.1	-13.4	2.8
NMX8670	Real Estate Investment Trusts		33.8	-36.5	-44.7	6.2	2.7	-12.6	25.7	15.1	20.2	1.1
NMX5330	Food & Drug Retailers	3.8	23.6	20.2	-22.5	12.5	1.8	-3.6	-12.0	6.5	-35.6	-0.5
NMX8350	Banks	7.3	10.0	-21.3	-56.8	23.8	-0.1	-29.6	34.5	7.8	-9.5	-3.4

SECTOR PROFILES OF THE FTSE 100 AND FTSE 250

The chart below shows the FTSE 350 sector weightings in the FTSE 100 and FTSE 250.

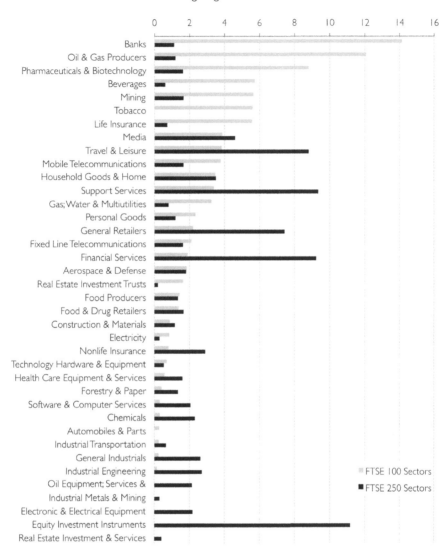

Note: Figures as of August 2015.

Observations

1. The top four FTSE 350 sectors (banks, oil and gas producers, pharmaceuticals and beverages) together account for 41% of the total market capitalisation of the FTSE 100. (In 2006, the top sectors accounted for 55% of the index capitalisation.)

2. In the last year, beverages has displaced mining in the top four sectors.

3. In 1935, the FT 30 index was dominated by engineering and machinery companies. Today, the sector isn't represented at all in the FTSE 100.

4. The FTSE 100 is still dominated by the old industries of oil, mining and banks, while the FTSE 250 has proportionately a greater representation of service (support, financial and computer) companies.

COMPANIES

COMPANY RANKINGS

On the following pages companies are ranked according to various criteria. The tables are grouped into the following categories:

1. FTSE 350

2. AIM

3. Investment Trusts

Table index

A summary of the tables is given below:

1. 10 largest companies by **market capitalisation** [FTSE 350]

2. 10 companies with largest average **daily trade value** [FTSE 350]

3. 5-year **share performance** 2011-2015 [FTSE 350]

4. 10-year **share performance** 2006-2015 [FTSE 350]

5. 10 companies with highest **turnover**

6. 10 companies with greatest **turnover growth** in 5 years to 2015 [FTSE 350]

7. 10 companies with highest **ROCE** [FTSE 350]

8. 10 companies with highest **profits**

9. 10 companies with greatest **profit growth** in the 5 years to 2015 [FTSE 350]

10. 10 companies with highest **operating margins** [FTSE 350]

11. 10 companies with highest **EPS growth** in the 5 years to 2015 [FTSE 350]

12. 10 companies with highest **dividend growth** in the 5 years to 2015 [FTSE 350]

13. 10 companies paying the most **tax** in last year

14. 10 companies with largest **market capitalisation** [AIM]

15. 10 companies with largest average **daily trade value** [AIM]

16. 5-year **share performance** to 2015 [AIM]

17. 10 companies with largest **turnover** [AIM]

18. 10 companies with largest **profits** [AIM]

19. 10 companies with highest **ROCE** [AIM]

20. 10 largest investment trusts by **capitalisation** [Investment Trusts]

21. 10 **best performing** investment trusts 2011-2015 [Investment Trusts]

22. 10 investment trusts with highest average **daily trading value** [Investment Trusts]

Note: All figures accurate as of August 2015.

FTSE 350

Size, volume and performance

Table 1: 10 largest companies by market capitalisation

Rank	Company	TIDM	Capital (£m)
1	Royal Dutch Shell	RDSB	110,206
2	HSBC Holdings	HSBA	105,645
3	British American Tobacco	BATS	68,174
4	BP	BP.	67,181
5	GlaxoSmithKline	GSK	67,085
6	Vodafone Group	VOD	62,386
7	Lloyds Banking Group	LLOY	56,385
8	AstraZeneca	AZN	53,579
9	SABMiller	SAB	52,111
10	Barclays	BARC	44,946

Table 2: 10 companies with largest average daily trade value

Rank	Company	TIDM	Average daily trade value (£m)
1	HSBC Holdings	HSBA	155
2	BP	BP.	148
3	Rio Tinto	RIO	139
4	Vodafone Group	VOD	137
5	GlaxoSmithKline	GSK	130
6	BHP Billiton	BLT	124
7	Lloyds Banking Group	LLOY	115
8	AstraZeneca	AZN	113
9	Royal Dutch Shell	RDSB	111
10	Glencore	GLEN	100

Table 3: 5-year share performance 2011-2015 [FTSE 350]

Rank	Company	TIDM	5-yr change (%)
1	Ashtead Group	AHT	912
2	Sports Direct International	SPD	669
3	Taylor Wimpey	TW.	642
4	IP Group	IPO	618
5	Howden Joinery Group	HWDN	614
6	Barratt Developments	BDEV	572
7	Ted Baker	TED	534
8	Rightmove	RMV	527
9	Persimmon	PSN	524
10	Galliford Try	GFRD	505

Table 4: 10-year share performance 2006-2015 [FTSE 350]

Rank	Company	TIDM	10-yr change (%)
1	JD Sports Fashion	JD.	1,489
2	Domino's Pizza UK & IRL	DOM	800
3	Ashtead Group	AHT	763
4	Croda International	CRDA	669
5	ARM Holdings	ARM	659
6	Shire	SHP	645
7	Micro Focus International	MCRO	636
8	Telecom plus	TEP	634
9	Aveva Group	AVV	631
10	Ted Baker	TED	574

Turnover

Table 5: 10 companies with highest turnover

Rank	Company	TIDM	Turnover (£m)
1	Royal Dutch Shell	RDSB	270,600
2	BP	BP.	227,200
3	Glencore	GLEN	142,000
4	Tesco	TSCO	62,280
5	Vodafone Group	VOD	42,230
6	BHP Billiton	BLT	39,460
7	Unilever	ULVR	37,850
8	SSE	SSE	31,650
9	Rio Tinto	RIO	30,620
10	Centrica	CNA	29,410

Table 6: 10 companies with greatest turnover growth in 5 years to 2015 [FTSE 350]

Rank	Company	TIDM	Turnover 5-yr growth (%)
1	Dixons Carphone	DC.	9000+
2	IP Group	IPO	1,793
3	Centamin	CEY	1,105
4	Nostrum Oil & Gas	NOG	600
5	Petra Diamonds Ltd	PDL	558
6	Redefine International	RDI	369
7	BTG	BTG	273
8	Londonmetric Property	LMP	257
9	Playtech	PTEC	250
10	SuperGroup	SGP	249

Table 7: 10 companies with highest ROCE [FTSE 350]

Rank	Company	TIDM	ROCE (%)
1	Hargreaves Lansdown	HL.	883
2	Just Eat	JE.	157
3	Wizz Air Holding	WIZZ	117
4	Clarkson	CKN	85
5	WH Smith	SMWH	84
6	Jardine Lloyd Thompson Group	JLT	75
7	Howden Joinery Group	HWDN	74
8	Next	NXT	74
9	PayPoint	PAY	74
10	Domino's Pizza UK & IRL	DOM	69

Profits

Table 8: 10 companies with highest profits

Rank	Company	TIDM	Profit (£m)
1	Royal Dutch Shell	RDSB	18,191
2	BHP Billiton	BLT	13,056
3	HSBC Holdings	HSBA	12,002
4	Rio Tinto	RIO	6,137
5	Unilever	ULVR	5,974
6	British American Tobacco	BATS	4,848
7	SABMiller	SAB	3,262
8	BP	BP.	3,180
9	GlaxoSmithKline	GSK	2,968
10	Diageo	DGE	2,933

Table 9: 10 companies with greatest profit growth in the 5 years to 2015 [FTSE 350]

Rank	Company	TIDM	5-yr profit growth (%)
1	Ashtead Group	AHT	9,771
2	Nostrum Oil & Gas	NOG	3,563
3	Aberdeen Asset Management	ADN	3,277
4	Bovis Homes Group	BVS	2,683
5	ITV	ITV	2,320
6	Jupiter Fund Management	JUP	2,122
7	Moneysupermarket.com Group	MONY	1,972
8	Workspace Group	WKP	1,285
9	CLS Holdings	CLI	1,180
10	Mondi	MNDI	1,012

Table 10: 10 companies with highest operating margins [FTSE 350]

Rank	Company	TIDM	Operating Margin (%)
1	Great Portland Estates	GPOR	758
2	Shaftesbury	SHB	501
3	Capital & Counties Properties	CAPC	473
4	Workspace Group	WKP	445
5	Derwent London	DLN	445
6	CLS Holdings	CLI	316
7	Land Securities Group	LAND	304
8	Londonmetric Property	LMP	300
9	British Land Co	BLND	262
10	Tritax Big Box REIT	BBOX	244

Table 11: 10 companies with highest EPS growth in the 5 years to 2015 [FTSE 350]

Rank	Company	TIDM	EPS 5-Yr Growth (%)
1	Great Portland Estates	GPOR	9000+
2	Ashtead Group	AHT	9000+
3	Vesuvius	VSVS	7,911
4	Old Mutual	OML	2,827
5	Moneysupermarket.com Group	MONY	2,120
6	CLS Holdings	CLI	1,358
7	Elementis	ELM	1,242
8	Tullow Oil	TLW	1,104
9	Segro	SGRO	1,000
10	Bovis Homes Group	BVS	988

Dividends

Table 12: 10 companies with highest dividend growth in the 5 years to 2015 [FTSE 350]

Rank	Company	TIDM	5-yr Div Growth (%)
1	RIT Capital Partners	RCP	643
2	Bellway	BWY	478
3	Big Yellow Group	BYG	443
4	Ashtead Group	AHT	426
5	St James's Place	STJ	418
6	Old Mutual	OML	408
7	Galliford Try	GFRD	388
8	Grafton Group	GFTU	381
9	Rio Tinto	RIO	368
10	Mondi	MNDI	336

Tax

Table 13: 10 companies paying the most tax in the last year

Rank	Company	TIDM	Tax paid (£m)
1	Royal Dutch Shell	RDSB	8,730
2	BHP Billiton	BLT	4,120
3	HSBC Holdings	HSBA	2,550
4	Rio Tinto	RIO	1,960
5	Royal Bank of Scotland Group (The)	RBS	1,910
6	Unilever	ULVR	1,670
7	British American Tobacco	BATS	1,450
8	Barclays	BARC	1,410
9	Glencore	GLEN	1,160
10	Standard Chartered	STAN	983

AIM

Table 14: 10 companies with largest market capitalisation [AIM]

Rank	Name	TIDM	Capital (£m)
1	ASOS	ASC	2,712
2	New Europe Property Investments	NEPI	2,052
3	GW Pharmaceuticals	GWP	1,560
4	BCA Marketplace	BCA	1,377
5	Optimal Payments	OPAY	1,351
6	Abcam	ABC	1,224
7	Hutchison China Meditech Ltd	HCM	1,064
8	MarketTech Holdings Ltd	MKT	1,056
9	James Halstead	JHD	862
10	Clinigen Group	CLIN	808

Table 15: 10 companies with largest average daily trade value [AIM]

Rank	Name	TIDM	Average daily trade value (£m)
1	ASOS	ASC	24
2	Optimal Payments	OPAY	9
3	Quindell	QPP	8
4	Plus500 Ltd	PLUS	4
5	Monitise	MONI	3
6	Abcam	ABC	3
7	Sirius Minerals	SXX	2
8	Tungsten Corp	TUNG	2
9	boohoo.com	BOO	2
10	GW Pharmaceuticals	GWP	2

Table 16: 5-year share performance to 2015 [AIM]

Rank	Name	TIDM	5-yr share price (%)
1	Energy Technique	ETQ	5,552
2	Concha	CHA	3,229
3	Cloudbuy	CBUY	2,278
4	Staffline Recruitment Group	STAF	1,464
5	Gemfields	GEM	1,344
6	Quindell	QPP	1,320
7	Solid State	SOLI	1,304
8	AdEPT Telecom	ADT	1,297
9	Scapa Group	SCPA	1,067
10	Trakm8 Holdings	TRAK	969

Table 17: 10 companies with largest turnover [AIM]

Rank	Name	TIDM	Turnover (£m)
1	Datatec Ltd	DTC	4,180
2	Total Produce	TOT	2,084
3	Vertu Motors	VTU	2,075
4	Ambrian	AMBR	1,854
5	ISG	ISG	1,483
6	Origin Enterprises	OGN	1,415
7	Impellam Group	IPEL	1,323
8	Dart Group	DTG	1,253
9	Marshall Motor Holdings	MMH	1,086
10	ASOS	ASC	976

Table 18: 10 companies with largest profits [AIM]

Rank	Name	TIDM	Profit (£m)
1	Bankers Petroleum Ltd	BNK	139
2	Secure Income REIT	SIR	133
3	Globalworth Real Estate Investments Ltd	GWI	96
4	New Europe Property Investments	NEPI	95
5	Datatec Ltd	DTC	91
6	Plus500 Ltd	PLUS	89
7	Summit Germany Ltd	SMTG	74
8	Origin Enterprises	OGN	74
9	Asian Growth Properties Ltd	AGP	62
10	Abbey	ABBY	49

Table 19: 10 companies with highest ROCE [AIM]

Rank	Name	TIDM	ROCE
1	Gfinity	GFIN	35900
2	32Red	TTR	30800
3	Styles & Wood Group	STY	17200
4	Wishbone Gold	WSBN	5680
5	Kennedy Ventures	KENV	3720
6	TyraTech Inc	TYR	3070
7	TyraTech Inc	TYRU	3070
8	Netdimensions (Holdings) Ltd	NETD	2970
9	Sacoven	SCN	2790
10	Plethora Solutions Holdings	PLE	2790

Investment Trusts

Table 20: 10 largest investment trusts by capitalisation

Rank	Investment Trust	TIDM	Capital (£m)
1	Land Securities Group	LAND	10,340
2	British Land Co	BLND	8,788
3	Hammerson	HMSO	5,248
4	3i Group	III	4,965
5	Intu Properties	INTU	4,520
6	Derwent London	DLN	4,193
7	Segro	SGRO	3,415
8	Scottish Mortgage Investment Trust	SMT	3,311
9	Great Portland Estates	GPOR	2,996
10	Alliance Trust	ATST	2,661

Table 21: 10 best performing investment trusts 2011-2015

Rank	Investment Trust	TIDM	5-yr price change (%)
1	Premier Veterinary Group	PVG	1684
2	Biotech Growth Trust (The)	BIOG	421
3	Workspace Group	WKP	395
4	Strategic Equity Capital	SEC	343
5	Inland Homes	INL	308
6	International Biotechnology Trust	IBT	306
7	EPE Special Opportunities	ESO	267
8	New Europe Property Investments	NEPI	242
9	Marwyn Value Investors Ltd	MVI	221
10	Northern Investors Company	NRI	216

STATISTICS – COMPANIES

Table 22: 10 investment trusts with highest average daily trading value

Rank	Investment Trust	TIDM	Average daily trade value (£m)
1	Land Securities Group	LAND	26.03
2	British Land Co	BLND	25.68
3	Hammerson	HMSO	13.97
4	Intu Properties	INTU	9.04
5	3i Group	III	8.25
6	Derwent London	DLN	6.84
7	Segro	SGRO	6.30
8	Great Portland Estates	GPOR	5.28
9	Shaftesbury	SHB	4.39
10	Scottish Mortgage Investment Trust	SMT	3.36

TEN BAGGERS

The term 'ten bagger' was coined by Peter Lynch, the legendary manager of the Fidelity Magellan fund, in his book *One Up on Wall Street*. Ten bagger comes from baseball and Lynch used it to describe stocks that rise ten times in value.

The table below shows the UK stocks that rose ten times or more in the ten years to August 2015.

UK ten baggers over ten years to August 2015

Company	TIDM	Price increase 10Y (%)	Capital (£m)	Sector	Index
Accesso Technology Group	ACSO	13,378	170	Technology	AIM All-Share
ASOS	ASC	4,571	2,728	Consumer Services	AIM All-Share
Advanced Medical Solutions Group	AMS	1,547	314	Health Care	AIM All-Share
Judges Scientific	JDG	1,514	95	Industrials	AIM All-Share
JD Sports Fashion	JD.	1,477	1,689	Consumer Services	FTSE Mid-250
Solid State	SOLI	1,463	73	Industrials	AIM All-Share
First Derivatives	FDP	1,433	322	Technology	AIM All-Share
Walker Greenbank	WGB	1,406	138	Consumer Goods	AIM All-Share
Staffline Recruitment Group	STAF	1,215	389	Industrials	AIM All-Share
Brooks Macdonald Group	BRK	1,104	251	Financials	AIM All-Share
Character Group (The)	CCT	1,065	110	Consumer Goods	AIM All-Share
Renew Holdings	RNWH	1,050	201	Industrials	AIM All-Share

Observations

1. The table above does not include those companies that rose ten times in the interim, only to see their share prices fall back again. For example, Ashtead, Aveva, Babcock Intl, Domino's Pizza, Dragon Oil, Goodwin and Randgold Resources, have all been ten baggers at some point.

2. Jim Slater's comment that "elephants don't gallop" would seem to hold true. Many of the above ten baggers were small companies ten years ago.

3. It can be seen that the ten baggers come from quite a wide range of sectors. In other words, it's not necessary to look for ten baggers in just a few glamour sectors. For example, only two of the above ten baggers are in the technology sector.

As Peter Lynch says:

"The very best way to make money in a market is in a small growth company that has been profitable for a couple of years and simply goes on growing."

ANNOUNCEMENT DATES OF COMPANY RESULTS

Companies listed on the London Stock Exchange are required to release certain information to the public. Some of these statements are one-offs and unpredictable, such as news of takeovers or board changes, while others follow a more regular timetable. For investors, two important regular announcements each year are:

1. **interim results** (known as *interims*): usually reported about eight months into a company's financial year, they relate to the unaudited headline figures for the first half of the company's year.

2. **preliminary results** (known as *prelims*): unaudited figures published prior to the full annual report at the end of the company's financial year. (Note: although these are termed 'preliminary' they are very much the real final results.)

These announcements are watched very carefully and have the potential to significantly move the share price of a company.

FTSE 100

The following chart plots the frequency distribution of the dates of these announcements for FTSE 100 companies.

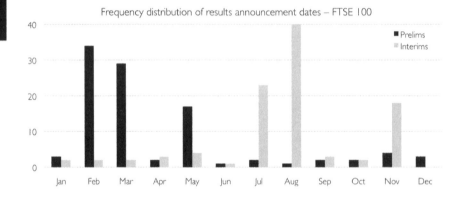

Frequency distribution of results announcement dates – FTSE 100

As can be seen, the majority of interim results are announced in July and August, while preliminary results are clustered in February and March (61 companies announce their prelims in this two-month period).

FTSE 250

The following chart is similar to that above, except this time the companies are in the FTSE 250.

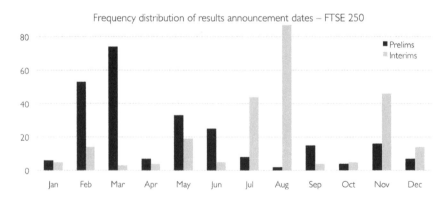

Frequency distribution of results announcement dates – FTSE 250

For the FTSE 250 companies, the announcements are a little more evenly distributed throughout the year, but the main months are the same as those for the FTSE 100: July/August being the busiest two-month period for interims – along with November – and February/March the busiest for the prelims.

LONG TERM

CORRELATION BETWEEN UK AND US MARKETS

The previous edition of the Almanac looked at the weekly correlation of the UK and US equity markets. In this edition we will look at the correlation not of weekly but of monthly returns.

The following charts plot the correlation of monthly returns of the FTSE All-Share and S&P 500 indices for each decade since the 1960s.

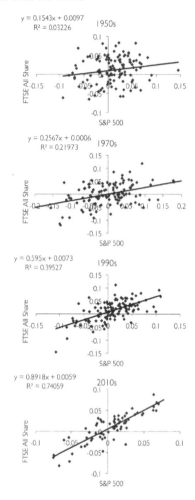

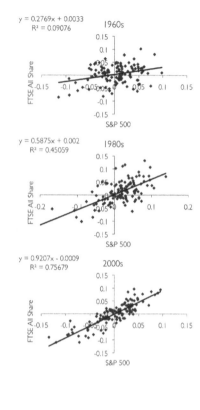

The trend of increasing correlation throughout the decades that was seen for weekly returns is repeated here. In the 1960s and 1970s there was negligible correlation (measured by the R^2 value in the charts) between the UK and US markets on a monthly basis. The US equity market might rise one month and the UK might at the same time rise or fall – there was no connection. In the 1970s some evidence of correlation can be seen for the first time – although it was still very weak.

But in the 1980s the monthly correlation of the two markets jumped and became statistically significant. There could be many reasons for this increase in correlation, but one contributing factor was undoubtedly the increasing presence of computers in trading rooms. And, of course, the October crash in 1987 would have alerted many for the first time to the scale of the inter-connectedness of worldwide markets.

Correlation increased somewhat again in the 1990s, but then increased hugely in the 2000s. This can be clearly seen in the last two charts, where the points are closely aligned along the line of best fit.

The correlation of monthly returns for the two markets since 2010 has been a high 0.74.

CORRELATION BETWEEN UK AND WORLD MARKETS

In the previous edition of the Almanac we looked at the correlation of monthly returns for the FTSE All-Share index and a range of international equity markets. Here we update that study with the most recent data.

The charts on this page show the correlation of monthly returns between the FTSE All-Share and six international indices for the period 2000-2015.

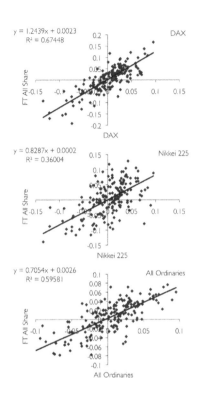

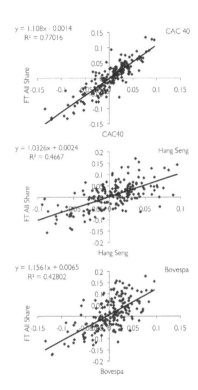

Analysis

The first observation is that all the markets are positively correlated with the UK market. The next question is how closely?

The table on the right summarises the R^2 values for the correlation between the FTSE All-Share and the six international indices. The values are also given for the previous two years. The higher the R^2 figure, the closer the correlation (R-Squared is a measure of correlation – in effect, how close the points are to the line of best fit).

Index	R^2 (2015)	R^2 (2014)	R^2 (2013)
CAC 40	0.77	0.78	0.79
DAX	0.67	0.69	0.70
All Ordinaries	0.60	0.61	0.62
Hang Seng	0.47	0.48	0.49
Bovespa	0.43	0.45	0.47
Nikkei 225	0.36	0.37	0.39

By visual inspection it can be seen that in the charts of CAC 40 and DAX the points are more closely distributed around the line of best fit. This is confirmed in the table where it can be seen these two markets have the highest R^2 values (the CAC 40 value of 0.77 is now higher than that of 0.74 for the S&P 500). Among the sample the index with the lowest correlation with the UK market is the Nikkei.

The practical impact of this is that if a UK investor is looking to internationally diversify a portfolio they would do better by investing in markets at the bottom of the table (low R^2) than at the top. And the good news for investors looking for diversification is that the correlation between the UK market and all the international markets in this study has slightly fallen in the past two years.

THE LONG-TERM FORMULA

The chart below plots the FTSE All-Share index from 1946 to the present day.

1. The Y-scale is logarithmic, which presents percentage (rather than absolute) changes better over long periods, and so is more suitable for long-term charts.

2. The straight line is a line of best fit calculated by regression analysis.

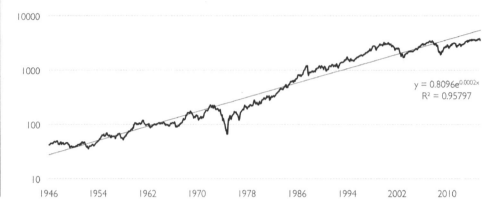

$$y = 0.8096e^{0.0002x}$$
$$R^2 = 0.95797$$

Observations

1. The R^2 for the line of best fit is 0.96, which is impressively high for such a simple model (i.e. the line of best fit fairly accurately approximates the real data points).

2. The FTSE All-Share fluctuated closely around the trend line (line of best fit) from 1946 to 1973; it then traded consistently below the trend line until 1983, when it crossed over to trade above the trend line until 2001. From 2001 the index was close to the trend, but then in 2008 fell significantly below it and has yet to revert to the long-term trend line.

Forecasts

The equation of the line of best fit in the chart above (with a little more precision) is:

$$y = 0.809649e^{0.000209x}$$

This equation allows us to make forecasts for the FTSE All-Share. It is, in effect, the Holy Grail, the key to the stock market – as simple as that!

For example, at the time of writing the FTSE All-Share is 3576; while the above equation forecasts a value today (according to the long-term trend line) of 5518. This suggests the index is currently underpriced relative to the long-tem trend line. But as can be seen in the above chart, the index can spend long periods trading above or below the long-term trend line.

Now, if we think that the trend of the market in the last 70 years will broadly continue, then we can use the equation to forecast the level of the FTSE All-Share index in the future. And this is what has been done in the table on the right. Forecasts for the FTSE 100 have also been given.

Date	FTAS forecast	FTSE 100 forecast	Change (%)
Dec 2016	6,127	11,197	71
Dec 2020	8,315	15,195	133
Dec 2030	17,837	32,597	399
Dec 2040	38,274	69,944	970

- The equation says that the trend line value for the FTSE 100 at the end 2016 will be 11,197 (71% above its current level in August 2015).

- By end 2020 the forecast is for a FTSE 100 level of 15,195 (+133%), and by end 2040 the equation forecasts a FTSE 100 value of 69,944 (+970%).

THE MARKET'S DECENNIAL CYCLE

The following table shows the annual performance of the FTSE All-Share index since 1801. The table is arranged to compare the performance of the market for the same year in each decade. For example, in the third year of the 1801-1810 decade (1803), the market fell 21.9%, while in the third year of the 1811-1820 decade (1813), the market fell 0.2%. Years are highlighted in which the market fell.

Decade	1st	2nd	3rd	4th	5th	6th	7th	8th	9th	10th
1801-1810	11.0	1.4	-21.9	10.3	8.5	0.7	3.5	4.7	10.4	-9.2
1811-1820	-14.6	-7.5	-0.2	2.4	-6.2	-12.2	32.6	5.5	-8.3	3.2
1821-1830	4.5	9.4	9.2	90.7	-22.7	-20.1	4.6	-14.5	3.3	-14.8
1831-1840	-15.7	2.2	16.5	-9.3	5.0	5.2	-8.5	-3.6	-12.7	3.1
1841-1850	-9.7	7.1	12.3	16.5	-2.1	-1.8	-13.9	-13.5	-7.3	14.4
1851-1860	-0.2	9.6	-6.8	-3.2	-3.4	5.4	-5.9	6.5	-2.0	11.1
1861-1870	3.1	16.6	12.8	5.0	1.4	-22.4	-2.2	6.8	7.4	8.6
1871-1880	18.9	4.0	3.6	-5.2	-7.9	-2.4	-9.6	-11.0	12.1	4.9
1881-1890	-0.6	-6.3	-5.0	-2.1	0.2	0.6	-3.6	5.8	13.1	-6.2
1891-1900	0.7	-0.1	1.6	6.0	11.2	22.0	5.2	0.3	-2.0	-0.9
1901-1910	-4.9	-1.3	-5.6	2.5	6.2	-0.4	-14.7	8.1	4.8	-2.5
1911-1920	0.3	-0.9	-6.7	-6.9	-5.1	0.5	-10.5	11.0	2.4	-13.3
1921-1930	-5.4	17.6	2.0	9.5	4.4	2.4	8.3	8.1	-7.4	-19.4
1931-1940	-23.5	5.6	27.2	8.3	7.8	13.9	-19.3	-14.3	0.8	-13.0
1941-1950	22.6	18.6	8.1	10.7	-0.6	18.1	-2.7	-4.0	-13.9	6.4
1951-1960	2.4	-5.1	16.0	34.5	1.6	-9.0	-3.3	33.2	43.4	-4.7
1961-1970	-2.5	-1.8	10.6	-10.0	6.7	-9.3	29.0	43.4	-15.2	-7.5
1971-1980	41.9	12.8	-31.4	-55.3	136.3	-3.9	41.2	2.7	4.3	27.1
1981-1990	7.2	22.1	23.1	26.0	15.2	22.3	4.2	6.5	30.0	-14.3
1991-2000	15.1	14.8	23.3	-9.6	18.5	11.7	19.7	10.9	21.2	-8.0
2001-2010	-15.4	-25.0	16.6	9.2	18.1	13.2	2.0	-32.8	25.0	10.9
2011-2020	-6.7	8.2	16.7	-2.1						
Analysis										
Since 1810										
Positive (yrs):	11	14	15	13	14	12	10	14	13	9
Average (%):	1.3	4.6	5.5	5.8	9.2	1.6	2.7	2.9	5.2	-1.2
Since 1921										
Positive (yrs):	5	7	9	6	8	6	6	6	6	3
Average (%):	3.6	6.8	11.2	2.1	23.1	6.6	8.8	6.0	9.8	-2.5
Since 1951										
Positive (yrs):	4	4	6	3	6	3	5	5	5	2
Average (%):	6.0	3.7	10.7	-1.0	32.7	4.2	15.5	10.6	18.1	0.6

Observations

1. Since 1801, the strongest years have been the 2nd, 3rd and 5th years in decades. The market has risen 14 out of the 21 decades in these years, with an average annual return over 4%. But the single year champion has got to be the 5th year in each decade, which has risen an average of 9.2%.

2. The standout weakest year in the decade since 1801 has been the 10th – this is the only year to have risen less than ten times in the 21 decades, and also the only year to have a negative average return (-1.2%).

3. Generally, performance in the more recent decades has not changed too much from the long-term picture. In the six decades since 1951, the strong years are still the 3rd and 5th years, although now also joined by the 7th and 9th years. The dominance of the 5th year is greater than ever – it is the only year to rise in every decade since 1951. And the 10th year continues to be weakest, with positive returns only twice in the past six decades.

4. Concerning 2016, the sixth year of decades is one of the weaker years, with an average return of just 1.2% since 1800.

BUY AND HOLD

The last decade or so has not been the best for buy-and-hold investors. At the time of writing (August 2015), the FTSE 100 is at 6367, which is 50 points below where it closed on 6 April 1999 – over 16 years ago.

The question must be asked: is buy and hold dead?

Such thinking inspired Richard Bernstein to write a paper[1] in July 2012 called, appropriately, "Is buy and hold dead?" In the paper, which advocates longer-term investing, Bernstein says:

> "There are sound economic reasons why extending one's time horizon can benefit investment returns. Changes within the economy tend to be very gradual, and significant adjustments rarely happen within a short period of time. Certainly, there is plenty of daily news, but how much of that news is actually important and worth acting on? The data suggest very little of that information is meaningful and valuable. Most of it is simply noise."

He also writes:

> Investment returns can be significantly hurt by strategies based on short-term, noise-driven strategies. The data clearly and consistently showed that extending one's investment time horizon was a simple method for improving investment returns.

In the paper he presents a chart showing the probability of sustaining a loss over different time horizons for an investment in the S&P 500.

The chart on this page does the same for the FTSE All-Share index. The analysis was carried out on daily data for 1970 to 2015.

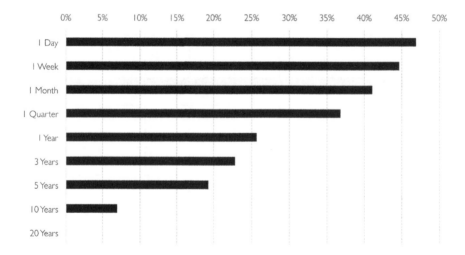

The analysis found that if an investment was made in the index on any day since 1970, the chance of the index being lower one week later (i.e. five trading days later) was 45%. Similarly, since 1970, investing on any day would see a 41% chance the market would be lower a month later.

As can be seen in the chart, the longer the time horizon of an investment, the lower the chance of loss. Conversely, the shorter the time horizon, the closer the probability of loss tends to 50/50 (i.e. the closer it becomes to a simple coin toss). By the time one gets to a holding period of ten years, the chance of loss is down to 7%; and is zero at a holding period of 20 years (based on the historic behaviour since 1970).

Finally, Bernstein's paper makes the interesting point that while longer time horizons tend to progressively improve investment returns in many financial assets (e.g. shares), this is not necessarily the case for real assets such as gold and other commodities.

---

1. www.rbadvisors.com

ULTIMATE DEATH CROSS

A previous edition of the Almanac showed a chart with the FTSE All-Share poised to make an ultimate death cross (when the 50-month moving average moves down through the 200-month moving average). Readers were left hanging with the comment, "If the 50-month average does fall below the 200-month average will that signal lost decade(s) for the UK market as in Japan?"

So, what happened?

The chart below updates the action.

As can be seen (just), the 50M MAV narrowly avoided crossing the 200M MAV. We were saved. And, in fact, the narrow avoidance of an ultimate death cross in the past has been a strong buy signal for an ensuing massive bull market.

The last time the FTSE All-Share made an ultimate death cross was 1945. So this signal is fairly rare. But this has not always been the case. The following chart plots the FTSE All-Share with 50-month and 200-month moving averages for the period 1845-1945.

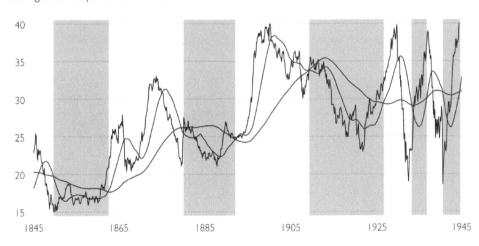

As can be seen, for the 100 years prior to 1945, ultimate death crosses were not uncommon. In fact, the 50-month MAV was below the 200-month MAV for 51 of the 100 years (these years are shaded in the chart).

SINCLAIR NUMBERS

SINCLAIR NOS – DAY, WEEK & MONTH MARKET BEHAVIOUR

By analysing past share price data it is possible to calculate the historic average returns on all days, weeks and months of the year. For example, since 1984 the LSE has traded 23 times on 8 January with an average return (of the FTSE 100) of -0.03%. Similarly, over the same period the FTSE 100 has had an average return of -0.49% in the second week of the year.

Sinclair Numbers

The Almanac has conducted such analysis of the historic behaviour for four stock indices:

1. FTSE 100 [from 1984]

2. FTSE 250 [from 1985]

3. S&P 500 [from 1950]

4. Nikkei 225 [from 1984]

The analysis produces three numbers (the Sinclair Numbers) for each day, week and month of the year:

1. **Positive(%)**: The proportion of historic returns on the day/week/month that were positive. For example, since 1984 the FTSE 100 has risen 15 times and fallen 6 times on 28 July; it therefore has a Positive(%) value of 71%. If you look at week 30 in the Diary section you will see this figure of 71% in the Sinclair table on the right for the FTSE 100 on 28 July.

2. **Average Return(%)**: The average (mean) return of the index on the day/week/month. For example, since 1984 the FTSE 100 has risen an average of 0.3% in the fourth week of the year. If you look at week 4 in the Diary section you will see the second figure on the top line is 0.3.

3. **StdDev**: This is the standard deviation of the returns for the day/week/month. In the above example, the average return for the fourth week was seen to be 0.3% and the standard deviation for that week is 2.0, which means that 68% of all returns in the fourth week have been in the range -1.7% (0.3 - 2.0) to 2.3% (0.3 + 2.0). The standard deviation measures how closely all the returns in the period cluster around the average return. A high number for the standard deviation suggests that clustering is not close and therefore confidence in forecasting future returns being close to the average is decreased. Conversely, a low standard deviation suggests good clustering and increases the confidence in forecasting future returns being close to the historic average.

These Sinclair Numbers are referred to often in the Almanac. An explanation of their occurrence in the Diary section can be found in the Introduction (page xii).

The rest of this section provides a comprehensive listing of the Sinclair Numbers calculated for the FTSE 100 for all the days, weeks and months of the year. The best and worst performing days/weeks/months in the year are also highlighted.

MARKET BEHAVIOUR – BY DAY

The two tables below list the historic ten strongest and weakest days for the market since 1984. The tables are ranked by the Positive (%) value – the percentage of years that the market has a positive return on the day.

10 strongest days in the year

Date	Positive (%)	Avg Change (%)	Std Dev
27 Dec	86	0.5	1.1
24 Dec	83	0.2	0.5
23 Dec	82	0.5	0.5
26 Jan	81	0.7	1.0
1 Apr	78	0.6	1.1
2 May	78	0.5	0.8
16 Dec	77	0.7	0.8
17 Feb	77	0.4	0.9
29 Jul	77	0.4	1.3
29 Dec	76	0.4	1.1

10 weakest days in the year

Date	Positive (%)	Avg Change (%)	Std Dev
30 May	21	-0.4	1.2
8 Apr	24	-0.3	0.6
9 Sep	27	-0.3	0.8
10 Aug	29	-0.6	1.3
4 Aug	29	-0.3	0.9
19 Nov	30	-0.5	1.5
8 Jul	30	-0.2	1.0
4 Dec	30	-0.1	0.7
23 Sep	32	-0.3	1.1
11 Sep	32	-0.1	0.9

Note: The above best and worst days for the market are marked in the Diary section by their performance data being in bold in the Sinclair numbers table to the right of the day's entry.

Historically, the very best day of the whole year has been 27 December; the market has risen on this day in 86% of all years. And on this day the market has risen by an average of 0.5.%. The second strongest day of the year is 24 December.

Considering a combination of the average change on days and their standard deviation, the strongest day of the year could be considered 23 December.

A small observation to make is that most of the ten strongest days occur in the first or last week of months.

On the downside, the worst day of the year is 30 May – the market has only risen on this day in 21% of previous years and has fallen by an average of 0.4% on this day.

Analysis of all days

Average Positive (%) [Std Dev]	52.6 [10.9]
Average Return (%) [Std Dev]	0.03 [0.24]

Since 1984 the market has risen on 53% of all days with an average daily return of 0.03%.

The standard deviation is 11 for the average Positive (%) value, which means that:

- days that have a Positive (%) value over 64 (the average plus one standard deviation) can be considered strong days, and

- days that have a Positive (%) value under 42 (the average minus one standard deviation) can be considered weak days.

The tables beginning on the next page list the Sinclair Numbers for all days in the year. The rows for the ten strongest [weakest] days are highlighted light grey [dark grey].

Date	Up (%)	Avg Change (%)	Std Dev
2 Jan	53	0.33	1.10
3 Jan	72	0.33	1.06
4 Jan	57	0.19	1.35
5 Jan	43	-0.15	1.03
6 Jan	57	0.26	0.88
7 Jan	35	-0.17	0.95
8 Jan	43	-0.03	0.78
9 Jan	41	-0.15	0.95
10 Jan	41	-0.10	0.82
11 Jan	38	-0.18	0.70
12 Jan	43	-0.32	0.68
13 Jan	41	-0.15	0.82
14 Jan	57	-0.23	1.45
15 Jan	65	0.28	1.23
16 Jan	57	0.19	0.87
17 Jan	59	0.19	0.84
18 Jan	62	0.22	1.08
19 Jan	43	-0.15	0.79
20 Jan	36	-0.38	0.77
21 Jan	43	-0.35	1.31
22 Jan	48	0.07	1.19
23 Jan	41	-0.31	0.84
24 Jan	59	0.41	1.21
25 Jan	38	-0.15	0.69
26 Jan	81	0.67	1.02
27 Jan	45	0.08	1.24
28 Jan	61	0.10	0.98
29 Jan	39	-0.17	0.90
30 Jan	52	0.21	1.05
31 Jan	59	0.18	0.75
1 Feb	67	0.66	0.96
2 Feb	76	0.30	0.84
3 Feb	50	0.33	1.12
4 Feb	39	-0.30	0.99
5 Feb	52	-0.11	1.15
6 Feb	61	0.04	0.86
7 Feb	55	0.01	1.10
8 Feb	57	0.20	0.95
9 Feb	52	0.02	0.71
10 Feb	36	-0.29	0.79
11 Feb	61	0.40	0.93
12 Feb	45	-0.05	1.12
13 Feb	65	0.19	0.54
14 Feb	45	0.03	0.67
15 Feb	62	0.06	0.64
16 Feb	43	0.15	1.01
17 Feb	77	0.41	0.89
18 Feb	43	0.06	0.69
19 Feb	48	-0.01	1.02
20 Feb	50	-0.24	1.02
21 Feb	45	-0.08	0.81
22 Feb	43	-0.10	0.61
23 Feb	43	-0.16	0.91
24 Feb	45	-0.02	0.88
25 Feb	65	0.33	1.05
26 Feb	57	0.16	0.83

Date	Up (%)	Avg Change (%)	Std Dev
27 Feb	48	-0.12	0.84
28 Feb	45	-0.17	1.07
29 Feb	40	-0.06	1.23
1 Mar	67	0.25	1.02
2 Mar	48	-0.07	1.34
3 Mar	50	0.01	1.02
4 Mar	61	0.43	1.12
5 Mar	55	0.07	1.19
6 Mar	52	0.18	0.93
7 Mar	45	-0.22	0.76
8 Mar	67	0.12	0.73
9 Mar	43	-0.05	0.72
10 Mar	64	0.17	1.39
11 Mar	48	-0.17	0.94
12 Mar	43	-0.31	1.26
13 Mar	39	0.01	1.52
14 Mar	59	0.27	1.22
15 Mar	48	0.08	0.95
16 Mar	48	0.07	1.23
17 Mar	59	0.03	1.34
18 Mar	52	0.19	1.11
19 Mar	61	0.09	0.71
20 Mar	48	0.08	0.96
21 Mar	48	0.05	0.97
22 Mar	43	-0.38	1.12
23 Mar	48	0.15	0.94
24 Mar	45	-0.21	1.26
25 Mar	45	0.18	1.09
26 Mar	57	0.17	0.93
27 Mar	45	-0.03	0.95
28 Mar	42	-0.26	0.70
29 Mar	56	0.17	0.76
30 Mar	48	-0.38	1.13
31 Mar	40	-0.05	1.36
1 Apr	78	0.56	1.06
2 Apr	71	0.65	1.10
3 Apr	39	-0.33	1.01
4 Apr	55	0.06	0.86
5 Apr	67	0.20	0.74
6 Apr	63	0.18	0.72
7 Apr	45	0.25	1.08
8 Apr	24	-0.28	0.62
9 Apr	70	0.37	0.72
10 Apr	59	0.36	1.56
11 Apr	39	-0.21	0.89
12 Apr	55	0.07	0.68
13 Apr	59	0.14	0.60
14 Apr	35	-0.27	0.86
15 Apr	61	0.26	0.86
16 Apr	55	0.07	1.14
17 Apr	55	-0.02	1.07
18 Apr	48	0.03	0.95
19 Apr	57	0.21	0.69
20 Apr	63	-0.03	1.17
21 Apr	42	-0.04	0.48
22 Apr	45	0.09	0.76

Date	Up (%)	Avg Change (%)	Std Dev
23 Apr	42	-0.10	0.95
24 Apr	57	0.10	1.02
25 Apr	59	0.06	0.52
26 Apr	68	0.27	0.61
27 Apr	52	-0.19	1.09
28 Apr	50	0.08	1.01
29 Apr	50	0.25	0.86
30 Apr	58	0.15	0.63
1 May	60	0.14	0.71
2 May	78	0.52	0.81
3 May	61	-0.17	1.06
4 May	53	-0.09	1.17
5 May	47	-0.03	0.99
6 May	65	0.24	0.88
7 May	37	-0.41	0.84
8 May	57	0.18	1.12
9 May	39	-0.07	0.63
10 May	45	0.27	1.39
11 May	50	0.07	1.06
12 May	55	-0.06	0.86
13 May	61	0.19	0.86
14 May	42	-0.43	1.28
15 May	50	0.11	0.81
16 May	43	0.08	0.54
17 May	50	-0.16	1.23
18 May	59	0.16	0.89
19 May	55	-0.16	1.28
20 May	52	-0.15	0.96
21 May	63	0.01	0.73
22 May	54	0.02	0.95
23 May	39	-0.36	1.14
24 May	41	-0.13	0.80
25 May	53	-0.18	1.06
26 May	53	0.21	0.81
27 May	47	0.05	1.03
28 May	60	0.16	0.70
29 May	63	0.15	0.85
30 May	21	-0.41	1.19
31 May	56	0.06	0.61
1 Jun	59	0.35	1.03
2 Jun	52	0.14	0.91
3 Jun	59	0.12	0.75
4 Jun	50	-0.02	0.98
5 Jun	48	-0.03	0.90
6 Jun	57	-0.01	1.01
7 Jun	50	0.01	0.82
8 Jun	38	-0.13	0.83
9 Jun	45	0.13	0.77
10 Jun	48	-0.01	0.72
11 Jun	50	-0.09	0.94
12 Jun	42	-0.21	0.85
13 Jun	52	-0.19	0.77
14 Jun	45	-0.06	1.04
15 Jun	45	-0.13	0.94
16 Jun	59	0.14	0.51
17 Jun	65	0.25	0.88

Date	Up (%)	Avg Change (%)	Std Dev
18 Jun	46	-0.22	0.68
19 Jun	50	-0.04	0.89
20 Jun	39	-0.41	0.97
21 Jun	55	0.02	0.74
22 Jun	45	-0.22	0.93
23 Jun	36	-0.26	0.75
24 Jun	39	-0.38	0.85
25 Jun	54	0.06	0.82
26 Jun	42	-0.45	0.96
27 Jun	61	0.17	0.79
28 Jun	64	0.15	0.86
29 Jun	55	0.00	1.22
30 Jun	55	-0.06	0.90
1 Jul	70	0.41	1.39
2 Jul	58	-0.01	1.04
3 Jul	63	0.18	1.15
4 Jul	57	0.35	0.96
5 Jul	41	0.05	0.98
6 Jul	50	0.05	0.99
7 Jul	55	0.26	1.00
8 Jul	30	-0.17	0.96
9 Jul	58	0.13	0.80
10 Jul	38	-0.33	0.93
11 Jul	57	-0.19	1.36
12 Jul	36	-0.17	0.72
13 Jul	73	0.35	0.89
14 Jul	62	0.32	0.96
15 Jul	45	-0.08	1.55
16 Jul	48	0.10	0.74
17 Jul	61	0.22	1.24
18 Jul	43	-0.10	1.03
19 Jul	50	-0.10	1.19
20 Jul	43	-0.11	0.80
21 Jul	43	-0.16	0.83
22 Jul	45	-0.40	1.43
23 Jul	57	-0.05	1.03
24 Jul	48	-0.36	1.05
25 Jul	39	0.10	1.13
26 Jul	55	0.05	0.95
27 Jul	57	0.12	0.93
28 Jul	71	0.20	0.60
29 Jul	77	0.43	1.30
30 Jul	57	0.29	0.85
31 Jul	43	0.17	0.94
1 Aug	57	-0.17	1.29
2 Aug	73	0.52	1.04
3 Aug	43	-0.12	1.17
4 Aug	29	-0.34	0.90
5 Aug	50	-0.20	1.17
6 Aug	39	-0.23	1.29
7 Aug	61	0.16	0.94
8 Aug	61	0.06	1.18
9 Aug	59	0.14	0.96
10 Aug	29	-0.57	1.31
11 Aug	48	0.03	1.28
12 Aug	64	0.35	0.99

Date	Up (%)	Avg Change (%)	Std Dev
13 Aug	61	0.19	1.01
14 Aug	70	0.24	0.96
15 Aug	57	-0.03	1.15
16 Aug	59	-0.11	1.05
17 Aug	62	0.08	1.18
18 Aug	57	0.06	1.42
19 Aug	45	-0.24	1.20
20 Aug	48	0.04	0.69
21 Aug	65	0.14	1.13
22 Aug	52	0.22	0.94
23 Aug	55	0.03	0.80
24 Aug	75	0.25	0.88
25 Aug	69	0.03	1.01
26 Aug	50	-0.06	0.76
27 Aug	56	0.13	1.03
28 Aug	42	-0.31	1.28
29 Aug	53	0.03	0.77
30 Aug	67	0.26	0.99
31 Aug	59	0.18	0.92
1 Sep	67	0.28	1.11
2 Sep	57	0.10	0.94
3 Sep	57	0.01	1.39
4 Sep	61	-0.03	0.92
5 Sep	48	-0.31	1.02
6 Sep	68	0.15	1.08
7 Sep	52	0.11	1.39
8 Sep	38	-0.06	1.08
9 Sep	27	-0.31	0.77
10 Sep	43	-0.25	1.09
11 Sep	32	-0.07	0.85
12 Sep	48	-0.22	1.12
13 Sep	50	0.08	0.80
14 Sep	57	0.03	1.39
15 Sep	48	-0.17	1.31
16 Sep	59	-0.06	1.13
17 Sep	43	0.07	1.49
18 Sep	48	-0.10	1.30
19 Sep	57	0.28	2.14
20 Sep	45	-0.15	1.26
21 Sep	33	-0.39	0.92
22 Sep	48	-0.29	1.31
23 Sep	32	-0.31	1.05
24 Sep	43	-0.08	1.23
25 Sep	43	-0.10	1.04
26 Sep	57	0.21	1.35
27 Sep	73	0.59	1.09
28 Sep	52	0.13	1.15
29 Sep	43	-0.32	1.28
30 Sep	41	-0.21	1.25
1 Oct	70	0.36	1.39
2 Oct	35	-0.17	1.20
3 Oct	61	0.26	0.96
4 Oct	64	0.12	1.02
5 Oct	76	0.27	1.63
6 Oct	57	0.29	2.26
7 Oct	45	-0.03	0.66

Date	Up (%)	Avg Change (%)	Std Dev
8 Oct	39	-0.32	1.42
9 Oct	39	-0.23	1.15
10 Oct	43	-0.26	2.09
11 Oct	67	0.37	1.20
12 Oct	48	0.22	1.21
13 Oct	62	0.69	1.93
14 Oct	50	0.14	1.05
15 Oct	48	-0.38	2.05
16 Oct	43	-0.69	1.83
17 Oct	70	0.49	1.47
18 Oct	55	-0.06	0.83
19 Oct	48	-0.20	1.67
20 Oct	48	-0.27	3.10
21 Oct	64	0.45	1.82
22 Oct	39	-0.51	1.63
23 Oct	57	-0.13	1.30
24 Oct	48	-0.17	1.39
25 Oct	41	-0.27	0.73
26 Oct	43	-0.33	1.58
27 Oct	52	0.02	1.24
28 Oct	68	0.13	1.20
29 Oct	57	0.58	2.03
30 Oct	70	0.36	1.29
31 Oct	74	0.41	1.02
1 Nov	59	-0.08	0.89
2 Nov	57	0.20	0.85
3 Nov	52	0.10	1.20
4 Nov	41	0.38	1.52
5 Nov	61	-0.04	1.11
6 Nov	61	-0.12	1.33
7 Nov	48	-0.17	0.94
8 Nov	59	0.14	0.64
9 Nov	43	-0.25	1.08
10 Nov	52	0.03	0.54
11 Nov	59	0.16	1.39
12 Nov	52	0.22	1.17
13 Nov	48	-0.14	0.96
14 Nov	57	0.22	0.73
15 Nov	59	0.14	0.68
16 Nov	62	0.08	0.89
17 Nov	43	-0.19	1.06
18 Nov	64	0.14	0.75
19 Nov	30	-0.46	1.49
20 Nov	48	-0.01	1.15
21 Nov	57	0.00	1.20
22 Nov	45	-0.14	0.94
23 Nov	57	0.35	1.22
24 Nov	52	0.58	2.22
25 Nov	64	0.01	0.92
26 Nov	43	-0.20	1.03
27 Nov	61	0.18	0.75
28 Nov	48	0.07	1.13
29 Nov	68	0.11	0.71
30 Nov	43	-0.18	1.42
1 Dec	55	0.05	1.83
2 Dec	50	0.12	0.92

Date	Up (%)	Avg Change (%)	Std Dev
3 Dec	48	0.01	0.74
4 Dec	30	-0.14	0.69
5 Dec	57	0.33	1.12
6 Dec	55	-0.03	0.73
7 Dec	45	-0.01	0.66
8 Dec	57	0.35	1.54
9 Dec	50	0.03	0.99
10 Dec	35	-0.20	0.66
11 Dec	39	-0.17	0.92
12 Dec	43	-0.36	0.96
13 Dec	64	0.04	0.92
14 Dec	52	-0.05	0.83
15 Dec	48	-0.08	0.82
16 Dec	77	0.73	0.83
17 Dec	43	-0.12	0.91
18 Dec	70	0.26	0.89
19 Dec	61	0.00	0.89
20 Dec	64	0.15	0.86
21 Dec	57	0.40	0.94
22 Dec	71	0.34	0.56
23 Dec	82	0.47	0.54
24 Dec	83	0.21	0.54
27 Dec	86	0.47	1.07
28 Dec	62	0.19	0.48
29 Dec	76	0.43	1.13
30 Dec	55	0.14	0.89
31 Dec	57	0.05	1.02

MARKET BEHAVIOUR – BY WEEK

The two tables below list the historic ten strongest and weakest weeks for the market since 1984. The tables are ranked by the Positive (%) value – the percentage of years that the market has a positive return on the week.

10 strongest weeks in the year

Week	Positive (%)	Avg Change (%)	Std Dev
51	81	1.1	1.7
52	74	0.5	1.4
34	74	0.4	1.8
7	71	0.5	1.9
31	71	0.3	2.9
27	69	0.9	2.0
5	68	1.0	2.0
16	66	0.6	1.3
18	66	0.5	2.3
14	65	0.6	1.8

10 weakest weeks in the year

Week	Positive (%)	Avg Change (%)	Std Dev
2	39	-0.5	2.0
38	39	-0.5	2.7
25	41	-0.6	1.9
21	41	-0.3	2.0
12	42	0.0	2.5
26	44	-0.2	1.9
36	45	-0.3	2.3
3	45	-0.2	2.3
30	45	-0.2	1.9
49	45	0.0	2.2

Note: The above best and worst weeks for the market are marked in the Diary section by their performance data at the top of the week's page being in bold.

The strongest week of the whole year – when the market has historically increased the most – is the 51st; in this week the market has risen in 81% of recent years, with an average return of 1.1%. It is worth noting that week 53 has a Positive (%) of 83%, but there have only been six occurrences of a week 53 since 1984 and so its data sample is smaller than for the other weeks. For this reason, week 53 has been excluded from the rankings.

The week with the worst record is the 2nd week. This is perhaps not surprising: the market is correcting after the historically strong final and first weeks of the year. The market has only risen in this week 39% of years and has an average return of -0.5%.

Analysis of all weeks

Average Positive (%) [Std Dev]	55.2 [10.8]
Average Change (%) [Std Dev]	0.17 [0.52]

Since 1984 the market has risen 55% of weeks with an average weekly return of 0.17%.

The standard deviation is 11 for the average Positive (%) value, which means that:

- weeks that have a Positive (%) value over 66 (the average plus one standard deviation) can be considered strong weeks, and

- weeks that have a Positive (%) value under 44 (the average minus one standard deviation) can be considered weak weeks.

The table on the following page lists the Sinclair Numbers for all weeks in the year. The rows for the ten strongest [weakest] weeks are highlighted light grey [dark grey].

Week	Up (%)	Avg Change (%)	Std Dev
1	55	0.63	2.27
2	39	-0.49	1.95
3	45	-0.17	2.27
4	58	0.26	1.98
5	68	1.01	2.00
6	53	-0.12	1.61
7	71	0.52	1.91
8	52	0.04	1.68
9	55	0.34	2.36
10	48	0.14	2.18
11	58	0.24	2.14
12	42	-0.03	2.49
13	48	0.11	2.03
14	65	0.58	1.81
15	47	0.08	2.24
16	66	0.65	1.29
17	53	0.06	1.79
18	66	0.48	2.28
19	50	-0.09	1.85
20	63	-0.06	2.20
21	41	-0.25	1.99
22	47	0.28	1.85
23	56	0.07	1.84
24	47	-0.47	1.90
25	41	-0.64	1.86
26	44	-0.16	1.87
27	69	0.87	1.99
28	47	-0.12	2.75
29	52	-0.22	2.18
30	45	-0.21	1.92
31	71	0.28	2.85
32	48	0.06	2.11
33	65	0.18	2.11
34	74	0.45	1.84
35	52	0.30	2.04
36	45	-0.34	2.28
37	48	-0.33	2.28
38	39	-0.49	2.66
39	48	0.10	2.78
40	65	0.99	2.17
41	55	-0.70	4.61
42	61	-0.16	3.65
43	48	-0.24	2.62
44	61	0.74	3.32
45	65	0.41	1.53
46	52	0.09	1.64
47	52	-0.06	2.96
48	55	0.63	3.32
49	45	0.02	2.23
50	52	-0.11	2.43
51	81	1.14	1.69
52	74	0.52	1.44
53	83	2.32	2.94

MARKET BEHAVIOUR – BY MONTH

The table below ranks the 12 months by their historic performance since 1984. The table is ranked by the Positive (%) value – the percentage of years that the market has a positive return on the month.

Month	Positive (%)	Avg Change (%)	Std Dev
December	84	2.3	3.0
October	74	0.7	6.5
April	71	1.8	3.4
February	61	1.1	3.9
November	58	0.7	3.7
August	58	0.5	4.5
January	58	0.4	5.1
July	56	1.0	4.2
March	55	0.4	3.4
May	50	-0.2	4.3
September	45	-1.0	5.6
June	38	-1.0	3.5

The best month of the whole year – when the market has historically increased most often – is December. The proportion of years when the market has increased in December is 84% and on average the market increases 2.3% in this month (with a low-ish standard deviation).

Surprisingly, perhaps, the second strongest month is October – but note the very high standard deviation, indicating the volatility of the market in this month.

The month with the worst record is June. The market has only risen in June in 38% of all years and the average return is -1.0%.

The following two charts plot the Positive (%) and Average Return (%) values from the above table.

FTSE 100 monthly positive returns (%)

FTSE 100 average month

3.
REFERENCE

CONTENTS

REFERENCE

STOCK INDICES

FT Ordinary Share Index (FT 30)

The FT 30 was first calculated in 1935 by the *Financial Times*. The index started at a base level of 100, and was calculated from a subjective collection of 30 major companies – which in the early years were concentrated in the industrial and retailing sectors.

For a long time the index was the best known performance measure of the UK stock market. But the index become less representative of the whole market. Also the index was price-weighted (like the DJIA), and not market-capitalisation-weighted. Although the index was calculated every hour, the increasing sophistication of the market needed an index calculated every minute and so the FT 30 has been usurped by the FTSE 100.

FTSE 100

Today, the FTSE 100 (sometimes called the "footsie") is the best known index tracking the performance of the UK market. The index comprises 100 of the top capitalised stocks listed on the LSE, and represents approximately 80% of the total market (by capitalisation). It is market capitalisation weighted and the composition of the index is reviewed every three months. The FTSE 100 is commonly used as the basis for investment funds and derivatives. The index was first calculated on 3 January 1984 with a base value of 1000.

The FTSE 100, and all the FTSE indices, are calculated by FTSE International – which started life as a joint venture between the *Financial Times* and the London Stock Exchange, but is now wholly owned by the LSE.

FTSE 250

Similar in construction to the FTSE 100, except this index comprises the next 250 highest capitalised stocks listed on the LSE after the top 100. It's sometimes referred to as the index of 'mid-cap' stocks, and comprises approximately 18% of the total market capitalisation.

FTSE 350

The FTSE 350 is an index comprising all the stocks in the FTSE 100 and FTSE 250.

FTSE Small Cap

Comprised of companies with a market capitalisation below the FTSE 250 but above a fixed limit. This lower limit is periodically reviewed. Consequently the FTSE Small Cap does not have a fixed number of constituents. In mid-2015, there were 288 companies in the index, which represented about 2% of the total market by capitalisation.

FTSE All-Share

The FTSE All-Share is the aggregation of the FTSE 100, FTSE 250 and FTSE Small Cap indices. Effectively it is comprised of all those LSE listed companies with a market capitalisation above the lower limit for inclusion in the FTSE Small Cap. The FTSE All-Share is the standard benchmark for measuring the performance of the broad UK market and represents 98% to 99% of the total UK market capitalisation.

FTSE Fledgling

This index comprises the companies that do not meet the minimum size requirement of the FTSE Small Cap and are therefore outside of the FTSE All-Share. There are fewer than 200 companies in the FTSE Fledgling.

FTSE All-Small

This consists of all the companies in the FTSE Small Cap and FTSE Fledgling indices.

FTSE TMT

Reflects the performance of companies in the Technology, Media and Telecommunications sectors.

FTSE techMARK All-Share

An index of all companies included in the LSE's techMARK sector.

FTSE techMARK 100

The top 100 companies of the FTSE techMARK All-Share, under £4bn by full market capitalisation.

FTSE AIM UK 50

Comprises the 50 largest UK companies quoted on the Alternative Investment Market (AIM).

FTSE AIM 100

Comprises the 100 largest companies quoted on the Alternative Investment Market (AIM).

FTSE AIM All-Share

All AIM-quoted companies.

STOCK INDICES – INTERNATIONAL

Dow Jones Industrial Average (DJIA)

The DJIA is the oldest continuing stock index of the US market and probably the most famous in the world. Created in 1896, it originally comprised 12 stocks, but over the years has expanded to reach the point where today it includes 30 stocks. The index is weighted by price, which is unusual for a stock index. It is calculated by summing the prices of the 30 stocks and dividing by the divisor. Originally the divisor was 30, but this has been adjusted periodically to reflect capital changes such as stock splits, and is currently about 0.13. This means that companies with high stock prices have the greatest influence on the index – not those with large market values. The longest established company in the index is General Electric, which joined in 1907.

Standard & Poor's 500 (S&P 500)

This is the main benchmark index for the performance of the US market. The index is weighted by market value and constituents are chosen based upon their market size, liquidity and sector. The index was created in 1957, although values for it have been back-calculated several decades.

NASDAQ 100

This index tracks the performance of the 100 largest stocks listed on the NASDAQ exchange. The index is calculated using a modified capitalisation weighting method ("modified" so that large companies like Apple don't overwhelm it). NASDAQ companies tend to be smaller and younger than those listed on the NYSE and although there is no attempt to select technology stocks, it is regarded as the tech stock index. The index can be traded as there's an ETF associated with it (the most actively traded ETF in the US). The ETF has the symbol QQQ and is sometimes referred to as the "Qs" or "Qubes".

Nikkei 225

The Nikkei 225 is owned by the Nihon Keizai Shimbun ("Nikkei") newspaper. It was first calculated in 1949 (when it was known as the Nikkei-Dow index) and is the most widely watched stock index in Japan. It is a price-weighted index of 225 top-rated Japanese companies listed in the First Section of the Tokyo Stock Exchange. The calculation method is therefore similar to that of the Dow Jones Industrial Average (upon which it was modelled).

TOPIX

The TOPIX is calculated by the Tokyo Stock Exchange. Unlike the Nikkei 255, TOPIX is a market capitalisation-weighted index. TOPIX is calculated from all members of the First Section of the Tokyo SE, which is about 1500 companies. For these reasons, TOPIX is preferred over the Nikkei 225 as a benchmark for Japanese equity portfolios.

Hang Seng

The Hang Seng was first calculated in 1964. Today it has 48 constituents representing some 60% of the total Hong Kong market by capitalisation.

CAC 40

The CAC 40 is the main benchmark for Euronext Paris (what used to be the Paris Bourse). The index contains 40 stocks selected among the top 100 by market capitalisation and the most active stocks listed on Euronext Paris. The base value was 1000 at 31 December 1987.

DAX 30

The DAX 30 is published by the Frankfurt Stock Exchange and is the main real-time German share index. It contains 30 stocks from the leading German stock markets. The DAX is a total return index (which is uncommon), whereby it measures not only the price appreciation of its constituents but also the return provided by the dividends paid.

EPIC, TIDM, SEDOL, CUSIP AND ISIN CODES

This page describes the common codes associated with securities.

EPIC

Some time ago the London Stock Exchange devised a system of code names for listed companies. These provide a short and unambiguous way to reference stocks. For example, the code for Marks & Spencer is MKS. This is easier to use than wondering whether one should call the company Marks & Spencer, Marks and Spencer or Marks & Spencer plc. These codes were called EPIC codes, after the name of the Stock Exchange's central computer prior to 1996.

TIDM

After the introduction of the Sequence trading platform, EPIC codes were renamed Tradable Instrument Display Mnemonics (TIDMs), or Mnemonics for short. So, strictly, we should now be calling them TIDMs or Mnemonics – but almost everyone still refers to them as EPIC codes.

SEDOL

SEDOL stands for Stock Exchange Daily Official List. These are seven digit security identifiers assigned by the London Stock Exchange. They are only assigned to UK-listed securities.

CUSIP

CUSIP (Committee on Uniform Securities Identification Procedures) codes are nine-character alphanumeric identifiers used for Canadian and US securities.

ISIN

ISIN stands for International Securities Identification Number. These are 12-digit alphanumeric identifiers assigned by the International Standards Organisation (ISO) in order to provide standardisation of international securities. The first two letters represent the country code; the next nine characters usually use some other code, such as CUSIP in the United States or SEDOL in the UK, with leading spaces padded with 0. The final digit is a check digit.

DAILY TIMETABLE OF THE UK TRADING DAY

This table displays the basic structure of the UK trading day, with some comments from a trader.

07.00	**Regulatory News Services open** The period before the market opens at 08.00 is the most important hour of the day. By the time the opening auction begins at 07.50 traders will have a clear idea at what price any particular major stock should be opening at. Scheduled announcements are normally in the Regulatory News. Having a good idea of what companies are reporting for the forthcoming week is essential. Quite a few banks, brokers and websites provide comprehensive forward diaries. As well as checking the movement of the major stock indices overnight, check the early show for the futures contracts on the main indices, as well as any US company results that were released after hours. Unlike the UK, in the US it is common for companies to release results after the markets close.
07.50–08.00	**Pre-market auction** There are fewer opportunities in the opening auction than the closing auction, partly because there are lower volumes in the opening auction. It is safer to trade against an 'at-market' order than against several orders from several other participants that appear to be at the wrong price – almost certainly they have seen something that you haven't. Despite representing only a small proportion of the total day's volume, the opening uncrossing trade will often be (or very close to) the high or low trade of the day for that stock.
08.00	**UK market and FTSE 100 Index Futures open** By 08.00 as the UK market opens you should be fully prepared for the day's trading.
08.00–16.30	**Continuous trading** Trading is continuous until 16.30. During the day there is a calendar of key economic figures to look out for, as well as both ad-hoc and scheduled announcements. Some company-scheduled trading figures come out at midday, particularly companies that are dual-quoted. US index futures should be monitored throughout the day as well as other influential continental indices such as Germany's DAX. Traders will often concentrate on watching the high volatility shares as these provide the most trading opportunities, although many will add 'guest' stocks to their watch list and go to where the day's action is and join 'event' traders. Stocks to watch during the day include the biggest movers on the day (both risers and fallers), those experiencing high volume and constant gainers (popular with momentum players).
14.30	**US markets open** The US markets usually open at 14.30 UK time, although at certain times of the year, due to daylight saving, it may be an hour earlier or later. As the futures contracts on the US markets trade throughout morning trading in the UK, traders will always have a good idea where the US markets are due to open, subject to the release of economic figures at 13.30 UK time.
16.30–16.35	**Post-market auction** There can often be opportunities in the closing auction, particularly on the last business day of the month or when there are index constituent changes. The general strategy is to take the other side of a large 'at-market' order that is forcing the uncrossing price away from the day's trading range, in the anticipation that the stock will revert to the previous ('normal') level the following day.
17.30	**FTSE 100 Index Futures close**
18.30	**Regulatory News Services close** A number of key announcements can come out after the market close and although most newspapers will pick up any significant stories, it is worth scanning through the day's late announcements before the start of trading the following day.

Source: *The UK Trader's Bible* by Dominic Connolly.

FT 30 INDEX 1935 – WHERE ARE THEY NOW?

The FT 30 index was started by the *Financial Times* on 1 July 1935. Today the most widely followed index is the FTSE 100, but for many years the FT 30 (originally called the FT Ordinaries) was the measure everyone knew. The table below lists the original companies in the FT 30 index in 1935 – a time when brokers wore bowler hats and share certificates were printed on something called paper. It's interesting to see what became of the stalwarts of UK PLC from over 70 years ago.

Company	Notes
Associated Portland Cement	The name was changed to Blue Circle Industries in 1978, and then left the index in 2001 when it was bought by Lafarge.
Austin Motor	Left the index in 1947. In 1952 Austin merged with rival Morris Motors Limited to form The British Motor Corporation Limited (BMC). In 1966 BMC bought Jaguar and two years later merged with Leyland Motors Limited to form British Leyland Motor Corporation. In 1973 British Leyland produced the Austin-badged Allegro... (the story is too painful to continue).
Bass	Left the index in 1947. In 1967 merged with Charrington United Breweries to form Bass Charrington. In 2000 its brewing operations were sold to Interbrew (which was then instructed by the Competition Commission to dispose parts to Coors), while the hotel and pub holdings were renamed Six Continents. In 2003 Six Continents was split into a pubs business (Mitchells & Butlers) and a hotels and soft drinks business (InterContinental Hotels Group).
Bolsover Colliery	Left the index in 1947. The mines were acquired by the National Coal Board on nationalisation in 1947. Bolsover Colliery closed in 1993.
Callender's Cables & Construction	Left the index in 1947. Merged with British Insulated Cables in 1945 to form British Insulated Callender's Cables, which was renamed BICC Ltd in 1975. In 2000, having sold its cable operations, it renamed its contruction business Balfour Beatty.
Coats (J & P)	Left the index in 1959. Traded as Coats Patons Ltd after the takeover of Patons & Baldwins, then as Coats Viyella, finally as Coats plc. Finally taken over by Guinness Peat Group in 2004.
Courtaulds	Demerged its chemical and textile interests in the 1980s, with the former eventually being bought by Akzo Nobel and the latter by Sara Lee. Left the index in 1998.
Distillers	Purchased by Guinness in the infamous bid battle of 1986 when it left the index.
Dorman Long	Left the index in 1947. Joined British Steel following nationalisation in 1967.
Dunlop Rubber	Left the index in 1983 and was bought in 1985 by BTR (which became Invensys).
Electrical & Musical Industries	In 1971 changed its name to EMI and later that year merged with THORN Electrical Industries to form Thorn EMI but then de-merged in 1996. In 2007 EMI Group plc was taken over by Terra Firma Capital Partners but following financial difficulties ownership passed to Citigroup in 2011.
Fine Spinners and Doublers	Fell out of the index in 1938, and was later bought by Courtaulds in 1963.
General Electric	General Electric was re-named Marconi in 1999, suffered disastrous losses in the dot-com crash and was bought by Ericsson in 2006.
Guest, Keen & Nettlefolds	Guest, Keen is better known as GKN and is still in the FT 30 today.
Harrods	Left the index in 1959 when it was bought by House of Fraser, and then later by Mohamed Al Fayed.
Hawker Siddeley	Left the index in 1991, and was then bought in 1992 by BTR (which became Invensys).
Imperial Chemical Industries	Spun out of Zeneca in 1993, and the rump (called ICI) was sold to Akzo Nobel in 2007.
Imperial Tobacco	Still going strong.
International Tea Co Stores	Fell out of the index in 1947, was acquired by BAT Industries in 1972 and ended up as Somerfield in 1994.
London Brick	Replaced in the index by Hanson which bought it in 1984.
Murex	Left the index in 1967 due to "poor share performance". Acquired by BOC Group in 1967.
Patons & Baldwins	Left the index in 1960 when bought by J&P Coats.

Company	Notes
Pinchin Johnson & Associates	Left the index in 1960 when bought by Courtaulds.
Rolls-Royce	In 1971 RR was taken into state ownership, the motor car business was floated separately in 1973, and RR returned to the private sector in 1987.
Tate & Lyle	Still going strong, although its sugar refining and golden syrup business was sold to American Sugar Refining in 2010.
Turner & Newall	Left the index in 1982. The company was heavily involved with asbestos production, so it is not surprising that things ended badly. In 1998 the business was acquired by Federal-Mogul, which soon after filed for Chapter 11 protection as a result of asbestos claims.
United Steel	Left the index in 1951. The iron and steel works on nationalisation became part of British Steel Corporation (and now part of Tata Steel); while the mining interests passed to the National Coal Board (now closed).
Vickers	Left the index in 1986. Bought by Rolls-Royce in 1999.
Watney Combe & Reid	Left the index in 1972 when it was bought by Grand Metropolitan, which itself became part of Diageo.
Woolworth (FW)	Left the index in 1971. Bought by the forerunner of Kingfisher in 1982, and then de-merged and re-listed in 2001. But the remaining Woolworths stores all closed by January 2009.

Of the 30 companies only four exist today as listed companies: GKN, Imperial Tobacco, Rolls-Royce and Tate & Lyle (all of which are in the FTSE 100). And only GKN and Tate & Lyle are in today's FT 30.

The star performer from the original line-up has been Imperial Tobacco.

It's interesting to note the complete lack of representation of the four sectors that dominate the UK market today – no banks, telecom, oil or drug companies.

Index performance

Since 1935 the FT 30 has risen 1935% (which is a rather odd coincidence!); by comparison the FTSE All-Share over the same period has risen 8936%. The following chart plots the year-end values of the FT 30 against the FTSE All-Share (the latter has been rebased to start at the same value as the FT 30).

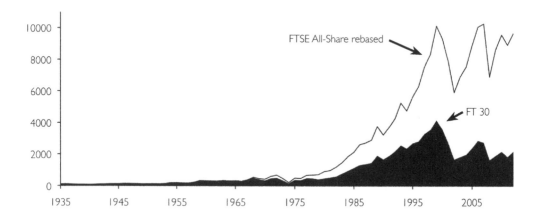

One of the reasons for the very large difference in performance is that the FT 30 is a price-weighted index (as are the Dow Jones Industrial Average and Nikkei 225), whereas most indices today (including the FTSE All-Share and FTSE 100) are weighted by market-capitalisation. When the FTSE 100 was introduced in 1984, if it had been price-weighted and performed in line with the FT 30, today it would have a value around 2805.

FTSE 100 INDEX – 1984

The FTSE 100 index was started on 3 January 1984 with a base level of 1000. The table below shows the original constituents. Of the initial 100 companies only 18 remain in the index today (indicated in bold, and with their new names in brackets) – a sign of the great changes in UK PLC in 31 years.

Allied – Lyons
Associated British Foods
Associated Dairies Group
Barclays Bank [Barclays]
Barratt Developments
Bass
BAT Industries
Beecham Group
Berisford (S. & W.)
BICC
Blue Circle Industries
BOC Group
Boots Co.
Bowater Corporation
BPB Industries
British & Commonwealth
British Aerospace
British Elect. Traction Co.
British Home Stores
British Petroleum [BP]
Britoil
BTR
Burton Group
Cable & Wireless
Cadbury Schweppes
Commercial Union Assurance [Aviva]
Consolidated Gold Fields
Courtaulds
Dalgety Distillers Co.
CJ Rothschild
Edinburgh Investment Trust
English China Clays
Exco International
Ferranti

Fisons
General Accident Fire & Life
General Electric
Glaxo Holdings
Globe Investment Trust
Grand Metropolitan
Great Universal Stores [Experian]
Guardian Royal Exchange
Guest Keen & Nettlefolds
Hambro Life Assurance
Hammerson Prop.Inv. & Dev. 'A'
Hanson Trust Harrisons & Crossfield
Hawker Siddeley Group
House of Fraser
Imperial Chemical Industries
Imperial Cont. Gas Association
Imperial Group
Johnson Matthey
Ladbroke Group
Land Securities
Legal & General Group
Lloyds Bank [Lloyds Banking Group]
Lonrho
MEPC
MFI Furniture Group
Marks & Spencer
Midland Bank
National Westminster Bank
Northern Foods
P & O Steam Navigation Co.
Pearson (S.) & Son [Pearson]
Pilkington Brothers
Plessey Co.
Prudential Corporation [Prudential]

RMC Group
Racal Electronics
Rank Organisation
Reckitt & Colman [Reckitt Benckiser Group]
Redland
Reed International [Reed Elsevier]
Rio Tinto – Zinc Corporation [Rio Tinto]
Rowntree Mackintosh
Royal Bank of Scotland Group
Royal Insurance
Sainsbury (J.)
Scottish & Newcastle Breweries
Sears Holdings
Sedgwick Group
Shell Trans. & Trad. Co. [Royal Dutch Shell]
Smith & Nephew Associated Co's.
Standard Chartered Bank
Standard Telephones & Cables
Sun Alliance & London Insurance
Sun Life Assurance Society
THORN EMI
Tarmac
Tesco
Trafalgar House
Trusthouse Forte
Ultramar
Unilever
United Biscuits
Whitbread & Co. 'A'
Wimpey (George)

The following table compares the market capitalisations of the top five largest companies in the index in 1984 and in 2015.

	Rank (1984)	Capital (£m)	Rank (2015)	Capital (£m)
1	British Petroleum Co.	7,401	Royal Dutch Shell	103,297
2	Shell Trans. & Trad. Co.	6,365	HSBC Holdings	99,098
3	General Electric Co.	4,915	British American Tobacco	63,849
4	Imperial Chemical Industries	3,917	GlaxoSmithKline	63,070
5	Marks & Spencer	2,829	BP	61,304

Oil is still there today, but industrial, chemical and retail have been replaced by bank, consumer goods and pharmaceutical.

COMPANY OLD NAMES

The following table shows a selection of companies listed on the LSE with their original names.

Note: Simple changes such as Reckitt Benckiser to Reckitt Benckiser Group have not been included.

Current name	TIDM	Previous name
I Spatial Holdings	SPA	Avisen
21st Century Technology	C21	TG21
365 Agile Group	365	Iafyds
4imprint Group	FOUR	Bemrose Corporation
7Digital Group	7DIG	UBC Media Group
88 Energy Ltd	88E	Tangiers Petroleum Ltd
Acacia Mining	ACA	African Barrick Gold Ltd
Accesso Technology Group	ACSO	Lo-Q
Active Energy Group	AEG	Cinpart
Advanced Oncotherapy	AVO	CareCapital Group
Aeorema Communications	AEO	Cheerful Scout
Afarak Group	AFRK	Ruukki Group
AGA Rangemaster Group	AGA	AGA Foodservice Group
Agriterra Ltd	AGTA	White Nile Ltd
Airea	AIEA	Sirdar
Alecto Energy	ALO	Cue Energy
Alliance Pharma	APH	Peerless Technology Group
Alpha Returns Group	ARGP	Shidu Group
Altitude Group	ALT	Dowlis Corporate Solutions
Amara Mining	AMA	Cluff Gold
Ambrian	AMBR	East West Resources
Amec Foster Wheeler	AMFW	AMEC
Amedeo Resources	AMED	Creon Corporation
Amerisur Resources	AMER	Chaco Resources
Andes Energia	AEN	Ragusa Capital
Anpario	ANP	Kiotech International
APC Technology Group	APC	Advanced Power Components
APR Energy	APR	Horizon Acquisition Co
Arbuthnot Banking Group	ARBB	Secure Trust Banking Group
Arcontech Group	ARC	Knowledge Technology Solutions
Armadale Capital	ACP	Watermark Global
Armstrong Ventures	AVP	iPoint Media
Artilium	ARTA	Future Internet Technologies
Asiamet Resources Ltd	ARS	Kalimantan Gold Corporation Ltd
ASOS	ASC	asSeenonScreen Holdings
AssetCo	ASTO	Asfare Group
Atlantic Coal	ATC	Summit Resources
Atlas Development & Support Services Ltd	ADSS	Africa Oilfield Logistics Ltd
AudioBoom Group	BOOM	One Delta
Aurasian Minerals	AUM	Triple Plate Junction
Avacta Group	AVCT	Readybuy
Avesco Group	AVS	InvestinMedia
Aveva Group	AVV	Cadcentre Group
Avingtrans	AVG	Usher (Frank) Holdings
Aviva	AV.	CGNU

Current name	TIDM	Previous name
Bahamas Petroleum Company	BPC	BPC
Baron Oil	BOIL	Gold Oil
BCA Marketplace	BCA	Haversham Holdings
BCB Holdings Ltd	BCB	BB Holdings Ltd
Belgravium Technologies	BVM	Eadie Holdings
Berendsen	BRSN	Davis Service Group (The)
Bezant Resources	BZT	Tanzania Gold
BHP Billiton	BLT	Billiton
Billington Holdings	BILN	Amco Corporation
Biome Technologies	BIOM	Stanelco
BMR Mining	BMR	Berkeley Mineral Resources
Booker Group	BOK	Blueheath Holdings
Boxhill Technologies	BOX	Weather Lottery (The)
BP	BP.	BP Amoco
Breedon Aggregates Ltd	BREE	Marwyn Materials Ltd
BSD Crown Ltd	BSD	Emblaze Ltd
BT Group	BT.A	British Telecommunications
Cable & Wireless Communications	CWC	Cable and Wireless
Camco Clean Energy Ltd	CCE	Camco International Ltd
Capital Management and Investment	CMIP	e-xentric
Carnival	CCL	P & O Princess Cruises
Castle Street Investments	CSI	Cupid
Castleton Technology	CTP	Redstone
Catalyst Media Group	CMX	Newsplayer Group
Centamin	CEY	Centamin Egypt Ltd
CEPS	CEPS	Dinkie Heel
Chamberlin	CMH	Chamberlin & Hill
China Nonferrous Gold Ltd	CNG	Kryso Resources Corp Ltd
Clarkson	CKN	Clarkson (Horace)
Clear Leisure	CLP	Brainspark
Cloudbuy	CBUY	@UK
Coal of Africa Ltd	CZA	GVM Metals Ltd
Coats Group	COA	Guinness Peat Group
Collagen Solutions	COS	Healthcare Investment Opportunities
Compass Group	CPG	Granada Compass
Coms	COMS	Azman
Concha	CHA	Hot Tuna (International)
Connect Group	CNCT	Smiths News
Conroy Gold And Natural Resources	CGNR	Conroy Diamonds & Gold
Consort Medical	CSRT	Bespak
Corero	CNS	Mondas
Craven House Capital	CRV	AIM Investments
Crawshaw Group	CRAW	Felix Group
Crimson Tide	TIDE	Cohen (A) & Co
Darty	DRTY	Kesa Electricals
DCD Media	DCD	Digital Classics

Current name	TIDM	Previous name
Dialight	DIA	Roxboro Group (The)
Distil	DIS	Blavod Wines and Spirits
Dixons Carphone	DC.	Carphone Warehouse
Dods (Group)	DODS	Huveaux
Doriemus	DOR	TEP Exchange Group
DS Smith	SMDS	Smith (David S) (Holdings)
Eastbridge Investments	EBIV	China Wonder Ltd
Ebiquity	EBQ	Thomson Intermedia
Eckoh	ECK	Eckoh Technologies
Eco Animal Health Group	EAH	Lawrence
ECR Minerals	ECR	Electrum Resources
Edenville Energy	EDL	TV Commerce Holdings
EKF Diagnostics Holdings	EKF	International Brand Licensing
Elecosoft	ELCO	Eleco
Elektron	EKT	Bulgin
EMED Mining Public Ltd	EMED	Eastern Mediterranean Resources Public Ltd
Emerging Markets Minerals	EMM	LP Hill
Environmental Recycling Technologies	ENRT	3DM Worldwide
Essentra	ESNT	Filtrona
European Wealth Group Ltd	EWG	EW Group Ltd
Evocutis	EVO	Syntopix Group
Fairpoint Group	FRP	Debt Free Direct Group
Fastjet	FJET	Rubicon Diversified Investments
Fastnet Oil & Gas	FAST	Sterling Green Group
Fidessa Group	FDSA	royalblue Group
Finnaust Mining	FAM	Centurion Resources
Finsbury Food Group	FIF	Megalomedia
First Property Group	FPO	Hansom Group
Fitbug Holdings	FITB	ADDleisure
Flowgroup	FLOW	Energetix Group
Flying Brands Ltd	FBDU	Flying Flowers Ltd
Formation Group	FRM	Proactive Sports Group
Fulcrum Utility Services Ltd	FCRM	Marwyn Capital I Ltd
G4S	GFS	Group 4 Securicor
Galliford Try	GFRD	Galliford
Gama Aviation	GMAA	Hangar 8
Gaming Realms	GMR	Pursuit Dynamics
GB Group	GBG	TelMe Group
GCM Resources	GCM	Global Coal Management
Gemfields	GEM	Gemfields Resources
Genel Energy	GENL	Vallares
GlaxoSmithKline	GSK	Glaxo Wellcome
Glencore	GLEN	Glencore International
Goldbridges Global Resources	GBGR	Hambledon Mining
Grafenia	GRA	Printing.com
Gusbourne	GUS	Shellproof Ltd
Guscio	GUSC	Talent Group
Hague and London Oil	HNL	Wessex Exploration
Harworth Group	HWG	Coalfield Resources
Hayward Tyler Group	HAYT	Specialist Energy Group
Helios Underwriting	HUW	Hampden Underwriting
Henderson Group	HGG	HHG
Hermes Pacific Investments	HPAC	Indian Restaurants Group

Current name	TIDM	Previous name
Highway Capital	HWC	Superframe Group
Homeserve	HSV	South Staffordshire Group
Howden Joinery Group	HWDN	Galiform
Hunter Resources	HUN	Gem Biofuels
Hvivo	HVO	Retroscreen Virology Group
Hydrodec Group	HYR	Vert-Eco Group
ICAP	IAP	Garban-Intercapital
IDOX	IDOX	i-documentsystems Group
Igas Energy	IGAS	Island Gas Resources
ImmuPharma	IMM	General Industries
Impact Holdings (UK)	IHUK	Nanotech Energy
IMPAX Asset Management Group	IPX	Impax Group
Impellam Group	IPEL	Carlisle Group Ltd
Infinity Energy SA	INFT	Global Brands S.A.
Informa	INF	T&F Informa
Infrastrata	INFA	Portland Gas
Inspiration Healthcare Group	IHC	Inditherm
Inspired Capital	INSC	Renovo Group
Inspirit Energy Holdings	INSP	KleenAir Systems International
Interbulk Group	INB	Interbulk Investments
InterContinental Hotels Group	IHG	Six Continents
International Consolidated Airlines Group SA	IAG	British Airways
International Mining & Infrastructure Corp	IMIC	India Star Energy
Interserve	IRV	Tilbury Douglas
IP Group	IPO	IP2IPO Group
IPPlus	IPP	County Contact Centres
Ironveld	IRON	Mercury Recycling Group
Ixico	IXI	Phytopharm
Jaywing	JWNG	Digital Marketing Group
JD Sports Fashion	JD.	John David Sports Group
Journey Group	JNY	Watermark Group
Judges Scientific	JDG	Judges Capital
K3 Business Technology Group	KBT	RAP Group
KCOM Group	KCOM	Kingston Communications (Hull)
Kellan Group	KLN	Berkeley Scott Group
Kemin Resources	KEM	GMA Resources
Kennedy Ventures	KENV	Managed Support Services
Ladbrokes	LAD	Hilton Group
Learning Technologies Group	LTG	In-Deed Online
LightwaveRF	LWRF	JSJS Designs
Lloyds Banking Group	LLOY	Lloyds TSB Group
M.P. Evans Group	MPE	Rowe Evans Investments
Management Consulting Group	MMC	Proudfoot Consulting
Manx Financial Group	MFX	Conister Financial Group
Marechale Capital	MAC	St Helen's Capital
Marlowe Holdings Ltd	MRL	Shellshock Ltd
Marston's	MARS	Wolverhampton & Dudley Breweries
MBL Group	MUBL	Air Music & Media Group
Metal Tiger	MTR	Brady Exploration

Current name	TIDM	Previous name
Mineral & Financial Investment Ltd	MAFL	Athol Gold Ltd
Mi-Pay Group	MPAY	Aimshell Acquisitions
Mirada	MIRA	YooMedia
Miton Group	MGR	MAM Funds
Mobile Tornado Group	MBT	TMT Group
Morgan Advanced Materials	MGAM	Morgan Crucible Company (The)
Mwana Africa	MWA	African Gold
MX Oil	MXO	Astar Minerals
MXC Capital	MXCP	2ergo Group
Mytrah Energy Ltd	MYT	Caparo Energy Ltd
Nakama Group	NAK	Highams Systems Services Group
Nanoco Group	NANO	Evolutec Group
National Grid	NG.	National Grid Transco
Nature Group	NGR	Nature Technology Solutions Ltd
NetPlay TV	NPT	Stream Group
Next Fifteen Communications Group	NFC	OneMonday Group
Norman Broadbent	NBB	Constellation Corporation
Nostra Terra Oil & Gas Company	NTOG	LHP Investments
Novae Group	NVA	SVB Holdings
Nyota Minerals Ltd	NYO	Dwyka Diamonds
Omega Diagnostics Group	ODX	Quintessentially English
OpSec Security Group	OSG	Applied Optical Technologies
OptiBiotix Health	OPTI	Ducat Ventures
Optimal Payments	OPAY	NEOVIA FINANCIAL ORD 0.01P
Orogen Gold	ORE	MEDAVINCI ORD 0.1P
Orosur Mining Inc	OMI	Uruguay Mineral Exploration Inc
Ortac Resources Ltd	OTC	Templar Minerals Ltd
Oxaco	OXA	Oxford Advanced Surfaces Group
Paddy Power	PAP	Power Leisure
Palace Capital	PCA	Leo Insurance Services
Panmure Gordon & Co	PMR	Durlacher Corporation
Parallel Media Group	PAA	World Sport Group
Parkmead Group (The)	PMG	Interregnum
Patagonia Gold	PGD	HPD Exploration
Paternoster Resources	PRS	Viridas
Petards Group	PEG	Screen
Petroceltic International	PCI	Ennex International
Petropavlovsk	POG	Peter Hambro Mining
PhotonStar Led Group	PSL	Enfis Group
Pinnacle Telecom Group	PINN	Glen Group
Pires Investments	PIRI	Oak Holdings
Polemos	PLMO	PLUS Markets Group
Porta Communications	PTCM	TSE Group
Power Capital Global Ltd	PCGB	Sportswinbet Ltd
Powerhouse Energy Group	PHE	Bidtimes
Premaitha Health	NIPT	ViaLogy
President Energy	PPC	Meridian Petroleum
Prime Active Capital	PACC	Oakhill Group
Pro Global Insurance Solutions	PROG	Tawa
Progility	PGY	ILX Group

Current name	TIDM	Previous name
Progressive Digital Media Group	PRO	TMN Group
Provexis	PXS	Nutrinnovator Holdings
Publishing Technology	PTO	Ingenta
PZ Cussons	PZC	Paterson Zochonis
Quadrise Fuels International	QFI	Zareba
Quoram	QRM	Bluebird Energy
Rare Earth Minerals	REM	Zest Group
Reach4entertainment Enterprises	R4E	Pivot Entertainment Group
React Group	REAT	Verdes Management
red24	REDT	ARC Risk Management Group
Redde	REDD	Helphire Group
Redhall Group	RHL	Booth Industries Group
Regenersis	RGS	Fonebak
RELX	REL	Reed Elsevier
Renew Holdings	RNWH	Montpellier Group
Restaurant Group (The)	RTN	City Centre Restaurants
Restore	RST	Mavinwood
Richland Resources Ltd	RLD	Tanzanite One Ltd
Richoux Group	RIC	Gourmet Holdings
Rose Petroleum	ROSE	Vane Minerals
Royal Dutch Shell	RDSB	Shell Transport and Trading Co
Royal Dutch Shell	RDSA	Shell Transport and Trading Co
RSA Insurance Group	RSA	Royal & Sun Alliance Insurance Group
RTC Group	RTC	ATA Group
RWS Holdings	RWS	Health Media Group
Sable Mining Ltd	SBLM	BioEnergy Africa Ltd
SABMiller	SAB	South African Breweries
Satellite Solutions Worldwide Group	SAT	Cleeve Capital
Savannah Resources	SAV	African Mining & Exploration
Science Group	SAG	Sagentia Group
SciSys	SSY	CODASciSys
Servoca	SVCA	Multi Group
Severfield	SFR	Severfield-Rowen
Sierra Rutile Ltd	SRX	Titanium Resources Group Ltd
Sigma Capital Group	SGM	Sigma Technology Group
Signet Jewelers Ltd	SIG	Signet Group
Silence Therapeutics	SLN	SR Pharma
Sirius Petroleum	SRSP	Global Gaming Technologies
Sky	SKY	British Sky Broadcasting Group
Smiths Group	SMIN	Smiths Industries
Solid State	SOLI	Solid State Supplies
Solo Oil	SOLO	Immersion Technologies International
Source BioScience	SBS	Medical Solutions
Spectris	SXS	Fairey Group
Speedy Hire	SDY	Allen
Sportech	SPO	Rodime
Stallion Resources	SPSM	Sports Star Media
Stanley Gibbons Group (The) Ltd	SGI	Communitie.com Ltd

Current name	TIDM	Previous name
Starvest	SVE	Web Shareshop (Holdings)
Stellar Resources	STG	CSS Stellar
Sterling Energy	SEY	LEPCO
Stobart Group Ltd	STOB	Westbury Property Fund (The) Ltd
Stratmin Global Resources	STGR	Woodburne Square AG
STV Group	STVG	SMG
Summit Therapeutics	SUMM	Summit Corporation
Sweett Group	CSG	Cyril Sweett Group
Symphony Environmental Technologies	SYM	Symphony Plastic Technologies
Synectics	SNX	Quadnetics Group
Synety Group	SNTY	Zenergy Power
Synthomer	SYNT	Yule Catto & Co
Tanfield Group	TAN	comeleon
Tangent Communications	TNG	Documedia Solutions
Tavistock Investments	TAVI	Social Go
Taylor Wimpey	TW.	Taylor Woodrow
Teathers Financial	TEA	Sperati (C.A.) (Special Agency)
Tengri Resources	TEN	Commoditrade Inc
Tissue Regenix Group	TRX	Oxeco
TomCo Energy	TOM	Netcentric Systems
Toumaz Holdings Ltd	TMZ	Nanoscience Inc
TP Group	TPG	Corac Group
Tricor	TRIC	PNC Telecom
Trinity Exploration and Production	TRIN	Bayfield Energy Holdings
Tri-Star Resources	TSTR	Canisp
Tullett Prebon	TLPR	Collins Stewart Tullett
Turbo Power Systems Inc	TPS	Turbo Genset Inc
Tyman	TYMN	Lupus Capital

Current name	TIDM	Previous name
UBM	UBM	United Business Media
UK Mail Group	UKM	Business Post Group
UK Oil & Gas Investments	UKOG	Sarantel Group
UMC Energy	UEP	Uranium Mining Corporation
Urban & Civic	UANC	Terrace Hill Group
UTV Media	UTV	UTV
ValiRx	VAL	Azure Holdings
Vast Resources	VAST	African Consolidated Resources
Vela Technologies	VELA	Asia Digital Holdings
Velocys	VLS	Oxford Catalysts Group
Vernalis	VER	British Biotech
Verona Pharma	VRP	Isis Resources
Vesuvius	VSVS	Cookson Group
Vianet Group	VNET	Brulines (Holdings)
Vodafone Group	VOD	Vodafone Airtouch
Vp	VP.	Vibroplant
W Resources	WRES	Caspian Holdings
Walker Crips Group	WCW	Walker, Crips, Weddle, Beck
Water Intelligence	WATR	Qonnectis
Waterman Group	WTM	Waterman Partnership Holdings
Webis Holdings	WEB	betinternet.com
West African Minerals Corporation	WAFM	Emerging Metals Ltd
Xtract Resources	XTR	Resmex
Yolo Leisure and Technology	YOLO	Pentagon Protection
Zoltav Resources Inc	ZOL	Crosby Asset Management Inc
Zoo Digital Group	ZOO	Kazoo3D

Notes

Obviously, there are many reasons why companies change their names, but a quick scan of the above table reveals a few themes. Firstly, a great many companies have taken to adding Group to their names, while a few have moved to the next stage by removing the word. The move to acronyms is always popular (e.g. British Telecommunications to BT Group), but in some cases the move is reversed (e.g. HHG to Henderson Group).

Some companies are unwinding their dot-com names (e.g. Printing.com to Grafenia), while others are just escaping silly names (e.g. Lo-Q to Accesso Technology Group, @UK to Cloudbuy).

Some companies seem to believe that appearing early in an alphabetically-ordered list is important and so have changed their names to a nonsensical word beginning with an a (e.g. CGNU to Aviva, Future Internet Technologies to Artilium).

When companies merge, often the new company name is an awkward amalgam of the old names, but these are usually unwound after a face-saving period of a few years (e.g. BP Amoco to BP, Lloyds TSB Group to Lloyds Banking Group, Granada Compass to Compass Group).

Quite a few companies seem to be trying to jump on the green bandwagon by squeezing an environmentally-friendly word into a new name (e.g. Camco International Ltd to Camco Clean Energy Ltd, 3DM Worldwide to Environmental Recycling Technologies, and Symphony Plastic Technologies to Symphony Environmental Technologies – nice one!).

In some cases one feels the directors must have been bored one afternoon and changed one silly name for another just for the hell of it (e.g. Zenergy Power to Synety Group – wasn't Synety Group one of Simon Cowell's girlfriends?). In other cases, companies went from wacky straight to catatonically boring and instantly forgettable (e.g. e-xentric to Capital Management and Investment).

Sometimes country names can become an awkward appendage and so they have to go (e.g. Centamin Egypt Ltd to Centamin, South African Breweries to SABMiller).

And, finally, there are just the mistakes (e.g. British Airways to International Consolidated Airlines Group, and Paterson Zochonis to PZ Cussons).

Which brings us to Royal Mail, which (briefly) changed its name to…? Anyone?*